Like a Dark Rabbi

MODERN POETRY & THE JEWISH

M000274419

LIKE A DARK RABBI

Modern Poetry & the
Jewish Literary Imagination

Norman Finkelstein

HEBREW UNION COLLEGE PRESS

HEBREW UNION COLLEGE PRESS
© 2019 Hebrew Union College Press

Names: Finkelstein, Norman, 1954- author.
Title: Like a dark rabbi : modern poetry & the Jewish literary imagination /
Norman Finkelstein.
Other titles: Modern poetry & the Jewish literary imagination | Modern
poetry
and the Jewish literary imagination
Description: Cincinnati : Hebrew Union College Press, [2019] | Includes
bibliographical references and index.
Identifiers: LCCN 2019007078 | ISBN 9780878201730 (alk. paper)
Subjects: LCSH: American poetry--Jewish authors--History and criticism.
American poetry--20th century--History and criticism. | American
poetry--21st century--History and criticism. | Jews--United
States--Identity. | Jews in literature. | Judaism and literature--United
States. | Judaism in literature. | Jewish religious poetry,
American--History and criticism. | Judaism and secularism.
Classification: LCC PS153.J4 F55 2019 | DDC 811/.6093529924--dc23
LC record available at https://lccn.loc.gov/2019007078

Set in Arno Pro by Raphaël Freeman, Renana Typesetting

Cover Image from *A Contract with God and Other Tenement Stories: A
Graphic Novel by Will Eisner*. Copyright © 1978, 1985, 1989, 1995, 1996 by
Will Eisner. Copyright (c) 2006 by Will Eisner Studios, Inc. Used by per-
mission of W.W. Norton & Company, Inc.

Cover design by Paul Neff Design, LLC

Printed in the United States of America

...Like a dark rabbi, I
Observed, when young, the nature of mankind,
In lordly study.
      – Wallace Stevens,
      "Le Monocle de Mon Oncle"

In memory of Harvey Shapiro

"Take me safely through the Narrows to the sea."

Contents

Acknowledgments   xi

Preface   xv

1. Introduction: Two Shapiros: Thoughts on Poetry and Secular Jewish Culture   1

2. Ghosts of Yiddish; or, Postvernacularity in Jewish American Poetry   17

3. Charles Reznikoff: Modernism, Diaspora, and the Problem of Jewish Identity   37

4. Allen Grossman and the Poetry of Holiness   77

5. Michael Heller: Between the Sacred and the Profane   103

6. Chana Bloch: Surfaces and Depths   131

7. "The darker wisdom of the Jews": Henry Weinfield's Dialectical Irony   161

8. Rachel Tzvia Back: Between Israel and the Diaspora   193

9. Dark Rabbis and Secret Jews   219

10. Afterword: "Diasporas of Imperfection"   263

11. Bibliography   271

Index   281

Acknowledgments

I WOULD LIKE TO THANK HEBREW UNION COLLEGE PRESS, WHICH brought *Like a Dark Rabbi* into being. Special thanks go to David H. Aaron, who was instrumental in helping me conceive the project and provided invaluable insights along the way. As I explain in the Preface, this book grew out of various articles, reviews and talks about Jewish American poets and poetry, written over a relatively long period of time. David recognized that these pieces, along with new work on the subject, could be shaped into a coherent volume that might add to our understanding of how the Jewish literary imagination continues to flourish in the context of modern American poetry.

After years of sharing meals and talking books with my old friend Sonja Rethy, managing editor of the Press, it's been an unexpected delight to find us collaborating on this project. Her suggestions have improved my book immensely.

My wife Alice is by now quite familiar with the sight of me working away on a book. She hears me kvetch when it grows tedious, and kvells with me when the writing turns out right. She has been by my side for many of the adventures which have led to whatever insights I may have to offer about the poetry discussed herein. I am always grateful for her love.

I have lived closely with the poetry I discuss in this book; it is fundamental to who I am as a reader, a poet, and a Jew. So to all of the poets whom I consider here, I extend the deepest gratitude and respect.

I gratefully acknowledge the following for having given me permission to quote from published work:

Rachel Tzvia Back, for permission to quote from her books *Azimuth, A Messenger Comes, On Ruins and Return,* and *What Use Is Poetry, the Poet Is Asking.*

Autumn House Press, for permission to quote from Chana Bloch, *Swimming in the Rain: New and Selected Poems 1980–2015* and *The Moon Is Almost Full.*

Farrar, Straus and Giroux, for permission to quote Peter Cole, "For a Theophoric Figure" from *Hymns & Qualms: New and Selected Poems and Translations* by Peter Cole. Copyright © 2017 by Peter Cole. Reprinted by permission of Farrar, Straus and Giroux.

Joseph Donahue, for permission to quote from his books *Dark Church: Terra Lucida IX–XII, Dissolves: Terra Lucida IV–VIII, Red Flash on a Black Field,* and *Terra Lucida.*

University of California Press via the Copyright Clearance Center, for permission to quote from Robert Duncan, *The Collected Later Poems and Plays.*

New Directions Publishing Company, for permission to quote from Allen Grossman, as follows:

"The Piano Player Explains Himself." By Allen Grossman, from *The Ether Dome,* copyright ©1991 by Allen Grossman. Reprinted by permission of New Directions Publishing Corp.

"Poland of Death." By Allen Grossman, from *The Ether Dome,* copyright ©1991 by Allen Grossman. Reprinted by permission of New Directions Publishing Corp.

"Descartes' Loneliness." By Allen Grossman, from *Descartes' Loneliness,* copyright ©2007 by Allen Grossman. Reprinted by permission of New Directions Publishing Corp.

"At Sunset." By Allen Grossman, from *Descartes' Loneliness,* copyright ©2007 by Allen Grossman. Reprinted by permission of NewDirections Publishing Corp.

"The Famished Dead." By Allen Grossman, from *Descartes' Loneliness,* copyright ©2007 by Allen Grossman. Reprinted by permission of New Directions Publishing Corp.

Nightboat Books, for permission to quote from Michael Heller, *Dianoia*, and *This Constellation Is a Name: Collected Poems, 1965–2010*.

David R. Godine, Publisher, for permission to quote from Charles Reznikoff, *The Collected Poems of Charles Reznikoff, 1918–1975*, ed. S. Cooney, Copyright © Charles Reznikoff, 1996.

Wesleyan University Press, for permission to quote from Harvey Shapiro, *A Momentary Glory: Last Poems* and *The Sights Along the Harbor: New and Collected Poems*.

Penguin Random House LLC, for permission to quote from Wallace Stevens, "The Auroras of Autumn," and "Things of August" from *The Collected Poems of Wallace Stevens* by Wallace Stevens, copyright © 1954 by Wallace Stevens and copyright renewed 1982 by Holly Stevens. Used by permission of Alfred A. Knopf, an imprint of the Knopf Doubleday Publishing Group, a division of Penguin Random House LLC. All rights reserved.

Henry Weinfield, for permission to quote from his books *A Wandering Aramaean: Passover Poems and Translations* and *Without Mythologies: New & Selected Poems & Translations*.

Preface

LIKE A DARK RABBI IS AN EXPRESSION OF MY DEVOTION TO JEWISH American poetry. This devotion, this desire to explore where it has been and to look where it is going, is intimately related to the fact that for a great many years, I have been writing poetry which turns to, and turns upon, the matter of modern Jewish identity. Sometimes this matter is addressed directly in my poems, sometimes not. Perhaps more importantly, it inhabits my poetic unconscious, and may be found on the borders of my discourse. It shapes the poetic utterance in ways I may hardly perceive at all. The deep streams of my Jewishness rise up and appear on the surfaces of my poems, and then submerge; but rarely are they entirely unfelt. Small wonder then that in my critical writing, I return often to the subject of Jewish poetry, and to the poets who for me represent Jewish concerns in ways that I find the most moving and compelling.

Like a Dark Rabbi is the second book I have written about modern Jewish poetry. I think of it as a collection of essays, for although various thematic threads run through the chapters, it is not intended to have a comprehensive argument. My first book on the subject, *Not One of Them in Place: Modern Poetry and Jewish American Identity* (2001), offers a *vision* of Jewish poetry in the United States, which is to say, it examines how Jewish belief, thought, and culture have been shaped and articulated in modern American poetry. It is highly conscious of poetic style, and of how Jewish poets in the twentieth century accommodate themselves to and have been influenced by major tendencies in modernist and postmodernist poetics. It presents neither a historical survey nor a systematic theory of Jewish American poetry; rather, it relies on deep and close reading of individual poets and their poems. It is deeply invested in matters of poetic tradition and lineage. But it is equally concerned with the ways in which textual markers of Jewish identity – gestures, tropes, figures, allusions, historical references, verbal inflections, as well as bolder and more overt articulations of Jewish selfhood – come to *signify* in American poems, written in American English, by American poets who are profoundly but often problematically self-conscious of their Jewishness. The present book deepens this examination of Jewish American poetry by revisiting some of the poets and extending my analysis to others.

When I first discussed the possibility of a book with the editors of Hebrew Union College Press, I thought to rework various articles, reviews, and talks that I had written since *Not One of Them in Place*. But I also wanted to write a few new pieces, dealing with poets and themes I have thought about for some time, but had not had the opportunity to address. In the end, one older piece made the cut and has been expanded ("Ghosts of Yiddish"), and others have been woven together with new material (the chapters on Charles Reznikoff, Allen Grossman, and Michael Heller). The chapters on Chana Bloch, Henry Weinfield, Rachel Tzvia Back, and the chapter on non-Jews writing "Jewish" poetry ("Dark Rabbis and Secret Jews"), plus the Introduction and Afterword, have all been written expressly for this collection. Two more speculative pieces that are important to me as a poet have not been included: "Secular Jewish Culture and Its Radical Poetic Discontents" and "Total Midrash."[1] My hope is that these essays, which are as much about my poetic practice as they are about my Jewish identity, will be included in a collection of more personal reflections at some future date.

In his magisterial essay "The Truth and Life of Myth," the poet

---

1. "Secular Jewish Culture and Its Radical Poetic Discontents," *Radical Poetics and Secular Jewish Culture*, ed. Stephen Paul Miller and Daniel Morris (Tuscaloosa: University of Alabama Press, 2010), 225–44; "Total Midrash," *Religion and Literature* 43, no. 2 (Summer 2011): 156–63.

Robert Duncan, reflecting on the relations between religious and literary traditions, tells us that "what I speak of here in the terms of a theology is a poetics."[2] Ironically, he makes this declaration in the process of criticizing the exclusivism of Jewish monotheism, a critique that I will examine later in this book. Despite what I identify in my last chapter as Duncan's rather vexed philosemitism, his understanding of the complex psychic, cultural, and literary transactions that take place between theology (organized bodies of religious belief) and poetics (organized forms of verbal expression) is of great importance to my critical project. Duncan subtitles "The Truth and Life of Myth" "*An Essay in Essential Autobiography.*" When I first read the essay sometime in the nineteen-seventies, it was a revelation to me. I discovered a mode of writing that is simultaneously intimate and erudite, scholarly and shamanic. It captures the essence of Duncan's poetic sensibility, as does much of his *The H.D. Book,* which I read some years later. Reading theology as a poetics (and reading poetics as a theology) describes, to some extent, what I am doing in *Not One of Them in Place,* and it is even more the case in a book I wrote more recently, *On Mount Vision: Forms of the Sacred in Contemporary American Poetry,* which does not deal with Jewish poetry at all. Returning to Jewish poetry after writing about Calvinism, gnosticism, spiritualism, and shamanism, I am increasingly sensitive to the ways in which poems written from "inside" a particular religious tradition simultaneously occupy a space "outside" of that tradition by imaginatively, if not transgressively, transforming religious gestures, texts, and rituals into poetic utterance. And even more uncannily, it is often just these transformations which demonstrate the poem's devotion to the tradition out of which it comes and from which it would depart. I have felt this tension in my own poetry, and I find evidence for it over and over again in the revisionism, sometimes subtle, sometimes overt, in the poetry I consider here.

    Like a Dark Rabbi, therefore, is a personal book, even if it is not quite "essential autobiography." As I explore "modern poetry and the Jewish literary imagination," I continue to discover how the work of other Jewish

---

2. Robert Duncan, *Collected Essays and Other Prose,* ed. James Maynard (Berkeley: University of California Press, 2014), 154.

poets helps me understand my own. Perhaps that will be the case for the readers of this book if they turn at some point, as I hope they will, to my poems. Meanwhile, I will meditate, as does the late Harvey Shapiro, my dear friend and mentor, "On Some Words of Ben Azzai":

> You will be called by your name.
> You will be seated in your place.
> You will be given what is yours.
> The dream goes something like that
> For everyone, I suppose, except
> When it's happening and the world
> Comes true, the air, the sky.
> But all of yesterday and again today
> I knew the dream. Age will end it.[3]

---

3. Harvey Shapiro, *The Sights Along the Harbor: New and Collected Poems* (Middletown, CT: Wesleyan University Press, 2006), 86.

ONE

Introduction
Two Shapiros: Thoughts on Poetry
and Secular Jewish Culture

ON SEPTEMBER 21, 2004, A SYMPOSIUM WAS HELD AT THE CENTER
for Jewish History in New York City. It originated when the American
Jewish Historical Society contacted the poet and critic Stephen Paul
Miller, and asked him to host a poetry event. The event took a more dis-
tinctive turn when Miller consulted Charles Bernstein, who proposed a
gathering to be called "Secular Jewish Culture / Radical Poetic Practice,"
which, according to Daniel Morris, Bernstein considered "an alternative
that would facilitate the public life of imaginative and interpretive, as
opposed to fundamentalist, forms of religious life."[1] The participants in
the symposium, along with Miller and Bernstein, were Marjorie Perloff,
Jerome Rothenberg, Kathryn Hellerstein, and Paul Auster. Inspired by
the talks at the symposium, Miller and Morris put out a call for con-
tributions to an anthology; the book that resulted, *Radical Poetics and
Secular Jewish Culture*, was published by the University of Alabama Press
in 2010 as part of its Modern and Contemporary Poetics Series, which
is edited by Bernstein and yet another important Jewish poet and critic,
Hank Lazer. Over four hundred pages long, the book includes a variety
of historical, critical, theoretical, and reflective essays by twenty-seven

---

1. Daniel Morris, introduction to *Radical Poetics and Secular Jewish Culture*, 1.

poets, critics, and scholars. Clearly, there was, and still is, a great deal to be said about the relationship of poetry to secular Jewish culture.

In his essay for the volume, originally presented at the symposium, Bernstein gives us a list of questions which he believes should be addressed if the complexities of this relationship are to be unpacked. Among them are the following: "What is the relation of Jewish modernist and contemporary poets to the historical avant-garde and to contemporary innovative poetry? How do Jewish cultural life and ethnic and religious forms and traditions manifest themselves in the forms, styles and approaches to radical American poetry? What roles does a distinctly secular approach to Jewishness by poets and other Jewish artists mean for 'radical Jewish culture'?"[2] Morris notes that in calling for contributors to the essay collection, he and Miller added a set of additional considerations, including "traces of religious Jewish texts and practices in secular Jewish radical poetic practice...asking how Jewish poetry can be written by non-Jews...Jewish cultural life and ethnic and religious forms and traditions in experimental American poetry... the secular as a paradoxically religious and in some ways characteristic Jewish concern that is germane to radical poetic processes; Jewishness as an alternative to religious and cultural forms of classification..."[3] As one can tell from these excerpts (the whole list is a good deal longer), numerous possibilities arise when secular Jewish attitudes and practices are made manifest in poetry; those that I quote here, from both Bernstein and Morris, exemplify only the most urgent concerns that I address throughout this present volume. Perhaps Bernstein puts it best when he declares that "I am no more Jewish than when I set my Jewishness adrift from fundamentalist religious practice. I am no more Jewish than when I refuse imposed definitions of what Jewishness means. I am no more Jewish than when I attend to how such Jewishness lives itself out, plays tunes not yet played...Call it the civic practice of Jewishness."[4]

2. Charles Bernstein, "Radical Jewish Culture / Secular Jewish Practice," in *Radical Poetics and Secular Jewish Culture,* 12.

3. Morris, introduction, 2.

4. Bernstein, 13. I should explain that although I find the overall project of *Radical Poetics and Secular Jewish Culture,* and many individual pieces in the book, to be extremely important (indeed, as I note in the Preface, I contributed what I regard as an important

The impetus behind an expression of this sort, and the poetry that results from it, may be better understood if we step back and briefly consider the nature of Jewish secular thought. In his study of this tradition, David Biale considers the ways in which Jewish secularism develops over thousands of years in relation to changing concepts of God, Torah, and Israel, noting how, under the conditions of modernity, "Jewish secularism may be seen as the attempt to fashion a countertradition, an alternative to Judaism as a religion that has its own intellectual lineage. While it may sometimes seem as if the story of secularization is a narrative of the world we have lost, secularism is not only negative; it is also an effort to fashion a new identity out of the shards of the past."[5] This assertion accords with the attitude of the writers in *Radical Poetics and Secular Jewish Culture*. According to Biale, as nineteenth- and twentieth-century secularist ideologies fade, Jews (among others) find themselves "in a 'postsecular' age, meaning an age in which religion and its negation are no longer polar opposites. Religion is permeated with the secular, just as the secular is permeated with religion."[6] And as he concludes, "The secularism of American Jews today is not ideological...and perhaps that is why it is writers of fiction and memoirists rather than ideologues who are giving it expression."[7]

Naturally, I would include poets in this group too, but with one caveat: because of poetry's traditionally greater affinities to matters of the

---

essay of my own to the volume), I take issue with the use of "fundamentalist," which I would replace with the less inflammatory word "observant." I would also question the almost fetishistic focus on notions such as "radical," "experimental," or "avant-garde" poetry and poetics. Although these notions are occasionally useful (and have a long, vexed critical history), I tend to agree with Wallace Stevens' adage that "All poetry is experimental poetry" – which is to say that all forms of poetry can assume, quite unpredictably, an oppositional status, given changing historical circumstances.

5. David Biale, *Not in the Heavens: The Tradition of Jewish Secular Thought* (Princeton, NJ: Princeton University Press, 2011), 13–14. The term "countertradition" is first used by Biale in his earlier study of Gershom Scholem, referring both to Kabbalah and to the sort of historiography of Kabbalah which Scholem essentially created. Scholem is considered as a secular thinker in *Not in the Heavens* as well.

6. Ibid., 181. Cf. my discussion below, pp. 124–25 of Steven M. Wasserstrom's notion of "religion after religion" in relation to the work of Michael Heller.

7. Ibid., 192.

spirit, the secularism of modern Jewish poetry is often a perfect example of how, in Biale's terms, religion and the secular are "permeated" with each other. In an essay on the secular and the sacred in recent Jewish American poetry, Maeera Y. Shreiber observes that "The secular is one stop along a continuum that includes and depends upon the idea of the sacred. It is not the sacred's opposite, nor its negation; rather, secularism is part of a dynamic ontology that is generally important for making an account of Jewish identity, and specifically relevant to understanding the contemporary moment in Jewish American poetics."[8] This is what the editors of *Radical Poetics and Secular Jewish Culture* must mean when they inquire about "traces of religious Jewish texts and practices in secular Jewish radical poetic practice," and about "the secular as a paradoxically religious" cultural condition. This paradoxical condition, posing an important challenge to the binarisms of the religious and the secular, the sacred and the profane, is variously expressed in all of the poets I discuss in this book, with Charles Reznikoff serving as one of its earliest iterations. It is important to note, however, that whereas the modern negotiations of religious and secular traditions often result in a richly provocative poetry, they can also be the source of anxiety and existential doubt – anxiety and doubt which are not always explicit, but are nonetheless still palpable in some important and representative Jewish American poets.

Consider the decidedly non-experimental work of Karl Shapiro (1913–2000), whose great success in the American literary mainstream, and immense reputation in the first half of his career (he won the Pulitzer Prize in 1945 and served as the editor of *Poetry* from 1950–1956), dropped off in the second half, despite his continued publications. The attempt to reconcile religion and secularism can produce troubled results, none more so than in Shapiro's *Poems of a Jew* (1958), a collection which he assembled out of the first twenty years of his poetry in order to demonstrate, as he writes in the introduction, how "the undercurrent of most of my poems is the theme of the Jew."[9] Although this may be the case,

8. Maeera Y. Shreiber, "Secularity, Sacredness, and Jewish American Poets 1950–2000," in *The Cambridge History of Jewish American Literature*, ed. Hana Wirth-Nesher (New York: Cambridge University Press, 2016), 183.
9. Karl Shapiro, *Poems of a Jew* (New York: Random House, 1958), xi.

Shapiro reveals how vexed and complicated, if not actually confused, his understanding of Jewish identity really is, especially as it is expressed in his poems. As he puts it, "The Jewish Question, whatever that might be, is not my concern. Nor is Judaism. Nor is Jewry. Nor is Israel. The religious question is not my concern... The artist's contribution to religion must in the nature of things be heretical."[10] This is certainly a strong secular position. The last statement in particular could sum up the situation, with Shapiro deliberately setting his Jewish poems in opposition to Jewish observance (although they actually are much more nuanced in this regard). But Shapiro cannot content himself with the status of secular Jewish heretic. Instead, he goes on to assert that "No one has been able to define *Jew*, and in essence this defiance of a definition is the central meaning of Jewish consciousness... As everyone knows, a Jew who becomes an atheist remains a Jew. A Jew who becomes a Catholic remains a Jew. Being a Jew is the consciousness of being a Jew, and the Jewish identity, with or without religion, with or without history, is the significant fact."[11]

Frankly, I am not sure what Shapiro means by this, though it does remind me of the uncanny ending of Philip Roth's *The Counterlife*, when Nathan Zuckerman argues with Maria, his British gentile wife, about having their unborn child circumcised if it turns out to be a boy. Having moved to England to make her happy, and subsequently dealing with various forms of British antisemitism, Zuckerman declares himself "A Jew without Jews, without Judaism, without Zionism, without Jewishness, without a temple or an army or even a pistol, a Jew clearly without a home, just the object itself, like a glass or an apple."[12] Perhaps this Jew as object is a more humorous version of Shapiro's "Being a Jew is the consciousness of being a Jew," a sort of degree zero of Jewish identity, a "man essentially himself, beyond nationality, defenseless against the crushing impersonality of history."[13] Shapiro is reflecting at this point, as seems inevitable in such discussions, on the Shoah, and

10. Ibid., ix.
11. Ibid., ix–x. Cf. Bernstein's remark in "Radical Jewish Culture / Secular Jewish Practice": "at least in some sense, you can't really be a lapsed Jew" (12).
12. Philip Roth, *The Counterlife* (New York: Farrar, Straus & Giroux, 1986), 324.
13. *Poems of a Jew*, x.

how the genocide of European Jewry confirms the minimal but still fundamental Jewish difference that so wholly shapes Jewish fate under modern conditions. For Shapiro, the Jew becomes (like James Joyce's Leopold Bloom in *Ulysses*), the "man left over, after everything that can happen has happened."[14] This, I suppose, is "the significant fact" of Jewish identity.

Yet even a brief look at Karl Shapiro's poems indicates that this minimal vision of a secular Jewish identity cannot find expression except through an ambivalent engagement not only with Jewish history, but with Jewish belief and religious practice as well. The first stanza of "The 151st Psalm" directly addresses the Jewish God:

> Are you looking for us? We are here.
> Have you been gathering flowers, Elohim?
> We are your flowers, we have always been.
> When will You leave us alone?
> We are in America.
> We have been here three hundred years.
> And what new altar will you deck us with?[15]

"When will You leave us alone?" asks this self-styled heretical poet, who claims in his introduction that his poems "are not religious poems but the poems of a Jew."[16] Heretics, however, tend not to be so expressly bothered by the God against whom they turn. Furthermore, one would think that American Jews, assimilated and increasingly secular in their worldview, need not remind that same persistent deity that they have managed to avoid Him for three hundred years, and so He need not gather them to Him on some new altar. On the contrary: God will not disappear, nor even keep His distance; He is very much in the forefront of this Jewish speaker's consciousness, however much he may claim otherwise, and the American experience that has reshaped his relationship to Jewish tradition does not help the poet's struggle with his faith in the least:

---

14. Ibid., xi.
15. Ibid., 6
16. Ibid., ix.

Immigrant God, You follow me;
You go with me, You are a distant tree;
You are the beast that lows in my heart's gates;
You are the dog that follows at my heel;
You are the table on which I lean;
You are the plate from which I eat.[17]

When God Himself is an immigrant who presumably struggles to assimilate to American culture as Shapiro's immigrant grandparents once did, when He proves to be ubiquitous and ineluctable as the metaphors of this stanza indicate (and note how elevated the diction becomes, echoing, perhaps, the King James Bible), then the secularity of Shapiro's Jewishness becomes highly questionable. Indeed, in the poem's concluding lines, it turns out that the speaker cannot do without Him: "Shepherd of the flock of praise, / Youth of all youth, ancient of days, / Follow us."[18]

There is much to indicate in Shapiro's work that although he may yearn to dispense with Jewish tradition and belief, he feels fated to be dogged by the Jewish God and caught in the trammels of Jewish history. A longer poem called "The Synagogue" declares in its opening lines that "The synagogue dispirits the deep street, / Shadows the face of the pedestrian," while in the next stanza, by contrast, "The swift cathedral palpitates the blood, / The soul moves upward like a wing to meet / The pinnacles of saints."[19] The comparison that Shapiro elaborates in the poem is curious, to say the least: Jewish belief, Jewish custom, and the Jewish God himself all have a peculiarly insistent, even stubborn reality to them, as opposed to the ideal or fantasmic essence of Christianity. Shapiro's attitude toward his religion seems both proud and regretful, an ambivalence that marks every trope in the poem. Thus "The altar of the Hebrews is a house, / No relic but a place, Sinai itself, / Not holy ground but factual holiness / Wherein the living god is resident."[20] "Factual holiness" is a wonderful expression of the traditional Jewish religious

17. Ibid., 6.
18. Ibid.
19. Ibid., 8.
20. Ibid.

and cultural sensibility, but somehow it does not satisfy the poet, as he goes on to observe that

> The Jew has no bedecked magnificat
> But sits in stricken ashes after death,
> Refusing grace; his grave is flowerless,
> He gutters in the tallow of his name.
> At Rome the multiplying tapers sing
> Life endless in the history of art.[21]

It is always awkward to raise the highly contested idea of Jewish self-hatred; be that as it may, the Jewish voice in this poem comes close to ventriloquizing the sort of Christian antisemitism that sees "the Jew" as caught up in the flesh and in the legalisms that structure Jewish life (and death). "Refusing grace," the Jew "gutters in the tallow of his name" (probably an image of a yahrzeit candle), as opposed to the Christian spirit of transcendence with its "multiplying tapers," which, unlike the Jewish faith, has for centuries inspired magnificent works of art. Because, as he puts it, "Our wine is wine, our bread is harvest bread / That feeds the body and is not the body," Shapiro's "Jew" even seems willing to accept the Christian accusation of Christ-killer: "The immanent son then came as one of us," but "We were betrayed to sacrifice this man."[22] The poem ends on the same sustained note of ambivalence: God provides us with "our devious reward":

> For faith he gave us land and took the land,
> Thinking us exiles of all humankind.
> Our name is yet the identity of God
> That storms the falling altar of the world.[23]

The Jews epitomize both exile and radical monotheism; taken together, the truth of this identity "storms the falling altar of the world." But this is not an empowering diasporism, that fundamental concept in the formation of a more recent radical Jewish culture and secular life.

21. Ibid., 9.
22. Ibid., 9, 10.
23. Ibid., 10.

There is, rather, something almost lugubrious about Shapiro's vision of modern Jewish identity. On the one hand, Jewish observance appears to be spiritually lacking, arrested in history, and still regarded with suspicion by cultured gentiles (who seem, as much or even more than Jews, to be Shapiro's audience). On the other hand, Jewish secularism leaves Jews indefinable to themselves: existentially lacking, they appear to be historically bereft *luftmenschen* of the sort that, again, come close to confirming an unsympathetic if not altogether hostile gentile perspective.

I have just observed that, for Shapiro, secularism leaves Jews indefinable to themselves, but that is not completely the case: one unavoidable aspect of Jewish identity remains. Shapiro's anxiety extends to almost every aspect of Jewish life, including the Jewish male body and all that it signifies in terms of Jewish identity, both for Jews and non-Jews alike. In "The First Time," Shapiro gives us a scene in a bordello, where a "boy, who is no more than seventeen, / Not knowing what to do, takes off his clothes / As one might in a doctor's anteroom."[24] The poem is both clinical and lurid to the point of hysteria: there is a "lamp of iodine and rose / That stains all love with its medicinal bloom" and a "great bed drugged with its own perfume" that "Spreads its carnivorous flowermouth for all."[25] The prostitute herself is even younger than the boy, but "She watches him behind her with old eyes,"

> Transfixing him in space like some grotesque,
> Far, far from her where he is still alone
> And being here is more and more untrue.
> Then she turns round, as one turns at a desk,
> And looks at him, too naked and too soon,
> And almost gently asks: *Are you a Jew?*[26]

Does the girl "almost gently" asking her question indicate pity, not only for the boy's inexperience but also for his Jewishness? Presumably it is the boy's circumcised penis which has elicited the question, and he may have ejaculated even before walking into her room, since earlier

24. Ibid., 28.
25. Ibid.
26. Ibid., 29.

he "Feels love hysterically burn away, / A candle swimming down to nothingness / Put out by its own wetted gusts of flame."[27] In any case, it would appear that the terror of sexual initiation is equated with the stigma of Jewishness; both are seen as "grotesque," and the image of the girl turning "as one turns at a desk," like some judgmental official, only makes her gentle question all the more humiliating. The alluring but frightening sexuality of the *shiksa* unmans the Jew who desires her – like the secular world that he finds equally compelling but so difficult to enter.[28]

"As a Jew," writes Shapiro, "I grew up in an atmosphere of mysterious pride and sensitivity, an atmosphere in which even the greatest achievement was touched by a sense of the comic."[29] But it would appear that there is far more sensitivity than pride in Shapiro's Jewish vision, and if Jewish achievement in a secular American milieu is touched by a sense of the comic, it is a self-deprecating sense of the comic beyond even typical Jewish humor. There is very little that is funny in the scenarios of *Poems of a Jew*. Caught between Jewish tradition that is seen as untenable if not spiritually moribund, and secular life that is fraught with psychic and social dangers, the American Jew finds himself paralyzed – not merely, to use Shapiro's term, "man left over," but so riddled with doubt and anxiety that he seems ready, in that heyday of psychoanalysis, for Alexander Portnoy's Dr. Spielvogel. Perhaps a secular rabbi of that sort could help him adjust to Jewish American life. As Maeera Shreiber

---

27. Ibid., 28.

28. Cf. Charles Reznikoff's poem "Hellenist," a frequently discussed instance of Jewish secularism and assimilation focused on performance anxiety and the scorn of a gentile female – though here, it is linguistic performance, and the female is not a prostitute but a goddess:

> As I, barbarian, at last, although slowly, could read Greek,
> at "blue-eyed Athena"
> I greeted her picture that had long been on the wall:
> the head slightly bent forward under the heavy helmet,
> as if to listen; the beautiful lips slightly scornful.

The Poems of Charles Reznikoff 1918–1975, ed. Seamus Cooney (Boston: Black Sparrow / David R. Godine, 2005), 93.

29. Ibid., xi.

notes, "One of the most sorrowful examples of the poet suffering the effects of this cultural vise may be found in the unhappy poems of Karl Shapiro, who, at the end of his life, quips bitterly: 'I once published a book called Poems of a Jew / To get rid of my Jewish problem. / It only made it worse.'"[30]

Fast forward to the early twenty-first century, where we find another poet named Shapiro – Harvey Shapiro (1924–2013) – also thinking about Jewish masculinity in a secular world, and writing a poem called, appropriately, "The Generations":

> His son stood, holding and rocking the baby,
> swaying back and forth, combined
> with a little sideways shuffle,
> which he had never done in shul,
> since he never went to shul,
> though his father had and his father had,
> so the prayer that bound them all
> was still being said.[31]

"The Generations" exemplifies secular Jewish culture as I have come to understand it, and demonstrates the way poetry functions as a unique expression of that culture. Decidedly patrilineal (and keep in mind that, traditionally, Jewish identity is passed from one generation to the next matrilineally), the poem dwells on the seemingly unavoidable anxiety about who is a Jew and what makes a generation of Jews identifiably Jewish, though here, such anxiety is expressed through equal measures of wit, irony, sweetness, and linguistic self-consciousness. We are not told the gender of the baby, but somehow we intuit that it's a boy, since the poem seems so determined to maintain the hereditary line of fathers and sons. The poet looks at his son holding the baby and discovers that his son is *shuckling*, swaying as if in prayer.[32] His son is a secular Jew – so where could he have picked up such movement, "since he never went

---

30. "Secularity, Sacredness, and Jewish American Poets," 182–83.
31. *The Sights Along the Harbor*, 7–8.
32. For an overview of this practice, see Louis Jacobs, "Swaying in Prayer," *My Jewish Learning*, https://www.myjewishlearning.com/article/swaying-in-prayer/.

to shul"? The poet himself "had," just as *his* father "had." (Note the use of the past tense and the reference to himself, in relation to the son, as "his father," as if he is somehow looking back on himself from the other side of life.) This means that the poet's father took his son to shul, as opposed to the poet, who apparently did not take *his* son. Hence what appears to be the son's secular lifestyle. Is the poet feeling guilty about this? Perhaps he is considering that he has failed to teach his son the proper Jewish way to worship, the proper relationship to God, and just as importantly, to the Jewish community. This is expressed in his use of the homely Yiddish term *shul* (which literally means "school," thereby implying a process of education), rather than the more typically American "synagogue." Yet the motion of the son rocking the baby is the same motion he would make praying in shul if he were to go. How to account for this? Is it in his DNA? Are the ritualistic physical gestures of the Jewish male genetically passed from father to son? And is this sufficient to produce the continuity of Jewish culture, even as religion is abandoned and secular values replace it?

Apparently, for Shapiro, the answer is yes: "so the prayer that bound them all / was still being said." In regard to a traditional practice such as prayer, Jews do not need to be in shul – indeed, Jews do not need to be actually "praying" at all – for there to be cultural as well as biological continuity. Prayer as a communal ritual is replaced by what appears to be an individual's instinctive gesture, the son's shuckling with the baby, which still proves sufficiently binding for the continuation of Jewish culture. The prayer is "still being said," though presumably the son does not know the prayer at all. How can this be? My answer is that the prayer, embodied in the son's gesture, is *in* the poem and maintains its living presence *through* the poem. The poem with its image of the son and the baby, as a secular utterance, literary rather than liturgical, takes the place of the prayer for presumably secular readers. While it does not give us the prayer's content, it is still a vehicle for Jewish identity and Jewish continuity; thus the prayer is "still being said." The poem, while not religious per se, positions itself as a meaningful statement of modern Jewish life, and gives Jewish life its continued meaning.

Surely a religiously observant Jew would regard Shapiro's conclusion (and my interpretation) as impossible, indeed, strictly speaking, as *nonsense*, the sort of fiction that comes into being when modernity has emptied the forms of Jewish life of their traditional meaning. Such *narishkeit* (foolishness) could only be the invention of some scribbler who no longer follows halakhah, Jewish law, who has lost his way – or "the Way," since that is what the Hebrew word halakhah literarily means. But Shapiro knows this quite well.[33] He alludes to his situation, his having lost the Way, in a poem that is roughly contemporary with "The Generations," called "According to the Rabbis":

> According to the rabbis,
> when God asks Adam, Where are you?
> He's not looking for information.
> He wants Adam to consider where he is in his life,
> where he is NOW and where he intends to be.
> I could say that I'm on a bus, headed for New York,
> but that would be frivolous. I could say
> that I'm in the middle of a dark wood,
> that I'm always in the middle of a dark wood.
> But that would be despair.[34]

This poem, another provocative instance of how poetry functions today in secular Jewish culture, begins with commentary ("According to the rabbis…") and ends with an allusion to Dante, the greatest of all Christian poets: "Nel mezzo del cammin di nostra vita / mi ritrovai per una selva oscura, / ché la diritta va era smarrita." ("When I had journeyed half of our life's way, / I found myself within a shadowed forest, / for I had lost the path that does not stray.")[35] Like "The Generations," it is premised on the poet's doubt regarding his position vis-à-vis traditional Jewish life: after all, if he had trusted himself to follow the Way, he would not feel that he was "in the middle of a dark wood." Indeed, it is his secularism, exemplified in this case by his identification with a major work of "Western" (read: Christian) literature, that provides

---

33. See below, p. 74.
34. *The Sights Along the Harbor*, 7.
35. Dante Aligheri, *The Divine Comedy of Dante Aligheri: Inferno*, trans. Allen Mandelbaum (New York: Bantam Books, 1982), 2, 3.

him with a metaphor for this feeling of existential insecurity and loss. Perhaps if Shapiro had truly followed the rabbis, he would not have read the *Commedia* at all, and would not identify with Dante's dilemma at the outset of the poem. Then again, he apparently does know enough rabbinic literature to cite a commentary which in itself raises existential doubts – doubts which might beset even the most devout of Jews, especially given the skepticism which permeates traditional rabbinic inquiry.[36] Thus we can conclude that although a great deal of doubt and despair may be articulated *in* the poem, the expression *of* the poem, its utterance, still provides a connection to Jewish tradition, however modernized and inflected by another religious tradition that is opposed, if not downright inimical, to Jewish belief. But Shapiro is not interested (at least in this poem) in religious conflict. Rather, Shapiro's secular Jewish identity is to be found precisely at the point where the Talmud and the *Commedia* productively intersect, both informing his worldview, and just as importantly, the vision of Jewish life captured in his poems.

We will return to Harvey Shapiro a number of times in this book: his profound insights into Jewish American life, coupled with his brilliantly understated style, makes him, to my mind, not only a major voice among recent Jewish poets, but one who epitomizes the endlessly paradoxical questions and answers that secular Jewish life provokes. As I write in the introduction to *A Momentary Glory*, the posthumous volume of poems which I edited after reading the manuscripts that Shapiro left behind upon his death, he gives us "an updated version of wisdom literature, suffused with Jewish irony and compassion, often anecdotal and bordering on the parabolic."[37] Parable and paradox are always close to the heart of modern Jewish poetry, as in this poem, one of Shapiro's last. It

---

36. One source for this commentary is the Talmud, b. Sanhedrin 38b: "And Rav Yehuda says that Rav says: Adam the first man was a heretic, as it is stated: 'And the Lord called to the man and said to him: Where are you'? (Genesis 3:9), meaning, to where has your heart turned, indicating that Adam turned from the path of truth." https://www.sefaria.org/Sanhedrin.38b. My thanks to Dr. Andrew Klafter for pointing me to this passage.

37. Norman Finkelstein, introduction to *A Momentary Glory: Last Poems* (Middletown, CT: Wesleyan University Press, 2014), xiii.

is called "Book Group," and my guess is that most if not all the readers in the group are highly educated, worldly New York Jews:

> We read a book ostensibly
> about the Holocaust in which
> six million are killed, babies
> had their skulls bashed against
> the wall, an entire culture
> was wiped out, leaving only
> the vaudeville Jews of America
> and the critic in the group says
> the theme is survival and
> everyone cries paradox! paradox![38]

In the shadow of inconceivable loss and cultural transformation, those "vaudeville Jews" need their poets to reveal the paradoxes of their continued survival.

38. *A Momentary Glory*, 64.

TWO

Ghosts of Yiddish; or, Postvernacularity in Jewish American Poetry

I DO NOT KNOW YIDDISH; I CANNOT SPEAK IT, CANNOT READ IT. Like many American Jews of my generation, I grew up hearing Yiddish spoken, mainly by my grandparents, who spoke it to each other and to my parents. It was often used around me to prevent me from learning about some unsavory family matter deemed inappropriate for my young sensibility; this too was part of the Yiddish experience for many such as I. I managed to pick up a few Yiddish phrases and individual words, though for the most part they were curses, dirty words, or words having to do with food. My older sister remembers my grandfather reading books in Yiddish, and reading the newspaper to my grandmother, who was probably illiterate. Grandpa read the *Tog* every day (I was sometimes sent to the candy store to get his copy), and, when that newspaper ceased publication in 1971, he switched to the *Forverts*; but as my mother explained to me, he never liked it because it was too left wing. (He was a furrier, and eventually opened his own little shop in Manhattan, across the street from Macy's, where his clientele consisted of wealthy Jewish ladies from the Upper East Side.) I was always impressed by my cousin Nina, who would recite the Four Questions in Yiddish at every family seder. I never got even that far. Years later, when I was writing about the Yiddish modernists in comparison to the Objectivists in my book on Jewish American poetry, I had to make do with various translations, trying to decipher a bit of the original text with my rudimentary Hebrew

and even more rudimentary German. Without the vowels, it was a lost
cause. In short, in my childhood I experienced, as Merle Bachman puts it,
"the 'natural' rejection of Yiddish culture, occurring somewhere between
abandonment and suppression."[1]

As for the ghosts in the title of this chapter, I do not mean the spirits
of Yiddish-speakers, but rather the ghosts of the language itself – which
would imply that the language is dead. Happily, though, Yiddish is not a
dead language, nor even, arguably, is it a dying literary language.[2] When
I give my introductory lecture on Jewish American literature to my
predominantly Catholic students at Xavier University, I describe the
thriving Yiddish literary culture that existed in Europe and America prior
to the Holocaust, and mention the historical irony that in America today,
most of the Jews who are capable of reading Yiddish literature do not do
so, since they are ultra-Orthodox, and regard it as secular, scandalous,
treyf. But as Jeffrey Shandler points out in the last chapter of Adventures in
Yiddishland, his landmark study of modern Yiddish language and culture –
a chapter devoted entirely to the trope of Yiddish as dying or dead – the
status of Yiddish as a living tongue has been debated at least since the late
nineteenth century, long before the Holocaust and the death of half the
world's Yiddish speakers. After the Holocaust, the trope has served "as
a discursive frame for addressing the shifting stature and significance of
Yiddish in modern Jewish life."[3] Shandler goes on to argue that in itself,
the trope of Yiddish as dead (which leads, of course, to the inevitable
metaphor of ghosts) "has become an autonomous cultural phenome-
non; like a specter, it has taken on a 'life' of its own.... Therefore, when
people now speak of Yiddish as moribund, they invoke the language

1. Merle L. Bachman, *Recovering "Yiddishland": Threshold Moments in American Literature*
   (Syracuse, NY: Syracuse University Press, 2008), 9.
2. The first chapter of Bachman's book consists of a beautiful meditation on what one
   might call the life and afterlife of Yiddish, seen through the author's persona of "the
   Yiddish student," a Jewish American woman who makes the conscious choice of
   learning Yiddish and immersing herself in Yiddish culture after having been raised
   in a largely assimilated milieu (similar to my own). The idea of "ghosts of Yiddish"
   inevitably arises as she considers her situation; see especially Bachman, 19–21.
3. Jeffrey Shandler, *Adventures in Yiddishland: Postvernacular Language and Culture*
   (Berkeley: University of California Press, 2006), 180.

symbolically to address, albeit obliquely, the sense of a breach in Jewish cultural or social continuity at its most elemental level."[4]

Most readers, including most Jewish American readers, who are interested in Yiddish literature, must encounter it in translation. Since they are a self-selecting group to begin with, they are, at least to some extent, conscious of the breach to which Shandler refers, and no doubt their awareness of the dubious status of Yiddish haunts them as they read. Securing translation into English of Yiddish works and authors is therefore of the utmost importance. One thinks of Cynthia Ozick's brilliant tragi-comic novella "Envy; or Yiddish in America" (1969), which hinges on the issue of translation among a group of aging Yiddish writers in New York City. Edelshtein, the beleaguered, masochistic poet who is the protagonist of the tale (said to be modeled after Yankev Glatshteyn), is consumed with envy of Ostrover (unquestionably modeled on I.B. Singer), who achieves fame because he cunningly manipulates his translators and succeeds in entering the mainstream of American letters. Edelshtein, desperate to have his poems translated, humiliates himself continually, and by the end of the tale, is indeed virtually haunted by the specter of a vanishing Yiddish literary culture, soon to be forgotten, or so he has come to believe.

But how does Yiddish haunt Jewish American poets writing in English? And how are we to recognize, how are we to appreciate, a linguistically haunted poem? Here, I need to bring into play the central concept of Shandler's book, the "postvernacularity" of contemporary Yiddish. According to Shandler, Yiddish as a vernacular language "is narrowing in scope. At the same time its secondary, or meta-level of signification – the symbolic value invested in the language apart from the semantic value of any given utterance in it – is expanding. This privileging of the secondary level of signification of Yiddish over its primary level constitutes a distinctive mode of engagement with the language that I call *postvernacular* Yiddish."[5] This secondary level of signification manifests itself in a remarkably wide variety of literary and cultural practices, which Shandler analyzes at great length; what we need to keep in mind

4. Ibid., 182, 183.
5. Ibid., 4.

is that "in postvernacular Yiddish the very fact that something is said (or written or sung) in Yiddish is at least as meaningful as the meaning of the words being uttered – if not more so."[6]

Haunting or being haunted, therefore, are subtle and dialectically nuanced processes, at least in regard to poetry. As Shandler notes, "The tension between notions of Yiddish as lost and as enduring find resolution of a sort in the meta-language of poetry; linguistic self-consciousness both stymies the writer (who fears his own verse may, like that of his Yiddish forebears, become lost in translation) and stimulates his literary creativity."[7] I want to focus on this meta-linguistic aspect of Jewish American poetry, especially those moments when it self-consciously invokes the lost or ghostly dimension of Yiddish, and all that Yiddish, in its postvernacularity, has come to signify. This haunting (or perhaps, necromantic) process differs, depending on whether the poet being haunted actually knows the ghost language or not. In *Call It English: The Languages of Jewish American Literature*, Hana Wirth-Nesher carefully delineates the various linguistic possibilities which arise in the work of Jewish American writers in relation to both Yiddish and Hebrew, and the strategies that these writers have historically deployed when they bring these Jewish languages into play – or when these languages manifest themselves in the work, which is to say, haunt it. According to Wirth-Nesher,

> Those writers whose works reveal traces of Yiddish and Hebrew (or Aramaic), whether they are immigrant or native-born Americans, have either strongly identified with, even celebrated, this continuity in their writings, or they have kept their distance by ironic treatment of characters' speech or by self-conscious declarations of English exclusivity. My contention is that for many Jewish American writers subsequent to the immigrant generation, Hebrew and Yiddish are sources of self-expression and identity even if the authors cannot "remember" them in the sense of ever having possessed them as a means of communication....

6. Ibid., 22.
7. Ibid., 113.

Their remembering, therefore, is not the result of an essential Jewishness that hearkens back to some racial memory but the result of socialization where practices, expectations, and assumptions about the entanglement of language and identity linger in their consciousness.[8]

This comprehensive statement, which serves as the basis for Wirth-Nesher's nuanced analyses of Jewish American prose fiction, is equally applicable to Jewish American poetry, as her occasional glances at a few poems indicate. Regarding Yiddish in particular, I am struck by Wirth-Nesher's observation that "attitudes toward Yiddish in the Jewish American community have shifted away from comical belittling, as was often the case among second generation writers, toward romanticizing, even sanctifying the language" – an assertion that finds a good deal of backing in Shandler's research as well.[9] Both Wirth-Nesher and Shandler analyze Jacqueline Osherow's "Ch'vil Schreibn a Poem auf Yiddish," a poem in which, as Shandler puts it, "Osherow's yearning for Yiddish is implicitly juxtaposed with her native fluency in English. The expressive possibilities with which English provides her are taken as self-evident; they are only problematic in that they are somehow insufficient in relation to Yiddish, which lies beyond the poet's grasp (even in translation)."[10] In this poem, Yiddish, as Wirth-Nesher notes, "is a signifier of longing for an unattainable purity, the longing itself expressed in the phonetic twilight zone of transliteration – where the sound of Yiddish transcribed into the Roman alphabet of English is alien to *both* languages."[11]

Arguably, what Shandler sees as a sense of "insufficiency" when Osherow compares her fluent English with her almost non-existent Yiddish, and what Wirth-Nesher calls the poem's "sanctifying" attitude toward Yiddish, might ultimately add up to a certain sentimentality toward Yiddish, given its vexed history. If this is the case, it is a sentimentality of which Osherow herself is at least partly aware:

8. Hana Wirth-Nesher, *Call It English: The Languages of Jewish American Literature* (Princeton, NJ: Princeton University Press, 2006), 5.
9. Ibid., 30.
10. Shandler, 114.
11. Wirth-Nesher, 31.

Maybe I understand it perfectly;
maybe, in Yiddish, things aren't any clearer
than the mumbling of rain on cast off leaves …

Being pure poem, pure Yiddish poem,
my Yiddish poem is above such meditations
as I, were I fluent in Yiddish,
would be above wasting my time
pouring out my heart in Goyish metaphors.[12]

Given the appropriative nature of Yiddish in relation to other languages, and the multilingualism of most Yiddish speakers, it is indeed ironic that Osherow equates Yiddish with purity. Likewise, the claim that her "Goyish metaphors" (like "the mumbling of rain on cast off leaves") are a waste of time does not keep her from producing them in her attempt to write a Yiddish poem. In effect, these contradictions constitute the poem's weakness and its strength. But this is not to criticize the poem unduly: one of the questions I want to raise in this chapter is whether any Jewish American poem that is written in English and haunted by Yiddish can *ever* escape a feeling of insufficiency, and that sanctifying or sentimental attitude, even when, *simultaneously*, it engages in what Wirth-Nesher calls "comical belittling." It may well be, then, that such contradictions are inevitable whenever Yiddish makes itself felt in an English poem. If this is indeed the case, it has everything to do with the historical fate of Yiddish, both globally and in America specifically, where Jewish immigrants moved rapidly to jettison the language in their urgent push toward assimilation, and tended not to pass it on to subsequent generations, at least as a vernacular. Yiddish "signifying" in Jewish American literature may move between the two poles of humor and sanctification, but regardless of attitude or affect, a secret longing for what is irredeemably lost is constantly at work.

Consider, for instance, Harvey Shapiro's poem "For the Yiddish Singers in the Lakewood Hotels of My Childhood":

12. Jacqueline Osherow, *Dead Men's Praise* (New York: Grove Press, 1999), 3.

I don't want to be sheltered here.
I don't want to keep crawling back
To this page, saying to myself,
This is what I have.

I never wanted to make
Sentimental music in the Brill Building.
It's not the voice of Frank Sinatra
I hear.

To be a Jew in Manhattan
Doesn't have to be this.
These lights flung like farfel.
These golden girls.[13]

This is a remarkable poem, not least because of the way it exemplifies, in just a few lines, some important aspects of Jewish American social history of the first half of the twentieth century. Affectively and thematically, it is a poem about cultural ambivalence. Shapiro makes it clear that he wants to resist sentimentality, despite the fact that the entire utterance is premised on nostalgia, especially for the Yiddish culture of his childhood.

Shapiro was born in 1924. During his childhood, Lakewood, New Jersey was a well-established Jewish winter resort. In the 1890s, when a leading gentile hotel had turned away the department store magnate Nathan Straus because he was Jewish, Straus "promptly built next to it a hotel, *twice as large*, for Jews only. In a few years other Lakewood hotels sold out to Jewish operators, and kosher establishments multiplied on all sides."[14] In the *heymish* Lakewood hotels, like those of the Catskills, one could still hear Old World Yiddish entertainers, along with more contemporary American popular music of the sort produced by Jewish American songwriters working out of the Brill Building, a Manhattan center of the music industry from the thirties through the sixties. Yet

13. *The Sights Along the Harbor*, 100.
14. John Highman, "Social Discrimination Against Jews, 1830–1930," in *Anti-Semitism in America. American Jewish History* 6, ed. Jeffrey S. Gurock (New York: Routledge, 1998), 243.

whether the "sentimental music" is sung in Yiddish by Jewish singers in Lakewood, or in English by Frank Sinatra crooning a hit written by Jewish American songsmiths, Shapiro still feels trapped in memory, ironically "sheltered" by his past and continually "crawling back" to the page on which he inscribes his early history.

A proof text: in Philip Roth's *Portnoy's Complaint* (1969), the young Alex Portnoy is taken to a Lakewood hotel on a winter weekend getaway with his parents and their Gin Rummy club, and Alex is given a taste of nature and its poetry, walking with his hardworking, semi-literate, constipated father and breathing what his father calls "good winter piney air." Alex immediately declares (keeping in mind that the entire book consists of Portnoy's narration to his psychoanalyst while on the couch), "*Good winter piney air* – another poet for a parent! I couldn't be more thrilled if I were Wordsworth's kid!"[15] Nostalgia, childhood innocence, good parenting (which Portnoy usually claims he failed to receive), and the physical and spiritual benefits of nature are all set within the specifically Jewish context of Lakewood. All are in turn related to the poetry of William Wordsworth, which itself signifies, especially in the popular mind (including Portnoy's), the restorative powers of nature and the Romantic view of childhood innocence. Alex's father is momentarily transformed into a Jewish American Wordsworth, guiding his son, with whom he usually has little wisdom to share, in the simple pleasures of a Jewish American life.

But let us return to Shapiro's poem. The phrase "crawling back," connotes both defeat and infantilization, a problem, of course, that haunts Portnoy as well. Both Shapiro and Portnoy simultaneously long for and seek to escape from all that Jewish Lakewood suggests. The poet asserts that "To be a Jew in Manhattan / Doesn't have to be this," but everything in the poem indicates otherwise.

What, we must ask, is another way to be a Jew in Manhattan – and more specifically, a straight adult male Jew? The obvious answer has to do with the last line of the poem, not even a sentence but a descriptive assertion, a finger pointing at a new world of possibility: "These golden girls": *shiksa* goddesses of the type Portnoy also perpetually pursues.

15. Philip Roth, *Portnoy's Complaint* (New York: Modern Library, 1982), 29.

Farewell, Lakewood and its Yiddish singers; welcome, the sexual conquests of the fully assimilated, cosmopolitan Manhattanite. But wait: it is the penultimate line on which the poem turns. Looking down on the city at night, dreaming of love, does the poet see the Great White Way? No, he sees "These lights flung like farfel." *Farfel?* Farfel: "from Middle High German *varveln* (through Yiddish *farfl*); small pellet-shaped noodles, made of either flour mixed with egg or matzo. Farfel is most prevalent in Jewish cuisine, where it is a seasonal item used in Passover dishes."[16] Those golden girls, those city lights, shine, in the poet's imagination, like Mama's cooking on Pesach. This, then, is to be a Jew in Manhattan, haunted by the Yiddish language and the Yiddish past.

In another of Shapiro's poems, "Three Flights Down the Stairs," a Portnoy-like sexual adventurism is again literally flavored by what we might call a post-Yiddish worldview:

> Three flights down the stairs,
> south one block to Houston,
> cross the street and maybe a half-block
> west to Russ & Daughters.
> Take a number – why is that woman
> buying all that sturgeon? – for black
> Russian bread, 3 smoked fish, farmer
> cheese (the bulk kind) and nova.
> Retrace the route, up the stairs,
> and she's just getting out of the tub
> right by the kitchen sink, pink
> thighs rising slowly so you can
> get the whole flavor of it, water
> streaming from the red muff thick
> as bread. That was Sunday.[17]

In this poem, as is almost always the case in Shapiro's work, the powerful sense of immediacy is balanced by a remarkable economy of means and intelligence of arrangement: the stairs, the streets, the shop, the retraced

---

16. http://www.jewishrecipes.org/jewish-foods/farfel.html.
17. *The Sights Along the Harbor,* 221.

route, and the vision of the bath. The moment-to-moment pacing and
the insistent enjambment carry the poem, matching the exuberant sen-
suality, the unapologetic celebration of the appetites.

One of those appetites is satisfied by Russ & Daughters, the renowned
Jewish "appetizing" store in which part of the poem is set. Founded in
1914 and located since 1920 at 179 East Houston Street on the Lower
East Side, Russ & Daughters provides an excellent definition of the type
of food for which Shapiro and the "woman / buying all that sturgeon"
hunger. And as it happens, the company website offers a short Yiddish
lesson:

> "Appetizing," as a noun, is a Jewish food tradition that is most
> typical among American Jews, and it is particularly local to New
> York and New Yorkers. The word "appetizer" is derived from the
> Latin "appete," meaning "to desire, covet, or long for." Used as a
> noun, "appetizing" is most easily understood as "the foods one
> eats with bagels." Its primary components are a variety of smoked
> and cured salmon, homemade salads, and cream cheeses.
>
> Eastern European Jews started meals with cold appetizers,
> known in Yiddish as the "forshpayz." In New York, the popularity
> of forshpayzn among Eastern European Jewish immigrants led to
> the creation of the institution known as the appetizing store.
>
> Appetizing also originated from Jewish dietary laws, which
> dictate that meat and dairy products cannot be eaten or sold
> together. As a result, two different types of stores sprang up in
> order to cater to the Jewish population. Stores selling cured and
> pickled meats became known as delicatessens, while shops that
> sold fish and dairy products became appetizing stores.[18]

Note that no actual Yiddish words, or even the noun "appetizing"
(created, as we have just observed, from a Yiddish word translated into
English, which then becomes a Yiddishism in itself), appear in Shapiro's
poem. Yiddish makes itself felt as a palpable, a *sensual* absence, through
a set of missing signifiers, which nevertheless hover behind the actual
signifiers in the text: first the "black / Russian bread, 3 smoked fish,

18. http://www.russanddaughters.com/whatisappetizing.php.

farmer / cheese (the bulk kind) and nova," and then the transgressive simile, "the red muff thick / as bread. That was Sunday." Sex and farmer cheese, the pleasures of a Lower East Side weekend, are evidence of a particular connoisseurship which extends from the Yiddish-haunted images offered by the poet to the sensibility of a particular audience as well – an audience that would likewise savor what Russ & Daughters (and is it someone's Jewish daughter up those three flights of stairs?) has to offer.

Shapiro's attitude is knowing, ironic, and sometimes self-deprecating; his English is spare, precise, succinct; he is a master of pithy under-statement, the wry turn of phrase, the startling figure of speech. Like his older friend Charles Reznikoff, from whom he learned a great deal, his poems frequently turn on gestures of comic deflation and highly restrained pathos. Both poets spoke Yiddish as children; Shapiro gradually lost his Yiddish, while Reznikoff claimed that his Yiddish was "very bad." As he explains in an interview with Reinhold Schiffer, "my mother's discipline was we should learn English"; his mother also, apparently, would not allow him to study Hebrew in the local cheder, located "in the cellar, or a basement" where "a child who wasn't paying any attention was spanked."[19] As Maeera Shreiber discusses in her study of Jewish American poetry, Reznikoff was actively encouraged by his mother to discard his Yiddish: "Rather than a sentimental attachment to Yiddish (commonly known as the *mame loshen*, the mother tongue), or fostering a love for the transcendent and scholarly Hebrew (the holy tongue), Sarah Reznikoff, an immensely practical woman, insisted that her children lay claim to an unambiguously American identity."[20] The degree to which Reznikoff truly forgets the Yiddish of his childhood remains debatable, but it does not seem to leave any strong stylistic markers in his work.[21]

19. Charles Reznikoff and Reinhold Schiffer, "The Poet in His Milieu," *Charles Reznikoff: Man and Poet*, ed. Milton Hindus (Orono, ME: National Poetry Foundation, 1984), 124.
20. Maeera Y. Shreiber, *Singing in a Strange Land: A Jewish American Poetics* (Stanford, CA: Stanford University Press, 2007), 74.
21. See Stephen Fredman, *A Menorah for Athena: Charles Reznikoff and the Jewish Dilemmas of Objectivist Poetry* (Chicago, IL: University of Chicago Press, 2001), 24.

Reznikoff's linguistic longing, as we shall see in the next chapter, is fixated upon Hebrew, but I suspect that below the surface of his texts one may still detect Yiddish rhythms and inflections, as is probably the case for Shapiro as well. But on the surface, both poets continually address matters of Jewish culture, history, and belief in a meticulously measured (I want to say tailored) English, and thereby play a double game. As we have seen in Shapiro's case, however, they occasionally tip their hands. Here is Reznikoff, from his collection *By the Well of Living and Seeing* (1969):

> When I came for my laundry, I found a shirt missing.
> The laundryman – a Jew – considered the situation:
> "There are four ways of losing a shirt," he said
>   thoughtfully;
> "in the first place, it may never have been delivered by the
>   steam laundry;
> in the second place, it may be lying around here,
>   unpacked;
> in the third place, it may have been delivered and packed
>   in someone else's bundle;
> and in the fourth place it may be really lost.
> Come in again at the end of the week and I'll know what
>   has happened."
> And his wife, recognizing a fellow Jew,
> smiled and spoke up in Yiddish,
> "We won't have to go to the rabbi about it, will we?"[22]

This poem presents Yiddish as a tribal code, spoken ironically by the wife to maintain good relations with a customer. The laundryman, presumably, is speaking perfectly grammatical English, but his interpretation of the problem of the missing shirt is utterly talmudic, as if he were a yeshiva *bucher* (which he may have been in his youth) engaged in *pilpul*. He is identified as a Jew in the

---

As Fredman points out, Reznikoff may actually have "feigned his lack of competence in Yiddish."

22. Charles Reznikoff, *Poems of Charles Reznikoff*, 272.

second line of the poem, but even without such identification, at least part of Reznikoff's readership – the Jewish part – could recognize him from his discourse. Likewise, the wife recognizes the poet as a Jew (and the poet identifies himself as such), addressing him in Yiddish. In short, the entire poem is about identity and recognition in a potentially conflicted social situation, with the utterance of Yiddish at the poem's conclusion serving to confirm group membership. Here, the invocation of Yiddish – but not its actual utterance in the text – functions, to borrow the central concept of Sander Gilman's great work, as a "hidden language of the Jews."[23]

Yiddish, then, may function as a hidden language that returns in a ghostlike, uncanny fashion, even in the texts of those poets who do not fully know Yiddish, have repressed it, or have forgotten it. An awareness of this situation on both conscious and sub-conscious levels leads to the carnivalesque, Yiddish-inflected poems of Jerome Rothenberg's *Poland/1931* (1974). This groundbreaking book by a poet who identifies with various European and American avant-garde movements and makes extensive use of their tactics, is followed some years later by *Khurbn* (1989), Rothenberg's powerful engagement with the Holocaust, which brings Yiddish to bear upon the English verse to an even greater extent. As Rothenberg tells us in the "Postface" of *Triptych*, in which both volumes are reprinted, an important subtext of *Poland/1931*, "coming to surface in my mind, was a running translation into Yiddish – not a real translation but a pretended voicing in which I dreamed of myself as 'the last Yiddish poet.'"[24] This is a fascinating reversal of what we usually understand to be the relation of Yiddish to English in Jewish American literature. Unlike such prose writers as Henry Roth, Bernard Malamud or Saul Bellow, in whose work Yiddish grammar, voicings and lexicon reshape the English from within, Rothenberg writes his poems

---

23. Cf. Sander L. Gilman, *Jewish Self-Hatred: Anti-Semitism and the Hidden Language of the Jews* (Baltimore, MD: Johns Hopkins University Press, 1986).
24. Jerome Rothenberg, *Triptych* (New York: New Directions, 2007), 221.

in English while pretending or imagining that he is writing them in, or at least translating them into, Yiddish. The poet, in effect, is possessed by Yiddish, which functions as a dibbik. Rothenberg, like Reznikoff and Shapiro, spoke Yiddish as a child. As he writes in "Secular Jewish Culture / Radical Poetic Practice,"

> My parents…were avowedly secular, from late adolescence on, but my mother's mother, who lived with us from a month or two before my birth, was an orthodox Jew, though the relationship between her and them was never less than cordial. The outside world – in street and school – were emphatically secular, extending even to the Jewish school where I would go most afternoons for Yiddish lessons.[25]

The link between Yiddish and secular literature was made even stronger, given that both of his parents were avid readers:

> So books and poetry (however defined) were a value for them – Yiddish dominant, although my mother also read novels in English and both of them read English newspapers and magazines as well as Yiddish ones, the latter acting as conduits for recent poetry and fiction. A shelf of books held Yiddish classics, and my father, no longer a believer, continued to read the Bible and various commentaries thereon in both Yiddish and Hebrew. There was also some familiarity with nineteenth-century European fiction – Russian in particular – which they either knew by reputation or had read earlier, I assume, in Yiddish translation.[26]

Thus, in *Poland/1931*, by dreaming his way into an identity of "the last Yiddish poet," Rothenberg comes to terms with his Yiddish heritage – not only his linguistic heritage, but the entire cultural heritage of an imagined Jewish Poland, as if the tales of I.B. Singer were reinscribed by the avant-garde modernists toward whom Rothenberg looks back, such

---

25. Jerome Rothenberg, *Poetics and Polemics 1980–2005* (Tuscaloosa: University of Alabama Press, 2008), 56–57.
26. Jerome Rothenberg, interview with Mark Weiss, *Karaub Online*, http://www.kaurab .com/english/interviews/rothenberg.html.

as Tristan Tzara or Gertrude Stein. In describing his book, Rothenberg is fond of quoting the poet David Meltzer, who long ago called it "a surrealist Yiddish vaudeville."[27] But where exactly, one may ask, is the Yiddish in the book?

My answer would have to be "everywhere and nowhere." What makes *Poland/1931* such an uncanny volume is that almost all of it, as Rothenberg instructs us, must be imagined – and can be heard – as a translation of a Yiddish text that was never written, that never came into being. As Rothenberg tells us, in writing the poems "I was deeply aware of *holocaust* but almost never spoke of it as such, knowing that I had it anyway & that I couldn't dislodge it as a hidden subtext."[28] The ghostly spell of the book is broken only at the end, in the poem "Cokboy," which recounts the phantasmagoric coming of a magical Old World Jew to the American southwest. In this poem, the language of the book is violated by the poet's introduction of a Yiddish accent, indicating not the dream-speech of imaginary Yiddish, but the supposed actual speech of a non-native speaker of English. In his essay "Poets & Tricksters: Innovation & Disruption in Ritual & Myth," Rothenberg identifies Cokboy as a trickster figure, whose name, with its phallic implications, is bound "to strike an English reader as rather aberrant. Also aberrant is the yiddish [*sic*] accent that I use near the opening of the poem – exaggerated and very far from accurate. It is one of several voices I allow myself, the poem shifting unannounced from one voice to another: my own voice (perhaps) as narrator, the voice of a mythopoeic trickster, the voice of a fictitious explorer/conqueror, the voices of ancestral Jews and Indians, and so on."[29] Here are the opening lines of the poem:

> saddlesore I came
> a jew among
> the indians
> vot em I doink in dis strange place

27. *Triptych*, 221.
28. Ibid. For an extended analysis of *Poland/1931*, see *Not One of Them in Place: Modern Poetry and Jewish American Identity* (Albany: State University of New York, 2001), 87–106.
29. *Poetics and Polemics*, 43.

> mit deez pipple mit strange eyes
> could be it's trouble
> could be could be
> (he says) a shadow
> ariseth from his buckwheat
> has tomahawk in hand
> shadow of an axe inside his right eye
> of a fountain pen inside his left
> vot em I doink here
> how vass I lost tzu get here
> am a hundred men
> a hundred fifty different shadows
> jews & gentiles
> who bring the Law to Wilderness...

"Cokboy" is the end of Rothenberg's imaginary journey; it is the point at which the poet as traditional Polish Jew is transplanted into the violence of a modern "America disaster," declaring in the last line "guess I got nothing left to say."[30] Cokboy's Yiddish accent signifies a diminishment of the poet's visionary power, as the ghosts of the language withdraw, leaving him in silence.

When Rothenberg visits the actual Poland in 1987 and writes *Khurbn*, "the overwhelming imagery for me," he relates, "was that of emptiness & silence."[31] In this volume, he is haunted by actual dibbiks of the murdered Jews, which means, naturally, that their native tongue also manifests itself. And indeed, unlike *Poland/1931*, many of the poems in this collection bear titles in both Yiddish and English: "Das Oysleydikn (The Emptying)," "Dos Geshray (The Scream)," and so on. But it is only in the penultimate poem, "Die Toyte Kloles (The Maledictions)" does Rothenberg use Yiddish phrases. The poem, which employs a long anaphoric line in the fashion of Smart, Blake, and Whitman, moves through a long series of horrendous curses, leading at last to this:

30. *Triptych*, 148, 149.
31. Ibid., 223.

Let the dead cry for the destruction of the living until there is
    no more death & no more life
Let a ghost in the field put out the light of the sun (I have no
    arms he cries
My face and half my body have vanished & am I still alive?
But the movement of my soul through space & time brings me
    inside you
The immeasurable part of a language is what we speak he says
    who am I? dayn mamas bruder farshvunden in dem khurbn
    un muz in myn eygenem loshn redn loz mikh es redn durkh
    dir dos vort khurbn
Mayne oygen zaynen blind fun mayn khurbn ich bin yetst a
    peyger
Let the light be lost & the voices cry forever in the dark & let
    them know no joy
in it…
Let ghosts & dibbiks overwhelm the living
Let the invisible overwhelm the visible until nothing more is
    seen or heard[32]

Rothenberg translates the Yiddish in a note at the bottom of the poem. The speaker is his uncle, who had joined the partisans but killed himself when he learned that his wife and children had been murdered at Treblinka. In a moment of extreme rage and sorrow, the dead uncle possesses the poet, causing him to speak in ghostly *mamaloshen*: "your mother's brother vanished in the khurbn and must speak in my own tongue let me speak it through you the word khurbn // My eyes are blind from my khurbn I am now a corpse."[33] In contrast to *Poland/1931*, in which a Yiddish accent signifies powerlessness and silence, the uncanny visitation of the Yiddish-speaking dibbik in *Khurbn* signifies a reassertion of spiritual power, of the continued life of the seemingly annihilated past.

    I would like to conclude this chapter with a brief mention of my

32. Ibid., 187–88.
33. Ibid., 188.

own ghostly relation to Yiddish, which makes its way into my work in relation to the *heymish* and, I admit, the sentimental – keeping in mind, as Freud tells us, that every invocation of the *heymish* (in German, *heimlich*), the *canny*, is an invocation of the *uncanny* as well.[34] As has been the case throughout this chapter, we are considering what is dead but still living. An elegy for my father, for instance, is called "My Father's Yahrzeit," though every time I look back at it, I wonder if it concerns my own father or the Father whom Nietzsche pronounces dead. A section of "Passing Over," my poem based on the Haggadah, includes a verse from a Hasidic song about Moshiach, which I learned, not in my childhood, but from the Klezmatics' album *Rhythm and Jews* (1990). Yiddish words and grammatical inflections also appear in my unruly book of poems called, appropriately, *Inside the Ghost Factory*, where they become, practically, a secret code. Here is the poem "Disputation"; the title refers to the staged debates over the messianic status of Jesus held during the Middle Ages between rabbis and Christian churchmen, during which the Jews were often constrained for political reasons from fully and successfully arguing their position:

> *Let it be gathered, let it be folded.* What do
> the doves say? I don't know;
> I don't speak the language. All I do

34. As Freud observes, "among its different shades of meaning the word '*heimlich*' exhibits one which is identical with its opposite, '*unheimlich.*' What is *heimlich* thus comes to be *unheimlich*...In general we are reminded that the word '*heimlich*' is not unambiguous, but belongs to two sets of ideas, which, without being contradictory, are yet very different: on the one hand it means what is familiar and agreeable, and on the other, what is concealed and kept out of sight." Sigmund Freud, "The 'Uncanny,'" trans. James Strachey, *The Standard Edition of the Complete Psychological Works of Sigmund Freud*, Volume XVII (London: The Hogarth Press, 1955), 224. See also Nicholas Royle, *The Uncanny* (Manchester, UK: Manchester University Press, 2003), especially Chapter 1, which provides a magisterial anatomy and genealogy of the concept. Royle points out that, "As Freud's essay shows...the uncanny is – even (or especially) if *inter alia* – an experience of writing. And conversely, of reading. One tries to keep oneself out, but one cannot. One tries to put oneself in: same result. The uncanny is an experience of being *after oneself*..." (16). The same could be said of Yiddish in Jewish American literature.

is listen. It's all I've ever done.
Con artists and magicians, rabbis,
saints, beggars, and all the little

contraptions found on the stairs.
No fixed address. Yes, because it's
broken and cannot be mended. Schuster,

it speaks but not to you. Schuster,
this is a tree, this is a house, this is
the wind. Thump, thump. He speaks

Yiddish but with an Italian accent, or
vice versa efsher. What do the
stars say? This I know, they say

we're not speaking to you, we never
really liked you. They say forget it,
we are at bloody war, the welkin

is weeping and will keep on weeping.
Tom said so, and he's one of yours,
whether you like it or not. You do?

You think you can handle it? Then here
is the score. Not that messiah – this one.[35]

Efsher: maybe: Yiddish, but also Hebrew. Everything in the poem exists
in a state of uncertainty, indeterminacy, in between languages, beliefs,

---

35. Norman Finkelstein, *Inside the Ghost Factory* (East Rockaway, NY: Marsh Hawk
Press, 2010), 37. I would have to say that this poem is a highly *performative* instance
of postvernacular Yiddish in the sense that both Bachman and Shandler use the term.
See, especially, Bachman, 174–80.

cultures, worlds. To be sure, every Yiddish reference or gesture in my work is an instance of postvernacularity. But *efsher* it is more accurate to say, quite simply, that my work is haunted by ghosts of Yiddish.

THREE

Charles Reznikoff: Modernism, Diaspora, and the Problem of Jewish Identity

Introduction

Although largely neglected during his lifetime, Charles Reznikoff (1894–1976) has come to be regarded not only as one of the most important of the American modernist poets, but as a writer who embodies many of the most significant – and contradictory – qualities of Jewish-American literature. Reznikoff's participation during the 1930s in the short-lived but extremely influential group of poets known as the Objectivists is crucial to our understanding of his poetic. The Objectivist credo, as seen not only in Reznikoff, but in his colleagues, Louis Zukofsky (1904–1978) and George Oppen (1908–1984), emphasizes clarity of sight, immediacy of perception, precise verbal articulation, the significance of mundane experience, and above all, sincerity of utterance based on careful, detailed, personal witness.[1] But equally important to Reznikoff's poetry

---

1. The secondary material on the Objectivists is by now voluminous and extends over many years. Recent studies have tended to focus on individual poets in the movement, but for an excellent overview, see Mark Scroggins, "Objectivist Poets," in *A History of Modernist Poetry*, ed. Alex Davis and Lee M. Jenkins (New York: Cambridge University Press, 2015), 381–97. The most important single gathering of criticism is *The Objectivist Nexus: Essays in Cultural Poetics*, ed. Rachel Blau DuPlessis and Peter Quartermain (Tuscaloosa: University of Alabama Press, 1999). An early but still important study is Michael Heller, *Conviction's Net of Branches: Essays on the Objectivist Poets and Poetry*

is his career-long obsession with Jewish history and textuality, from the biblical period up until the Holocaust, which leads him to return to this subject in nearly every one of his books, despite what may be described as his fundamentally secular sensibility and lifestyle. As the poet and critic Michael Heller puts it in his essay "Remains of the Diaspora," thinking in particular of modern Jewish poets like Reznikoff, "The secular poet of the diaspora might well sense that meaning comes to him not from any unitary direction, but surrounds and even overwhelms him, and mostly comes to him 'through' other texts, entrained by other meanings and surfacings."[2] Because "the secular poet of the diaspora" is unable to find any "unitary" meaning (as in religious observance or halakhah), a dispersed, equally diasporic experience of historicity and textuality brings about an existential and literary condition of radical openness to discourse, or what Harold Bloom names "wandering meaning."[3] This decentered condition is congruent to what Yosef Hayim Yerushalmi identifies as "the modern effort to reconstruct the Jewish past, [which] begins at a time that witnesses a sharp break in the continuity of Jewish living and hence also an ever-growing decay of Jewish group memory.

(Carbondale: Southern Illinois University Press, 1985). In regard to Reznikoff, see Milton Hindus, ed., *Charles Reznikoff: Man and Poet* (Orono, ME: National Poetry Foundation, 1984); Fredman, *A Menorah for Athena: Charles Reznikoff and the Jewish Dilemmas of Objectivist Poetry*; Ranen Omer-Sherman, *Diaspora and Zionism in Jewish-American Literature* (Hanover, NH: Brandeis University Press / University Press of New England, 2002); and Shreiber, *Singing in a Strange Land*. My own work on Reznikoff, which serves as the foundation for the present essay, includes "Tradition and Modernity, Judaism and Objectivism: The Poetry of Charles Reznikoff" (*The Objectivist Nexus* 191–209) and *Not One of Them in Place: Modern Poetry and Jewish American Identity* (Albany: State University of New York Press, 2001).

2. Michael Heller, "Remains of the Diaspora: A Personal Meditation," in *Radical Jewish Poetics and Secular Jewish Culture*), 179.

3. "The wandering people has taught itself and others the lesson of wandering meaning, a wandering that has compelled a multitude of changes in the modes of interpretation available to the West." Harold Bloom, "Introduction," in Olivier Revault D'Allonnes, *Musical Variations on Jewish Thought* (New York: George Braziller, 1984), 6. For extensive considerations of this idea in relation to various American and continental figures, including Bloom himself, see Norman Finkelstein, *The Ritual of New Creation: Jewish Tradition and Contemporary Literature* (Albany: State University of New York Press, 1992).

In this sense, if for no other, history becomes what it had never been before – the faith of fallen Jews. For the first time history, not a sacred text, becomes the arbiter of Judaism."[4]

Reznikoff's faith, if we can use that term – and even more importantly, Reznikoff's poetic – while having some of their deepest roots in the tradition of biblical prophecy, are, as we shall see, thoroughly modern. And insofar as the Jewish experience of modernity is in some respects a reflection of the crisis of modernity itself, it is not only fallen Jews for whom history has become faith: it is the faith of all who have fallen, that is, who have experienced the ruptures of modernity. But history, unlike religion, is not an entity in which one can place faith. Whether one claims to have religious faith or not, in the modern period we are all compelled to "believe" in history, for history imposes itself on ordinary lives with unanticipated shock and unprecedented violence. It may be that Jews like Reznikoff understand this sooner and more deeply than most, so in this respect Reznikoff is "prophetic" indeed. But to be more exact, when history replaces the sacred text, *testimony*, as the Objectivists understand it, replaces prophecy. It is from this intuition that much of Reznikoff's greatest poetry comes.

The son of impoverished Russian-Jewish immigrants, Reznikoff, whose first language was Yiddish, grew up in a relatively observant home but came to feel increasingly distant from traditional religious and cultural practices.[5] Throughout his work, he frequently attests to the suffering and guilt that accompanied what he experienced, in spite of himself, as a serious loss. The love of English poetry that he developed as a teenager led him to the work of the first generation of modernists; rejecting the romanticism and symbolism of nineteenth-century poetry, he embraced the poetic innovations that came to be gathered under the rubric of Imagism and, like the other Objectivists, was strongly influenced by poets such as Ezra Pound, T.S. Eliot, and William Carlos

4. Yosef Hayim Yerushalmi, *Zakhor: Jewish History and Jewish Memory* (Seattle: University of Washington Press, 1982), 86.
5. At present, there is no full-length biography of Reznikoff. Biographical sketches and memoirs include a detailed "Chronology" in *Poems of Charles Reznikoff*, 381–92; Milton Hindus, *Charles Reznikoff: A Critical Essay* (Santa Barbara, CA: Black Sparrow Press, 1977); and various chapters in Hindus, *Charles Reznikoff: Man and Poet*.

Williams. He published most of his early books himself, printing a number of them on a letter press which he kept in his father's basement in Brooklyn. Trained as both a journalist and an attorney, he never practiced law, and got by much of the time writing for a legal encyclopedia (he was fired), doing freelance research and writing, and later working as an editor for various Jewish magazines (he hated journalism), virtually the only ones which would publish his poetry. Married in 1930 to Marie Syrkin, daughter of Nachman Syrkin and one of the foremost American Zionists of her generation, Reznikoff chose to remain in New York City while Syrkin taught for years at Brandeis; his work celebrating (but also critically scrutinizing) both urban life in America and the Jewish world of the diaspora may be read as an implicit but firm repudiation of the Zionist vision – to use the term that Michael Heller applies to all of the Objectivists, it is a prime instance of "Diasporic poetics." Ranen Omer-Sherman, who reads Reznikoff through the lens of "Diasporism," sums up the position neatly: "Above all, his poetry and prose argues for a history of cultural choices rather than an organic unfolding of a single cultural impulse – which was essentially his reason for rejecting Zionism as well."[6]

In this chapter, what I will do, essentially, is use the crucial, overlapping historical, philosophical and literary notions I have just introduced in order to open Reznikoff's Objectivist poetry and poetics (and to some extent, his exemplary Jewish-American life story). In doing so, I will address the great complexities and contradictions in the work of a poet for whom, as Charles Bernstein puts it, Jewishness is to be understood as "an inhering possibility for poetry and its testimony as engaged witness that *changes* – intervenes in – what it witnesses by its care in and for the world/word."[7] As we shall see, Reznikoff's pervasive concern with testimony, witness, and care for the world and the word, aligns him, however obliquely, with the traditions of Jewish prophecy

6. Omer-Sherman, 140.
7. Charles Bernstein, "Reznikoff's Nearness," in *The Objectivist Nexus*, 237. Bernstein's essay brilliantly presents the formal innovations of Reznikoff's poetry, what Bernstein calls his "cubo-seriality" (222), in terms of both broader trends in modernist poetics and the poet's Jewish identity.

and psalm, and with their reconceptualization in the poetic traditions of Britain and America. The prophetic tendency in Reznikoff's work makes sense, of course, given his equal identification with both the Anglo-American poetic tradition and with Jewish history and culture. Yet despite the calm, measured tone we hear so often in Reznikoff's poems, the psychic and cultural tensions in his work are palpable. L.S. Dembo, one of Reznikoff's earliest academic critics, understands these tensions when he writes of the poet that "Being himself... really meant not just a Jew or just an American but both and neither. When he wrote Objectivist poems he was an Objectivist; when he wrote of 'his people' he was, in a manner of speaking, a psalmist... An exile, he sits down by the waters of Manhattan to weep; a wry smile comes over his face, for he realizes that he is home. And then he really weeps."[8]

If we move from a sociological to a philosophical or theological register, the tensions and contradictions which so many of Reznikoff's readers have identified may be understood, as Walter Benjamin would say, as dialectical counterforces of the sacred and the profane. "Just as a force can, through acting, increase another that is acting in the opposite direction," writes Benjamin, "so the order of the profane assists, through being profane, the coming of the Messianic Kingdom. The profane, therefore, although not in itself a category of this Kingdom, is a decisive category of its quietest approach."[9] To attend to Reznikoff's poetry deeply – for like the poet himself, the reader must become a witness to the world's

8. L.S. Dembo, *The Monological Jew* (Madison: University of Wisconsin Press, 1988), 129. Dembo uses the term "psalmist" rather loosely, though it is true that in one of Reznikoff's finest volumes, *Jerusalem the Golden* (1934), the poet's persona is strongly identified with the figure of King David. However, I still prefer to apply the term "prophetic" to much of Reznikoff's Jewish poems, for reasons I will explain below, though the lyric impulse in his poems may well be identified with a psalmic voice too.

9. Walter Benjamin, *Reflections*, trans. Edmund Jephcott (New York: Schocken Books, 1986), 312. My understanding of such concepts, especially in relation to the Objectivist poets, is tremendously enriched by the critical essays of Michael Heller, who has read deeply in Benjamin and applies his ideas to the Objectivists (and in his own extraordinary poetry) on numerous occasions. See, for instance, such essays as "Diasporic Poetics," "Avant-garde Propellants of the Machine Made of Words," and "Aspects of Poetics," in *Uncertain Poetics: Selected Essays on Poets, Poetry and Poetics* (Cambridge, UK: Salt Publishing, 2005).

utterance through the word of poem – is to accept the Jewish insistence on the ongoing possibility of redemption, "the coming of the Messianic Kingdom," posed against a profane sense of contingent historicity. If we listen closely enough to Reznikoff, if we pay close attention to the everyday noise of his urban milieu, we may indeed discover Benjamin's decisive category, what he calls the quietest approach of the Messianic Kingdom. Reading the work, we discover that this religious impetus is reconfigured through a poetic sensibility that is rational, modern, and secular, yet still irreducibly Jewish. The Jewish prophetic tradition and its attendant messianic vision form an essential but highly volatile fold in Reznikoff's poetic sensibility – not because of any conventional religious belief on his part, but because of his fundamentally *historical* consciousness.

Reznikoff the Objectivist

Before exploring the relationship of Objectivist poetry and Jewish identity, history, and textuality in Reznikoff's work, I will present, from Reznikoff's perspective, a summary of what might be called "the Objectivist moment" in American literary history. Born in 1894, Reznikoff was at least ten years older than the other Objectivists, and about ten years or more younger than the first, breakthrough generation of modernists, such as Pound, Williams, Wallace Stevens, and H.D. (Hilda Doolittle). In a retrospective piece called "Obiter Dicta," Reznikoff writes about his initial experiences with writing verse and encountering poetic modernism. His explanation is worth quoting at length:

> ... when I grew older, twenty-one or so, I grew tired of regular meters and stanzas: they had become a little stale; the smooth lines and the rhymes I used to read with pleasure now seemed affected, a false stress on words and syllables. And yet I found prose unsatisfactory, too: without the burst of song and the sudden dancing, without the intensity that I wanted. I wanted to be brief and emphatic, as it seemed to me I could be best in verse.
>
> The brand-new verse some American poets were beginning to write, Ezra Pound and H.D. (Hilda Doolittle) for example, with sources in the French free verse other poets had been writing, as

well as in the irregular rhythms of Walt Whitman, perhaps in the King James translation of the Hebrew Bible, and perhaps too in the rough rhythm of Anglo-Saxon verse, seemed to me, when I first read it, just right: not cut to patterns, however cleverly, nor poured into ready molds, but words and phrases flowing as the thought; to be read just like common speech but for stopping at the end of each line – and this like a rest in music or a turn in the dance.[10]

In this passage (although he does not mention it specifically), Reznikoff is responding to the three principles of the "Imagist Manifesto," a crucial document of the movement, famously inscribed by Ezra Pound:

> In the spring or early summer of 1912, 'H.D.', Richard Aldington and myself decided that we agreed upon the three principles following:
> 1. Direct treatment of the "thing" whether subjective or objective.
> 2. To use absolutely no word that does not contribute to the presentation.
> 3. As regarding rhythm: to compose in the sequence of the musical phrase, not in the sequence of a metronome.[11]

Although Imagism as a movement soon splinters amongst various groups of poets, and comes to be regarded as passé, these fundamental principles are to have a lasting impact well beyond the vicissitudes of contemporary social formations. To be sure, they shape Reznikoff's practice from the beginning. When he starts submitting his poems to literary magazines in 1917, it is no accident that he sends work to Harriet Monroe, the founding editor of *Poetry*, one of the most important venues for this new poetry (she accepts three but he withdraws them before they appear). The following year, his first chapbook of poems, *Rhythms*, is privately

---

10. *Poems of Charles Reznikoff*, 371. This passage appears nearly word for word, set as verse, in Reznikoff's long autobiographical poem "Early History of a Writer," *Poems*, 328–29. It would appear then that Reznikoff wants this to be the "official" account of his initiation into modernist poetry.

11. Ezra Pound, "A Retrospect," in *Literary Essays of Ezra Pound* (New York: New Directions, 1935), 3.

published, and he will continue to produce small, mostly self-published volumes through the twenties. But it is in the *Menorah Journal* that his work appears most regularly, and it is at "one of the almost-weekly dinners of the *Menorah* group [that] Reznikoff meets the poet and critic Louis Zukofsky, ten years his junior and an ardent admirer of his work."[12]

Zukofsky, seeking entrée into the pages of the *Menorah Journal*, writes an essay on Reznikoff's poetry which is rejected by Elliot Cohen, the *Journal*'s editor. Zukofsky, however, has already found another mentor, whose support takes him and his essay in a distinctly different direction. That mentor is Ezra Pound, living in Rapallo, Italy, who, despite his increasing antisemitism, enthusiastically supports Zukofsky's poetry and comes to regard him almost as a son.[13] Pound arranges with Harriet Monroe for Zukofsky to guest-edit the February 1931 issue of *Poetry* – but only on the condition that the issue represent a new "movement" in poetry. Hence the Objectivist issue of *Poetry*, which includes Zukofsky's "Program: 'Objectivists' 1931," and a version of the essay originally intended for the *Menorah Journal*, now titled "Sincerity and Objectification: *With Special Reference to the Work of Charles Reznikoff*."[14] The latter presents, in addition to a good deal of close analysis of individual Reznikoff poems, what has become the single most important formulation of the Objectivist credo:

---

12. "Chronology," 385. The tremendous importance of the Menorah Association and the *Menorah Journal* in Reznikoff's career is beyond the scope of this essay, and is central to Fredman's reading of Reznikoff in *A Menorah for Athena*. See also Daniel Greene, *The Jewish Origins of Cultural Pluralism: The Menorah Association and American Diversity* (Bloomington: Indiana University Press, 2011). The *Menorah Journal* ran from 1915 to 1962; for a retrospective, see Robert Alter, "Epitaph for a Jewish Magazine," *Commentary*, 39, no. 5 (1965): 51–55.

13. The friendship of Pound and Zukofsky is one of the most problematic in modern American letters, as seen from their deeply unsettling correspondence. See *Pound/Zukofsky: Selected Letters of Ezra Pound and Louis Zukofsky*, ed. Barry Ahearn (New York: New Directions, 1987). For interpretations of the relationship, including its impact on Reznikoff's career, see *Not One of Them in Place*, 40–46; Fredman, 127–32; and Mark Scroggins, *Louis Zukofsky and the Poetry of Knowledge* (Tuscaloosa: University of Alabama Press, 1998), 134–35.

14. The entirety of this issue is available online at https://www.poetryfoundation.org /poetrymagazine/issue/70538/february-1931 – toc

In sincerity shapes appear concomitants of word combinations, precursors of (if there is continuance) completed sound or structure, melody or form. Writing occurs which is the detail, not mirage, of seeing, of thinking with the things as they exist, and of directing them along a line of melody. Shapes suggest themselves, and the mind senses and receives awareness...

Presented with sincerity, the mind even tends to supply, in further suggestion which does not attain rested totality, the totality not always found in sincerity and necessary only for perfect rest, complete appreciation. The rested totality may be called objectification – the apprehension satisfied completely as to the appearance of the art form as an object.[15]

Zukofsky's complicated and abstract formulation, derived, ironically, from Reznikoff's precise, carefully detailed, and unfailingly direct poems, has produced decades of nearly talmudic discussion (Stephen Fredman calls it "the Jewish language magic of Objectivist poetry"); Reznikoff himself, upon reading it, is bemused.[16] Keeping in mind, however, that Reznikoff's poetry represents an Objectivist ideal to the theoretically-minded Zukofsky, here is a poem by Reznikoff that Zukofsky cites in his essay:

> She sat by the window opening into the airshaft,
> And looked across the parapet
> At the new moon.
>
> She would have taken the hairpins out of her carefully coiled
>   hair,
> And thrown herself on the bed in tears;
> But he was coming and her mouth had to be pinned into a
>   smile.

15. Louis Zukofsky, *Prepositions+: The Collected Critical Essays*, ed. Mark Scroggins (Hanover, NH: Wesleyan University Press / University Press of New England, 2000), 194.
16. See Fredman, 134–43, for a highly nuanced discussion of Zukofsky's terms in relation to both his and Reznikoff's Jewishness.

If he would have her, she would marry whatever he was.
She who, slim and gentle once, would soon become clumsy,
   talking harshly.

A knock. She lit the gas and opened her door.
Her aunt and the man – skin loose under his eyes, the face
   slashed with wrinkles.
"Come in," she said as gently as she could and smiled.

Of the "tension of tragedy" in this poem, Zukofsky remarks that
"The total rhythm has been lulled to emphasize each word's particular
hush, with the result that objectification, inevitably recognized as the
complete satisfaction derived from melody in a poem, is missed. Yet
the lives of Reznikoff's people slowly occur in the sincerity of the craft
with which he has chosen to subdue them. One returns in the end not
to the aging girl at the window, nor to 'her aunt and the man', but to the
sincerity which has seen, considered, and weighed the tone these things
have when rendered, in only necessary words."[17] In other words, not
quite the "rested totality" of objectification, but very close, derived from
the "sincerity" of the poem's relation to its subject matter. That subject
matter – "Reznikoff's people" – are, as it happens, very much Zukofsky's
people too: Yiddish-speaking Jewish immigrants from eastern Europe
living mainly on Manhattan's Lower East Side, and their rapidly assimi-
lating American-born children. With Reznikoff's poetry placed front and
center in Zukofsky's essay, the distinctly Jewish American dimension of
Objectivist poetry unabashedly asserts itself.

   As Zukofsky's formulations imply, there is a connection between

17. *Prepositions+*, 199–200. This untitled poem, number 11 from *Poems* (1920), continues
   to attract the attention of poets, marking it as a crucial instance of Reznikoff's early
   formal achievement. In a recorded session of a class on Reznikoff taught by Allen
   Ginsberg at the Naropa Institute in Boulder, Colorado, in the seventies, Ginsberg
   observes "that is one of the great narrative poems of the 20th century...a complete
   lifetime, a complete moral lifetime, complete emotional growth indicated...You can
   condense whole cycles of generations into five or six lines that tell a complete story
   of the development of character and are a complete presentation of an economic,
   social, living situation..." Allen Ginsberg, "Reznikoff's Poetics," *Charles Reznikoff:
   Man and Poet*, 140.

Reznikoff's Objectivist method and his Jewish immigrant subject matter. In the poem, we see a totalizing procedure: the sincerity of the poet giving his testimony results in the objectification of emotion through the precision of the images and the careful choice of detail in a miniaturized narrative. Not only is the episode recounted in the poem treated with dignity and restraint, it inevitably raises the moral questions that are embedded in the narrative but never stated outright. This is arguably a development out of Imagism but also a crucial step beyond it. As the poet Robert Hass puts it in an essay on George Oppen,

> The great discovery of the objectivist poets . . . was that what was really going on at the level of prosody was not a presentation of the image as a picture but an analysis of the constitutive elements of the image as it is being presented. As soon as they found ways to render this subtle shift in emphasis, it became clear that an image is not a picture of a thing, but a picture of a mind perceiving a thing. And as soon as it became the picture of the mind perceiving the thing, then the morality of perception came to be an issue.[18]

Despite such important poetic innovations, the momentum of Objectivist poetry in the thirties proved to be short-lived. In 1932, George Oppen (who comes from a very wealthy and much more assimilated German Jewish family with roots on both coasts) and his wife Mary, while living in France, started the publishing house To Press, with Zukofsky as editor. They published An "Objectivist" Anthology, an expanded version of the February 1931 issue of Poetry. When the Oppens returned from France the following year, they joined with Zukofsky and Reznikoff to form the Objectivist Press, a venture that will last until 1936; among the most significant books they published were Oppen's first collection, Discrete Series (1934), William Carlos Williams' Collected Poems: 1921–1931 (1934), and four books by Reznikoff: the first version of his long serial poem Testimony (1934), Jerusalem the Golden (1934), In Memoriam: 1933 (1934), and Separate Way (1936).

---

18. Robert Hass, *What Light Can Do: Essays on Art, Imagination, and the Natural World* (New York: HarperCollins Publishers, 2012), 56.

Unfortunately, *Separate Way* proves appropriately titled, for it was the last book that the Objectivist Press released. With the United States in a period of political and economic crisis, George and Mary Oppen made the momentous decision that shaped the remainder of their lives: they severed their ties with their artistic friends, deliberately stopped practicing their art (Mary was a painter and writer), and became active members in the Communist Party USA. George did not return to writing poetry until the late fifties. Zukofsky, at first strongly influenced by Marxism and a CP "fellow traveler," did not join the Party, and as he worked for many years on his epic poem *"A"*, gradually drifted away from his early leftism, becoming, in terms of both his writing and his life, increasingly hermetic. From 1947 until his retirement in 1966, he taught English to engineering students at Brooklyn Polytechnic Institute. Along with his wife Celia, with whom he occasionally collaborated, he became deeply involved in the career of his son Paul, a violin prodigy. As for Reznikoff's politics, although sympathetic to the left in the thirties, he maintained what could be called a liberal political perspective. Yet *Testimony*, based on court records from the late nineteenth through the early twentieth centuries and written over the course of at least thirty years, may be read as a scathing indictment of systemic American injustice, violence, racism, and worker exploitation. Continuing to labor steadily on his poetry and prose, Reznikoff, irregularly employed and living modestly in Manhattan, periodically published his poems in Jewish magazines and his books in small editions, either privately or through little presses, but remained largely obscure until well into the sixties.

As Mark Scroggins observes, "Far more remarkable than the Objectivists' brief moment of collective activity in the early 1930s was their return to public prominence thirty years later."[19] Oppen, returning from exile in Mexico, where he and his family had fled in 1950 rather than being forced to give testimony to the House Un-American Activities Committee, resumed writing, eventually producing one of the greatest bodies of post-war American poetry. His sister, June Oppen Degnan, editing the *San Francisco Review*, entered into a collaboration with James Laughlin's famous New Directions Publishing, leading to the publication of Oppen's

19. Scroggins, "Objectivist Poets," 388.

The Materials (1962) and Reznikoff's *By the Waters of Manhattan: Selected Verse* (1962) and *Testimony: The United States 1885–1890: Recitative* (1965). In 1968, the literary critic L.S. Dembo invited Reznikoff, Zukofsky, Oppen, and Carl Rakosi, another important Objectivist from the original issue of *Poetry* who had recently returned to writing, to a symposium at the University of Wisconsin. When this plan proved unfeasible, Dembo interviewed each of them separately, leading to the publication of "The 'Objectivist' Poet: Four Interviews" in *Contemporary Literature* (not surprisingly, when asked to define "Objectivist," there is little consensus among the four poets).[20] Most importantly, younger generations of poets became aware of the Objectivists, read them intently, and variously assimilated Objectivist poetics to their new work. Reznikoff was championed by such writers as Allen Ginsberg, Robert Creeley, Harvey Shapiro, David Ignatow, Paul Auster, and Michael Heller. In 1973, John Martin of Black Sparrow Press entered into an agreement with Reznikoff leading to the eventual publication of nearly his complete works. He gave retrospective readings of his poetry at the 92nd Street Y, the Poetry Center at San Francisco State University, at SUNY-Buffalo, and at the National Poetry Festival.[21] On January 21, 1976, shortly before suffering the massive heart attack that killed him, he told Marie Syrkin "with a sweetness and serenity not usual for him, 'You know, I never made money but I have done everything I most wanted to do.'"[22] On his tombstone is inscribed "Charles Reznikoff, Maker, 1894–1976" ("maker" being the archaic English term for "poet"), and a line from his poem "Heart and Clock": "and the day's brightness dwindles into stars."[23]

Multilingual Awareness and Primal Scenes

In his interview with L.S. Dembo, Reznikoff proposes this definition of an Objectivist writer: one "who does not write directly about his

20. L.S. Dembo, "The 'Objectivist' Poet: Four Interviews," *Contemporary Literature* 10, no. 2 (Spring 1969): 155–311.
21. Recordings of these events may be found on the Reznikoff page of Penn Sound, the online archive of modern poetry, http://writing.upenn.edu/pennsound/x/Reznikoff.php.
22. Marie Syrkin, "Charles: A Memoir," in *Charles Reznikoff: Man and Poet*, 65.
23. *Poems of Charles Reznikoff*, 153.

feelings but about what he sees and hears; who is restricted almost to the testimony of a witness in a court of law; and who expresses his feelings indirectly by the selection of his subject matter and, if he writes in verse, by its music." He also quotes from the introduction to an anthology of ancient Chinese verse: "Poetry should be precise about the thing and reticent about the feeling."[24] As for the "music" of the verse itself, he notes in "Obiter Dicta," "Clarity, precision, order, but the answer is intensity: with intensity we have compression, rhythm, maybe rhyme, maybe alliteration. The words move out of prose into verse as the speech becomes passionate and musical instead of flat."[25] This reticent and austere position, derived, as we have seen, from Imagism, is intended to achieve a linguistic and formal purity, or what Zukofsky would call a "rested totality." Stylistically, it results in a highly refined, deliberately phrased American English – produced by a writer whose first language (as is true of Zukofsky) is not English at all, but, as discussed in the previous chapter, Yiddish. Stephen Fredman, after analyzing Reznikoff's methods for achieving the purity of his style, asserts that "Although the poems are written in idiomatic English, their language appears to be bulging at the seams with an unaccustomed weight, as though there were Hebrew words confined within."[26]

How is this the case? Reznikoff is an instance of a first-generation Jewish-American writer who, to return briefly to Hana Wirth-Nesher's argument, demonstrates intense "multilingual awareness."[27] Let us recall that as Wirth-Nesher puts it, "for many Jewish American writers subsequent to the immigrant generation, Hebrew and Yiddish are sources of self-expression and identity even if the authors cannot 'remember' them in the sense of ever having possessed them as a means of communication.... Their remembering, therefore, is not the result of an essential Jewishness that hearkens back to some racial memory but the result of socialization where practices, expectations, and assumptions about the

24. Charles Reznikoff, "A Talk with L.S. Dembo," in *Charles Reznikoff: Man and Poet*, 98–99, 97.
25. *Poems of Charles Reznikoff*, 373.
26. Fredman, 30–31.
27. Wirth-Nesher, 3.

entanglement of language and identity linger in their consciousness."[28] Though he is kept largely ignorant of the language while growing up (his mother kept him from studying at the neighborhood *cheder*), Reznikoff actively studies Hebrew as an adult. In his interview with Schiffer, he says that "I began to pick it up when I was in my twenties," while in his interview with L.S. Dembo, he claims that "No, I wasn't taught Hebrew, you see, as children frequently are, and I began picking it up in my thirties."[29] In her memoir of Reznikoff, Marie Syrkin recalls that "Each evening he read a few pages of the Old Testament in the original Hebrew and in two translations, English and Luther's German."[30]

As we can see, Reznikoff tends to return to certain family events and personal memories which have shaped his relationship to language, to poetic vocation, and to Jewish identity. These episodes invariably weave together issues of kinship with matters of linguistic knowledge, difference and performance, frequently combined with the threat of antisemitism or the guilt of assimilation. Fredman calls one such instance "the primal scene of poetry for Charles Reznikoff": the family story of Reznikoff's maternal grandfather Ezekiel, a sales agent in Russia who died of influenza away from home years before Reznikoff was born. Ezekiel wrote poetry in Hebrew, but all his work was burned after his death by his wife, for fear that it would lead the authorities to suspect the family of "nihilism." As Fredman observes, it is a story that is "related by Reznikoff obsessively in interviews and in family histories he wrote in prose and verse."[31] For the American-born Reznikoff, who is named for this grandfather (in Hebrew, but not, significantly, in English), the story of the lost ancestral poetry serves as a rationale for his life-long habit of self-publication when no other outlet for his work was available.[32]

Let us consider another of these poetic "primal scenes." It too involves a grandfather, in this case the paternal grandfather, a Hebrew teacher

---

28. Ibid, 5.
29. "The Poet in His Milieu," 121; "A Talk with L.S. Dembo," 104.
30. Syrkin, 59.
31. Fredman, 41.
32. Fredman also analyzes the story of Reznikoff's names. When he is born, he is about to be named Chezkel, for his grandfather Ezekiel, but the attending physician, an assimilated German Jew, urges the family to "Call him Charles." Fredman, 13–18.

who had immigrated to the United States and whom Reznikoff knew as
a child. Reznikoff recounts the anecdote in his autobiographical "Early
History of a Writer" (1969):

I went to my grandfather's to say good-bye:
I was going away to school out West.
As I came in,
my grandfather turned from the window at which he sat
(sick, skin yellow, eyes bleary –
but his hair still dark,
for my grandfather had hardly any grey hair in his beard or on
    his head –
he would sit at the window, reading a Hebrew book).
He rose with difficulty –
he had been expecting me, it seemed –
stretched out his hands and blessed me in a loud voice:
in Hebrew, of course,
and I did not know what he was saying.
When he had blessed me,
my grandfather turned aside and burst into tears.
"It is only for a little while, Grandpa," I said
in my broken Yiddish. "I'll be back in June."
(By June my grandfather was dead.)
He did not answer.
Perhaps my grandfather was in tears for other reasons:
perhaps, because, in spite of all the learning I had acquired in
    high school,
I knew not a word of the sacred text of the Torah
and was going out into the world
with none of the accumulated wisdom of my people to guide
    me,
with no prayers with which to talk to the God of my people,
a soul –
for it is not easy to be a Jew or, perhaps, a man –
doomed by his ignorance to stumble and blunder.[33]

33. *Poems of Charles Reznikoff*, 323–24.

This extraordinary poem is often discussed in terms of religious and linguistic rupture, loss, and compensation. Obviously, the break in the generational process of scriptural education and cultural transmission is a source of chagrin and wrenching sorrow for both grandfather and grandson, compounded by the boy's departure to further his secular education. The ensuing death of the already ill grandfather, reported in hindsight by a flat parenthetical comment, heightens the pathos. In his reading of the poem, Fredman argues that "Eschewing religious purity, Reznikoff achieves a compensatory purity by poetic means: through scrupulous technique, simple diction, and the investment of emotion in the choice of subject matter rather than in 'self-expression.'"[34] Along similar lines, Milton Hindus, after quoting from the poem, suggests that "Reznikoff's study of the law of the United States seems to have become for him a substitute for the Jewish patrimony of knowledge of the sacred law which he had rejected when he was too young."[35]

What is surprising about these responses is that neither critic connects the dismay of both grandfather and grandson over the boy's failure to have acquired any of the "accumulated wisdom" of the Jews with the poet's adult study of biblical Hebrew, which is surely motivated in part by his desire to make up for this loss of family heritage and of Jewish tradition at large. In effect, the grandfather's blessing becomes a task and an obligation, which can only be fulfilled when the grandson learns to read the sacred texts. Perhaps this critical oversight is partly due to other important and frequently interpreted poems which indicate the poet's estrangement from and difficulty learning Hebrew. Ranen Omer-Sherman even asserts that "In spite of Reznikoff's oft-stated love for the learning of Hebrew, he much prefers to write lyrics that declaim the difficulties it causes him than to actually gain fluency in it.... Hebrew is frequently alluded to in his poetry, though chiefly as a trope of irrecoverable absence."[36]

Here are two of the lyrics that Omer-Sherman surely has in mind. The first is #14 from *A Fifth Group of Verse* (1927):

34. Fredman, 28.
35. Milton Hindus, "Introduction," *Charles Reznikoff: Man and Poet*, 25.
36. Omer-Sherman, 167, 169.

> How difficult for me is Hebrew:
> even the Hebrew for *mother,* for *bread,* for *sun*
> is foreign. How far have I been exiled, Zion.[37]

At first glance, this would appear to be solely a poem of loss, regret, and nostalgia. The poet declares how difficult it is for him to learn the holy tongue, and with the colon at the end-stopped first line, he sets up the reader to expect an explanation of that loss and difficulty. The words he then chooses all signify fundamental elements of life, implying primal warmth, comfort, and physical gratification.[38] In psychoanalytic terms, the poem presents a severing of the pre-Oedipal bond of mother and child, a severing that, in a subtle but ingenious formal gesture, is enacted in the enjambment between the second and third lines, when the lost words in Hebrew (given to us only through their English equivalents) are followed by the painfully direct phrase "is foreign." The period after "foreign" produces a full stop, a dramatic caesura, and the final statement, while maintaining the personal register of frustration, also opens the poem out into the cultural and historical registers through the resonant reference to exile and Zion – whereupon it ends. We see the modern Jewish poet as a prophet or psalmist in spite of himself, experiencing a compounded sense of exile that is psychological, linguistic, and cultural.

The words "mother," "exiled," and "Zion," appearing in a very brief, three-line poem, inevitably lead us to think of the figure of the Shekhinah.[39] Following a consideration of another Reznikoff poem

37. *Poems of Charles Reznikoff,* 58.
38. According to Fredman, "In Reznikoff's private lexicon, 'bread' stands for the gift of sustenance, over which one offers a (Hebrew) prayer; 'sun' represents the universal (nonparochial) supplier of illumination and warmth; and 'mother' symbolizes the fundament, with which the poet (having repudiated the *mameloshen*) must maintain contact at all costs." Fredman, 25.
39. The Shekhinah has been discussed at length in relation to Jewish-American poetry. In addition to Shreiber, see Allen Grossman, "Jewish Poetry Considered as a Theophoric Project," *The Long Schoolroom: Lessons in the Bitter Logic of the Poetic Principle* (Ann Arbor: University of Michigan Press, 1997), 159–67; Jerome Rothenberg, "Pre-Face," *A Big Jewish Book: Poems and Other Visions of the Jews From Tribal Times to Present,* ed. Jerome Rothenberg, Harris Lenowitz and Charles Doria (Garden City, NJ: Anchor Press / Doubleday, 1978), xxi–xlv; and Eric Murphy Selinger, "Shekhinah in America," *Jewish American Poetry: Poems, Commentary, and Reflections,* ed. Jonathan N. Barron

describing an episode from the poet's childhood, Maeera Shreiber offers the following interpretation:

> It is an exquisitely personal experience that opens out onto a matter of collective concern, as Reznikoff sounds a theme central to the Jewish psyche. One of the standard images surrounding an exilic condition, a foundational event in Jewish identity, is that of a paternalistic God who angrily casts his child(ren) away from him after they have violated his word. Indeed, in the wake of this severing, marked by the destruction of the Temple, only *Halacha*, the Law, remains as a bridge to the divine. As they begin their lengthy sojourn in exile, the children of Israel are accompanied by the Shekhinah, otherwise known as the Mother of Exile. [40]

However remote "Zion" (more as a cultural construct or even rhetorical trope, and less as a geopolitical entity) might be, and even when "mother" (the word, if not the pre-linguistic object) must be uttered in a language other than Hebrew, the poet still finds the means to articulate his (Jewish) experience. "Exile" may be read as maternal muse or existential condition, but in any case, for Reznikoff, as for his literary antecedents writing in whatever "Jewish" language, exile remains textually productive and empowering – which is why the poem, although certainly about loss, may also be about the condition of, or at least the potential for, cultural recovery or restoration.

I would argue that this is also the case with another lyric about language, exile, and the psychosexual disposition of the poet, the crucial opening poem of *Jerusalem the Golden* (1934), one of Reznikoff's most important volumes:

and Eric Murphy Selinger (Hanover, NH: Brandeis University Press / University Press of New England, 2000), 250–71.

40. *Singing in a Strange Land*, 65. The poem in question is from "Early History of a Writer." It describes a memory of Reznikoff as a child visiting a park with his mother and running away from her with a sense of freedom and abandon. The mother is then reprimanded by a (gentile) policeman, and the child is scolded in turn by his mother. See *Poems of Charles Reznikoff*, 295. Shreiber's extended analysis includes a comparison of the poem to Wordsworth's "Ode: Intimations of Immortality."

> The Hebrew of your poets, Zion
> is like oil upon a burn,
> cool as oil;
> after work,
> the smell in the street at night
> of the hedge in flower.
> Like Solomon,
> I have married and married the speech of strangers;
> none are like you, Shulamite.[41]

As in the previous poem, Hebrew – this time explicitly the Hebrew of the Jewish poetic tradition – is first presented as a source of comfort and gratification, at once sensual and healing. The image of the cooling oil has an ancient biblical resonance; the hedge flowering in the street after work is obviously more urban and contemporary.[42] And again, "Zion" is addressed not as a geopolitical entity, but as a cultural construct, with the same implication of separation and loss. But in this instance, rather than the implicit mothering presence of the Shekhinah, Reznikoff invokes the figure of the Shulamite, the beloved from the Song of Songs, or the Song of Solomon, since traditionally Solomon is sometimes credited with its authorship. But Reznikoff may also intend the Shunamite, Abishag, from 1 Kings, the beautiful young woman who serves David in his old age, though "the king knew her not."[43] And by invoking the Shunamite and King Solomon, Reznikoff, in the three last lines of the poem, produces a remarkably complex network of allusive meanings.

Reznikoff compares the Hebrew language to the Shunamite, the epitome of loveliness and sexual desirability. But like King David, who, as the traditional author of the Psalms, we may consider in effect to be the first great Jewish poet, Reznikoff, the modern Jewish poet, also cannot

41. *Poems of Charles Reznikoff*, 93.
42. As I argue in *Not One of Them in Place*, "*Jerusalem the Golden* draws a great deal of its verbal energy from this conflicted sense of identity: however much the poet seems at home in New York, on intimate terms with its most common sights and unassuming details, he still feels the accumulated weight of centuries of Jewish exile" (27).
43. 1 Kings 1:3. All biblical references are from the KJV; see below pp. 59–60 for my rationale for using this translation.

possess the Shunamite, because he does not write in Hebrew but in English, a "foreign" tongue. The image, therefore, would implicitly be one of impotence, a falling off of linguistic strength, except that rather than David, Reznikoff explicitly equates himself with David's son Solomon, the wisest of men and the builder of the First Temple.[44] At the beginning of Solomon's reign, Solomon's older brother Adonijah asks Bathsheba, Solomon's mother, to intervene on his behalf in his request to marry Abishag. Given that request, Solomon understands that Adonijah is a threat to his throne, since Adonijah seeks to demonstrate his power by possessing the Shunamite, the act that their father David was unable to perform. Solomon rejects Bathsheba's plea and has Adonijah killed: sex, political power, and for Reznikoff, linguistic ability, are inextricably intertwined. Solomon, furthermore, had seven hundred wives, whom he took mainly for political reasons. Because they were not Hebrew women, they led him astray, so that he tolerated the worship of false gods: "And Solomon did evil in the sight of the Lord, and went not fully after the Lord, as did David his father."[45] By declaring that he has "married and married the speech of strangers," Reznikoff therefore identifies himself with both the sexual power and the sinfulness of Solomon, which is to say that the modern Jewish poet possesses a linguistic potency that is also related to disobedience, dissension and, ultimately, exile – since Solomon's sins lead to the breaking of the Kingdom and all that follows, disastrously, in biblical history.

We may conclude, therefore, that in poems such as these, Reznikoff offers oblique explanations for his diasporic stance, which always has him looking backward through Jewish chronicle and history while simultaneously reflecting on his current circumstances. Drawing on his Objectivist principles (clarity, precision, order, intensity, etc.), while working with (and against) original texts, Reznikoff produces startlingly modern poetry that is also richly evocative of a providential sense of

---

44. In another poem in *Jerusalem the Golden*, Reznikoff compares modern New Yorkers gazing at the moon to King David gazing at Bathsheba, a more sexually charged moment in David's life, but also the event that alienates him from God. See *Poems of Charles Reznikoff*, 93.

45. 1 Kings 11:6.

Jewish history. Indeed, the poems, which result from his autodidactic study of the Jewish Scriptures are some of his most moving and culturally significant works. His resonant reworkings of both biblical and talmudic texts, in addition to those poems which, as we have seen, more indirectly allude to traditional figures and materials, are not only crucial to our understanding of this diasporic vision, but also lead us to see Reznikoff as a major poet of modern, secular Jewish life. As Ranen Omer-Sherman observes, "Reznikoff ironically *amalgamates* the cultural strata of ancient Israel and the *Galut*. Even when he poeticizes themes and motifs from the Bible, he frequently ironizes these through layers of cultural perspectives and attitudes acquired over centuries of diasporic living. And so the chief referent always remains his present position, not a distant landscape or a yearning for recovery."[46]

Revisionism and the Midrashic Impulse

As Omer-Sherman's formulation indicates, Reznikoff's treatment of traditional texts is inevitably ironized by his diasporic condition, which develops over long centuries and shapes the poet's "present position." And in regard to that position, Marie Syrkin notes that "Charles was always returning to Jewish themes, Biblical, historical or contemporary. Not that he was an observant Jew or a nationalist with political affiliations." Indeed, in describing life with her husband, Syrkin writes of "the typical home of an emancipated American Jew periodically moved by sentiment and ancestral memories."[47] Be that as it may, the ancient texts and the culture they represent remain fundamental to Reznikoff's Jewishness; he regards them as an inheritance and returns to them throughout his career. As we observed earlier, Syrkin herself attests to Reznikoff's biblical studies, which involved scrutinizing the original Hebrew and comparing it to English and German translations. A born revisionist, Reznikoff treats this material in a manner that is at once respectful and destabilizing. Reznikoff, therefore, may be regarded as a midrashic poet, and his contemporary stance, including his Objectivist

46. Omer-Sherman, 144.
47. Syrkin, 55.

methods, produces a unique vision: secular, contingent and historically self-conscious, but still deeply infused with redemptive possibility.[48]

How does this midrashic stance affect the poet's linguistic attitudes – his sense of poetic style, of diction, tone, and so on? When asked by Reinhold Schiffer about his reading of the King James Bible, Reznikoff responds as follows:

> Well, the King James version I delight in, and I dislike the modern. My argument there, and this I feel very strongly, is, if I were a Christian, or even not a Christian, to me, why should I talk the language of the streets? When I go into a temple or a synagogue or a church, I want to feel I'm off the street, and if I'm reading the King James version, I'm off the street, and if I'm reading it modernized I'm on the street again, and I haven't got that feeling of exaltation that I expect, and so I think the King James version is excellent.... Now in the Hebrew, when I hear the Hebrew praying, I'm annoyed, because it's so fast.... I want each word

48. In calling Reznikoff a midrashic poet, I am using a term that has become relatively common in discussions of modern Jewish literature since the nineteen-eighties (if not earlier), although it is sometimes contested, especially by experts in traditional midrash. While some of these scholars actively seek to apply the term to modern writing, others resist its use, arguing that the loss of historical and philological specificity when the term is appropriated in this fashion moves it far from its original function as a specific form of scriptural commentary. This is an ongoing debate among midrashic scholars, literary theorists, critics, and creative writers. My own thoughts on the subject (including what I take to be a consideration of the literature for the purposes of modern criticism) may be found in my essay "Total Midrash," cited in the Preface. This essay is part of a forum in *Religion and Literature*, edited by the poet and Jewish feminist scholar Alicia Ostriker. In her introduction to the forum, Ostriker argues that "What drives this kind of writing is an intimately personal insistence on wrestling with tradition – wrestling, as it were, for one's life, for one's identity. If traditional midrash is preoccupied with closing gaps in the biblical text, reconciling internal contradictions, and demonstrating that *halakha* and *haggadah* form a single body, contemporary midrashim – and midrashists – commonly rejoice in the gaps, foreground the contradictions, and explore issues that are psychological, political, philosophical or spiritual in a broad sense rather than halakhic or religious." Alicia Ostriker, introduction to "Turn It and Turn It: A Forum on Contemporary Midrash," *Religion and Literature* 43, no. 2 (Summer 2011): 113. These remarks inform my understanding of Reznikoff as a midrashic poet.

> stressed, and I see, each word, the meaning of it, and I'm very
> much moved by some of it.[49]

These comments shed a good deal of light on the kind of style Reznikoff
wishes to achieve in his scriptural poems. This is poetry which takes us
"off the street." It has a kind of formality which, while in no way violating
Reznikoff's Objectivist principles, conveys "that feeling of exaltation"
which the poet associates with "a temple or a synagogue or a church."
In other words, Reznikoff seeks for virtually religious sublimity in these
poems, but not the sublimity of traditional verse, which he describes in
"Early History of a Writer" (1969) as having "grown a little stale," "fake
flowers / in the streets in which I walked."[50] Note again the image of the
streets. Reznikoff was a famous walker; even in his old age, he was known
to cover many miles on his daily excursions through Manhattan. And of
course, many of his most well-known poems arise from his observations
of daily life in these Manhattan streets. But in these remarks, the biblical
style in both the English of the King James translation and in the original
Hebrew is associated with a careful stress, a meaningful dignity, that
takes us outside the realm of daily life and of casual modern discourse.
Indeed, even the liturgical Hebrew of the synagogue does not satisfy the
poet; the speed of the prayers memorized and recited by rote drains the
words of their significance, their deliberate weight.

The verbal weight and intensity of Reznikoff's scriptural poems,
their straightforward, dignified eloquence, may be related in turn to
the diasporic vision of Jewish history which unfolds in this work, and
additionally, as we have seen, to the crucial but always problematic
status of Hebrew and its translation into the languages of the diaspora,
including English, the language of the poems themselves. The status of
the Jews in the modern American diaspora, compounded not only with
the question of a "Jewish" language for poetry but also with the question
of a Jewish poetic *vocation*, precipitates in a very early work in which
Reznikoff wrestles with his sense of himself as a modern Jewish poet in
the prophetic line. The figure of the prophet as derived from the Hebrew

49. "The Poet in His Milieu," 123.
50. *Poems of Charles Reznikoff*, 327.

Scriptures is essential to poetry in the West, and of particular impor-
tance in the English tradition starting with John Milton.[51] Reznikoff
almost never sounds like a prophetic poet in the way of Milton and his
various Romantic descendants, such as William Blake, P.B. Shelley, or
in Reznikoff's own lifetime, W.B. Yeats. Nor does he bear much resem-
blance to the American poet-prophets, the line beginning with Walt
Whitman, and extending, with various revisions, through such figures as
Wallace Stevens, Hart Crane, or even Pound in his most lofty registers.[52]
But there is one Reznikoff poem in which this is not the case. It appears in
Reznikoff's first book, *Rhythms* (1918), a volume which consists of poems
which are mostly Imagist in their style and contemporary in their subject
matter. However, "Wringing, Wringing His Pierced Hands," poem #12
in the volume, is a symbolic text suffused with Romantic intensity, in

51. The locus classicus in Milton's case would be the opening lines of Book I of *Paradise
     Lost*, in which the poet invokes the "Heavenly Muse" who first inspired Moses on
     Sinai, so that he may now pursue "Things unattempted yet in prose or rhyme" and
     thereby "assert Eternal Providence / And justify the ways of God to men." In Blake's
     The Marriage of Heaven and Hell, the poet, in a "Memorable Fancy," dines with Isaiah
     and Ezekiel, and is instructed by the latter that "we of Israel taught that the Poetic
     Genius (as you now call it) was the first principle and all the others merely derivative,
     which was the cause of our despising the Priests and Philosophers of other countries,
     and prophesying that all Gods would at last be proved to originate in ours and to
     be the tributaries of the Poetic Genius. It was this that our great poet, King David,
     desired so fervently and invokes so pathetically..."
52. Whitman's concept of the poet-prophet is summed up in the following passage from
     the preface to the 1855 edition of *Leaves of Grass*: "There will soon be no more priests.
     Their work is done. They may wait awhile ... perhaps a generation or two ... dropping
     off by degrees. A superior breed shall take their place ... the gangs of kosmos and
     prophets *en masse* shall take their place. A new order shall arise and they shall be
     the priests of man, and every man shall be his own priest. The churches built under
     their umbrage shall be the churches of men and women. Through the divinity of
     themselves shall the kosmos and the new breed of poets be interpreters of men and
     women and of all events and things." When asked if Whitman had influenced him,
     Reznikoff responded that "I had read Whitman, but I don't particularly care for him."
     Janet Sternberg and Alan Ziegler, "A Conversation with Charles Reznikoff," in *Charles
     Reznikoff: Man and Poet*, 131. For a survey of canonical American poets' conceptions
     of the sacred in relation to the poetic vocation, see Norman Finkelstein, *On Mount
     Vision: Forms of the Sacred in Contemporary American Poetry* (Iowa City: University
     of Iowa Press, 2010), 7–26.

which Jewish history and identity collide with the English lyric tradition, a tradition which the young Reznikoff studied intensely yet with great ambivalence. Here is the poem in its entirety:

> Wringing, wringing his pierced hands,
> he walks in a wood where once a flood
> washed the ground into loose white sand:
> and the trees stand each a twisted cross,
> smooth and white with the loss of leaves and bark,
> together like warped yards and masts
> of a fleet at anchor centuries.
> No blasts come from the hollow of these dead;
> long since the water has gone from the stony bed.
> No fields and streets for him, his pathway runs
> among these skeletons, through these white sands,
> wringing, wringing his pierced hands.[53]

The degree of skill that the poem demonstrates is extremely impressive: in terms of meter, rhyme, tone and imagery, Reznikoff, in his early twenties, has already mastered the symbolist idiom of the late Romantics. Yet the explicit Christian imagery – pierced hands and trees like crosses – is unlike anything else in *Rhythms*, or for that matter, any other poem Reznikoff is to write throughout his career. In a provocative essay on this poem in relation to Reznikoff's Jewish identity, Henry Weinfield offers the following analysis:

> [I]f the crucifixion motif dominates "Wringing, wringing his pierced hands," Reznikoff's greatest lyric poem, this is not only because of the poet's necessary engagement with the Christian tradition, as mediated by the lyric, but also because of this poet's experience of *victimization* by that tradition. Jesus was a Jew; yet because antisemitism in the West could be justified on the grounds that the Jews were responsible for his crucifixion, the Jews themselves took on the role of "crucified" scapegoat. All this is implied in the symbolic chain of associations and condensations

---

53. *Poems of Charles Reznikoff*, 12.

that are present in the poem. But not only is Reznikoff, the Jew (standing here as a synecdoche for his people), crucified, as it were, by Christianity, but Reznikoff, the lyric poet, is crucified by a poetic tradition which, by virtue of his absorption in it, robs him of his Jewish identity. It was all too much to deal with at this stage of history, and Reznikoff had to move in another direction – away from lyric subjectivity, toward what we have come to refer to as "Objectivism."[54]

Reznikoff's situation as adumbrated here is prophetic in a number of senses. In "Wringing, wringing his pierced hands," we are presented with the modern Jew who aspires to write prophetic, visionary poetry in English – a predominantly Christian mode, to say the least – while maintaining his Jewish identity. Weinfield believes that this situation is actually too much to bear; in effect, Reznikoff was not strong enough to be the Jewish poet who would prophetically call out for justice against the (antisemitic) Christian lyric tradition while remaining stylistically rooted in that tradition. Like some of the Hebrew prophets, he seeks to evade this great, even overwhelming, and certainly contradictory task – and the name of that evasion is Objectivism. In some respects, this hypothesis is related to what Harold Bloom posits in his "The Sorrows of American Jewish Poetry," an essay which may be said to inaugurate the academic study of Jewish American poetry. In that essay, Bloom declares that Reznikoff "should have been the American-Jewish poet in whom younger writers could find a precursor of real strength" – but again, is unable to become that precursor, because of the style he ultimately adopts, an Objectivist style based on the poetics of Eliot, Pound, and Williams.[55] Following this line of argument, Reznikoff is undone as a poet-prophet because of this change of style, turning away from

54. Henry Weinfield, "'Wringing, Wringing His Pierced Hands': Religion, Identity, and Genre in the Poetry of Charles Reznikoff," *Sagetrieb* 13, no. 1–2 (1994): 226–27.
55. Harold Bloom, "The Sorrows of American Jewish Poetry," in *Figures of Capable Imagination* (New York: Seabury Press, 1976), 251. For a full discussion and critique of Bloom's crucial essay in relation to Reznikoff, see Finkelstein, *Not One of Them in Place*, 17–22. See also Jerome Rothenberg, "Harold Bloom: The Critic as Exterminating Angel," in *Poetics and Polemics 1980–2005*, 63–81.

the Romantic, visionary (and, ironically, Judaized) discourse – but his change of style is also inevitably the result of a particular psycho-historical failure.

This ostensible failure would have as much to do with the situation of Jewish Americans in the early twentieth century as it does with Reznikoff's personal experience, which begins with antisemitic violence in the poor ethnic enclaves of New York City, and goes on to a secular poetic career which is almost totally ignored by an American literary audience. The Jews of Reznikoff's generation fulfill their immigrant parents' desire to enter the American mainstream, but in many instances, they do so almost too well, sacrificing important aspects of Old World Jewish culture and belief: thus Reznikoff would indeed stand as a synecdoche for his people. "Wringing, wringing his pierced hands" may be regarded, therefore, as a poem of simultaneous election and crucifixion, a unique poem that could only have been written at that time by such an individual.

While it is undoubtedly true that Reznikoff hardly enters the late Romantic, visionary mode before turning from it, it can also be argued that the Objectivist program he adopts leads him more deeply into his Jewish identity and more strongly into his poetic vocation, while additionally confirming his sense of himself as a thoroughly American artist. For example, in "Samuel," the final poem from Reznikoff's *Five Groups of Verse*, the poet seems to speak simultaneously from the persona of the biblical prophet and from a modern persona very close to his own. Like the other poems we have considered which deal with exile, linguistic loss, and cultural rupture, "Samuel" treats the situation of the prophet with remarkable ambiguity, and the result is a poem of exquisite revisionary grace and intelligence:

> All day I am before the altar
> and at night sleep beside it;
> I think in psalms, my mind a psalter.
> I sit in the temple. From inside it
> I see the smoke eddy in the wind;
> now and then a leaf will ride it
> upward and when the leaf has spinned

its moment, the winds hide it.
Against their hurly-burly
I shut the window of my mind,
and the world at the winds' will,
find myself calm and still.

Reznikoff's poem begins, presumably, with the young Samuel, still serving Eli the high priest and tending the altar at Shiloh. Although God may well have revealed himself to Samuel already, the first stanza, with its preponderance of graceful feminine rhymes (altar / psalter; beside it / inside it / ride it / hide it) and gently lilting meter, is as self-contained as the mind of the poet-prophet who chants the lines. This is not yet the prophet and judge of Israel; he does not yet present himself as a public figure. Communing before the altar with his divine inspiration, Samuel closes himself away from the "hurly-burly" world of the wind-tossed leaves (symbolic, perhaps, of the strife and conflict of Israel) in order to "think in psalms, / my mind a psalter." But in the three subsequent stanzas, written in a looser free verse, his prophetic vision opens outward in surprising directions:

The days in this room become precious to others also,
as the seed hidden in the earth becomes a tree,
as the secret joy of the bride and her husband becomes a man.

Whatever unfriendly stars and comets do,
whatever stormy heavens are unfurled,
my spirit be like fire in this too,
that all the straws and rubbish of the world
only feed its flame.

The seasons change.
That is change enough.
Chance planted me beside a stream of water;
content, I serve the land
whoever lives here and whoever passes.[56]

---

56. *Poems of Charles Reznikoff*, 59.

In these lines, the meditative, self-enclosed youth of the first stanza is transformed not into ancient Israel's servant but into a *modern* prophetic figure, one more in line with Reznikoff himself, the ironic but still compassionate recorder of ghetto life in the New York City of the nineteen-twenties. This figure presents his inspiration in sexual terms, "as the secret joy of the bride and her husband becomes a man." If he is a prophet, he serves not only the God of Israel but "others also," drawing strength from the adversity of "unfriendly stars and comets," as his spirit grows "like fire in this too, / that all the straws and rubbish of the world / only feed its flame." The last stanza modulates to a more accommodating position, one of greater acceptance of the world as it is, a world unredeemed and in a state of exile – a world of Jewish diasporism. Stephen Fredman observes that the text "does not condemn the Diaspora, nor is there such an impulse anywhere in Reznikoff's work.... Instead of invoking 'Zion' as a means of indulging in nostalgia or as the basis for a Zionist politics, Reznikoff sees his job as making the condition of exile habitable."[57] Ranen Omer-Sherman puts this even more strongly: for him, the poem is one of Reznikoff's "unequivocal representations of Judaism as an extraterritorial culture, a textual landscape enriched by a living stream of ideas (even from antisemites), enlivened by its propinquity to other discourses."[58] In effect, the poem offers a revisionary perspective on the figure of the prophet: the burning spirit of righteousness is literally transplanted "beside a stream of water" (Fredman notes how this line contrasts with the rivers of Babylon in Psalm 137, where the Jewish exiles wept), and the poet-prophet declares that "content, I serve the land, / whoever lives here and whoever passes."[59] Yet in another respect, the universalism of these lines – and, perhaps, their American idealism – remains congruent with the biblical message of the prophets, which speaks of justice for all peoples, wherever God's voice is heard.

Diasporism, then, proves to be the motive force behind much of Reznikoff's midrashic poetry, and it is in that spirit Reznikoff is to be understood as a modern revisionist. One of the clearest instances of this

57. Fredman, 72.
58. Omer-Sherman, 121.
59. Fredman, 71.

is "Joshua at Shechem," again from *Jerusalem the Golden*. The poem is sub-
titled "*Joshua XXIV: 13*," which in the King James version (that source, let
us recall, of the poet's "delight" and "exaltation") reads as follows: "And
I have given you a land for which ye did not labour, and cities which ye
built not, and ye dwell in them; of the vineyards and olive-yards which ye
planted not do ye eat." XXIV is the last chapter in the Book of Joshua, in
which Joshua gathers the tribes together to reaffirm the covenantal rela-
tionship between God and the Children of Israel. This is done through
retelling their history, beginning with Terach, the father of Abraham,
leading up to their present circumstance in Canaan, and concluding
with the death of Joshua himself. The text reads much like a chronicle,
and as verse 13 (and most of Chapter XXIV) implies, settling the land
of Canaan is by no means the end of the Jewish story. The conquest of
the land is incomplete and the covenant between God and the people
remains unfulfilled, for the risk of the Israelites abandoning their God
to worship "the strange gods which are among you" (XXIV:23) remains a
serious problem. Although the Israelites assert their willingness to serve
God, and Joshua takes their word as witness, writing it in "the book of
the law" and setting a great stone beneath an oak to memorialize it, the
sense nevertheless remains that the people could break their word, as
they have done in times past. Furthermore, as verse 13 also indicates, the
Israelites in Canaan, with God's blessing, have appropriated the cities,
vineyards and olive-yards of other peoples, and have benefitted from
their previous labors – a concept which Reznikoff, given his diasporic
sympathies, could relate to the circumstances of modern American Jews,
adjusting to life in the New World and what it provides.

Thus, the overarching themes of Joshua XXIV are the covenantal
relationship between God and Israel, Israel's history of wandering, the
dissatisfaction which obtains due to the unfulfilled covenant, and the
ambiguity of Israel's situation in relation to other peoples as the Jews
enter and inhabit the Land. And as in Chapter XXIV, Reznikoff's poem
reads primarily as chronicle, retelling Jewish history with an emphasis
on a virtually timeless and repetitive sense of wandering. In both texts,
God is active in Jewish history, scattering the Jews every time they
become too comfortable in a particular place. But Reznikoff's poem
elides the actual gathering at Shechem and the explicit reaffirmation

of the covenant between God and the Israelites through the prophetic figure of Joshua. Each episode in Jewish history is recounted with a great sense of immediacy, as is clear from the opening lines:

> You Hebrews are too snug in Ur,
> said God; wander about in waste places,
> north and south leave your dead;
> let kings fight against you,
> and the heavens rain fire and brimstone
> on you. And it was so.[60]

As in Joshua, the first line of Reznikoff's poem alludes to the end of Genesis 11 and the beginning of Genesis 12, which recounts Terach's departure with his family from Ur to Canaan, and God's subsequent promise to Abram that He "will make of thee a great nation" (Genesis 12:2). But Reznikoff moves immediately to a generalized vision of disastrous wandering, apparently a punishment inflicted by God owing to the Hebrews being "too snug in Ur." There is no mention of God's promise to Abram, nor for that matter, any of the reaffirmations of the covenant which God makes to Isaac or Jacob. Rather, in Reznikoff's poem a strange pattern develops: wandering, imposed by God, becomes the defining Jewish experience and every location or haven is merely temporary. These temporary havens are all referred to as comfortable. When the Jews prove "rich in flocks and herds, / with jewels of silver / and jewels of gold," God declares "Be slaves / to Pharaoh. And it was so." But then,

> ... God looked again and saw
> the Hebrews at the fleshpots,
> with fish to eat,
> cucumbers and melons.
> And God said, Be gone
> and into the wilderness by the Red Sea
> and the wilderness of Shur and the wilderness
> of Shin; let Amalek come upon you,
> and fiery serpents bite you. And it was so.

60. *Poems of Charles Reznikoff*, 112.

> And God looked again and saw in a land of brooks and springs
> and fountains,
> wheat and barley,
> the Hebrews, in a land on which they did not labor,
> in cities which they did not build,
> eating of vineyards and olive trees which they did not plant.

The Hebrews' ability to recover from God's punishments and prosper in whatever situation they find themselves is almost comic: it is as if the worse the conditions of exile become, the more resilient the Hebrews prove to be, and the more capable they are of thriving "in a land on which they did not labor, / in cities which they did not build." The actual words of verse 13 take on a peculiarly modern irony here, and the polarity of homeland and diaspora is reversed, an idea that is confirmed and brought to an extraordinary conclusion in the last part of the poem:

> And God scattered them –
> through the cities of the Medes, besides the waters of Babylon,
> they fled before Him into Egypt, and went down to the sea in
> ships; the whales swallowed them,
> the birds brought word of them to the king;
> the young men met them with weapons of war,
> the old men with proverbs –
> and God looked and saw the Hebrews
> citizens of the great cities,
> talking Hebrew in every language under the sun.

Reznikoff's allusions in these lines are somewhat difficult to pin down. He may be referring to Jeremiah, who was taken from Babylon to Egypt; he may also refer to the Psalms, specifically Psalm 137 ("By the rivers of Babylon...") and 107 ("They that go down to the sea in ships..."). The image of being swallowed by whales certainly alludes to Jonah. Overall, the hardships of exile, the vicissitudes of history, and the difficulties of the prophetic vocation are all connected to God's punitive scattering of the Hebrews and their being driven from land to land. But when God looks in these final lines (and this is the fourth time Reznikoff uses a variation of the phrase "God looked again"), he sees the Hebrews as "citizens of the great cities / talking Hebrew in every language under the sun."

What does it mean for this severely judgmental deity – an ironic depiction of an "Old Testament" God in every respect – to see His Chosen People "talking Hebrew in every language under the sun"? It is unquestionably an assertion of the poet's diasporism, cosmopolitanism, secularism, and universalism, an assertion which Reznikoff extends to the Jews themselves throughout history. Stephen Fredman captures this position nicely when he observes that "Celebrating the survival of Jewish identity in poem after poem, he seems to accept scatteredness as an essential human destiny."[61] Jewish destiny is human destiny, and vice versa. This existential and historical condition is preeminently a linguistic condition as well. The Hebrew language, the *ursprache* which God spoke to bring Creation into being and the *lashon ha-kodesh* through which pious Jews commune with their Maker, is seen as *immanent* in all human speech. Conversely, this condition implies that for the Jews, Hebrew is inescapable, whether they actually speak the language or not. Thus, in Reznikoff's diasporic conception of Jewish history and identity, the Hebrew language – which may be taken in this instance as metonymic of Jewish culture in general and perhaps even of some essential "Jewishness" – *infiltrates* the world's great cities and languages, making them all more or less Jewish. To be Jewish is therefore to be capable of being at home *everywhere* and *nowhere*. To be Jewish is to *embody* and to *articulate* an impossible but imaginatively inspiring condition: an essential condition which resists any form of essentialism. What Reznikoff accomplishes in "Joshua at Shechem," as he does in so much of his midrashic poetry on Jewish subjects, exemplifies what Michael Heller will go on to assert in his extraordinary essay "Diasporic Poetics." After discussing the ways in which the Jewishness of the Objectivist poets have shaped his own thought and writing about Jewish identity, Heller declares that "obviously, from the view I have espoused above, there is no such stable category as Jewishness. That is, if the commonplace of Jewishness, of Jewish thought and poetry, involves textuality and commentary, it is also true that the poetics of Jewishness involves the

61. Fredman, 73.

undoing of text and comment, that textuality is a kind of traveling away, of departing, of heresy."[62]

Speculative Conclusion: Reznikoff and the Problem of Liturgical Poetry

> It would be a great relief to break with the idea of the sacred, and especially with institutions that claim to mediate it. Yet the institution of language makes every such break appear inauthentic.
>
> – Geoffrey Hartman[63]

The recently published Reform machzor, *Mishkan HaNefesh* (2015) contains, by my count, ten selections from the poetry of Charles Reznikoff, two in the volume for Rosh HaShanah and eight in the volume for Yom Kippur. *Mishkan HaNefesh* replaces *Gates of Repentance* (originally published in 1978 and reissued in a gender-neutral version in 1996), which also includes selections from Reznikoff's poetry. But the new machzor includes a great deal more poetry in general, by both Jews and non-Jews, almost all of it written within the last fifty years. Contemporary poetry, in fact, is a crucial component of the text; it serves as commentary upon the prayers and as prompts for reflection and meditation upon traditional themes related to the Days of Awe. In this respect, it extends the practice of appropriating "secular" literature for religious purposes that has been operative in Reform prayer books for many years. Having been raised in the Conservative tradition, I did not encounter this practice until I joined Wise Temple after moving to Cincinnati in 1980. Opening *Gates of Prayer*, I was surprised and intrigued to find modern poetry in a High Holy Days prayer book, and, skeptic that I am, I wondered how many of the congregants filling Plum Street Temple were engaged by this material, including the Reznikoff poems. Some years later, when I began to study Reznikoff closely, to teach him in my Jewish American Literature courses, and to write about his poetry

62. Michael Heller, "Diasporic Poetics," *Uncertain Poetries: Selected Essays on Poets, Poetry and Poetics* (Cambridge, UK: Salt Publishing, 2005), 168.
63. Geoffrey Hartman, *Criticism in the Wilderness: The Study of Literature Today* (New Haven, NJ: Yale University Press, 1980), 249.

in an academic context, I continued to ponder what the meaning of the work might be in a specifically liturgical context. By then, I was also immersed in the literary and cultural criticism of Harold Bloom, and had become deeply influenced by passages such as this:

> The scandal is the stubborn resistance of imaginative literature to the categories of sacred and secular. If you wish, you can insist that all high literature is secular, or, should you desire it so, then all strong poetry is sacred. What I find incoherent is the judgment that some authentic literary art is more sacred or more secular than some other. Poetry and belief wander about, together and apart, in a cosmological emptiness marked by the limits of truth and of meaning.[64]

Nor was my stake in this question merely academic or critical: I myself was writing midrashic poetry, culminating in *Passing Over*, the long poem based on the Haggadah and related Passover rituals to which I refer in Chapter 2. Indeed, one of my own poems, what to my mind is the ironically titled "Prayer," has now made its way into the Rosh HaShanah volume of *Mishkan HaNefesh*.[65]

As Bloom might ask (despite the "incoherence" he posits), what does it mean for a poem composed as a secular work of art to be placed in, or repurposed for, a religious context? What alchemical transformation takes place? I take Michael Heller very seriously when he declares that Jewish poetics constitutes a form of textuality that "is a kind of traveling away, of departing, of heresy." Reznikoff's poetry is surely imbued with a constant sense of departure, a traveling away from all forms of orthodoxy, whether religious, Zionist, or assimilationist. Just when it appears that his work is resolutely secular, his complicated, contradictory understanding of Jewish history and culture seems to wrap him in a prophetic

64. Harold Bloom, *Ruin the Sacred Truths: Poetry and Belief from the Bible to the Present* (Cambridge, MA: Harvard University Press, 1987), 4.

65. Norman Finkelstein, "Prayer," in *Mishkan HaNefesh: Machzor for the Days of Awe: Rosh HaShanah* (New York: CCAR Press, 2015), 187. To compound the irony, in the Sources and Permissions section, the author of the poem is identified as "Rabbi Norman Finkelstein" (348). "Prayer" originally appeared in *Restless Messengers* (Athens: University of Georgia Press, 1992), 42.

mantle – and just when he seems to assert a redemptive vision of the Jewish faith, that same complexity and contradictory understanding produces, as Heller would say, a deep textual "undoing." [66] If the undoing, or the radical interrogation of foundational Jewish premises, constitutes heresy, then Reznikoff's poems are certainly heretical, though that is probably not the way the editors of *Mishkan HaNefesh* read them.

Among the Reznikoff poems in the new Reform machzor are a number we have examined in this essay: "I went to my grandfather's to say good-bye...," "How difficult for me is Hebrew...," and "The Hebrew of your poets, Zion..." I have argued that texts such as these, however self-critical (or even *because* they are self-critical) come into their own poetically through Reznikoff's Objectivist principles working in tandem with a newly discovered Jewish American diasporism. Genuine regret over the loss of tradition vies with the vital insistence that to have "married and married the speech of strangers" can still result in an authentically Jewish poem – because Jewish authenticity is precisely what is at issue. During the Days of Awe, Jews are called upon to meditate upon the concept of *teshuvah*, turning or returning to the Jewish way, or halakhah. But in a modern, secular context, the way is always in the process of defining itself; the text must always find new commentary and be given new expression. In this respect, I suppose, Reznikoff's poems in the machzor may not become liturgical in any conventional sense, but they may be read as aids in the process of *teshuvah*, of returning to the way, however it may be redefined for modern Jews.

Among the many other poems in *Mishkan HaNefesh* is Harvey Shapiro's magnificent "Psalm," one of the most searching yet consoling Yom Kippur poems in the modern Jewish canon:

> I am still on a rooftop in Brooklyn
> on your holy day. The harbor is before me,
> Governor's Island, the Verrazano Bridge
> and the Narrows. I keep in my head
> what Rabbi Nachman said about the world

---

66. For a beautiful musical presentation of this notion, see The Klezmatics, "An Undoing World," *Possessed* (Xenophile, 1997).

being a narrow bridge and that the important thing
is not to be afraid. So on this day
I bless my mother and father, that they be
not fearful where they wander. And I
ask you to bless them and before you
close your Book of Life, your Sefer Hachayim,
remember that I always praised your world
and your splendor and that my tongue
tried to say your name on Court Street in Brooklyn.
Take me safely through the Narrows to the sea.[67]

Shapiro was a close friend of Reznikoff, and learned a great deal from
the older poet, as well as from the other first-generation Objectivists.
Like Reznikoff, Shapiro is a quintessential poet of New York, another
walker and observer of street life, who brings to bear a deeply diasporic
sensibility upon daily events in order to produce a sort of modern Jewish
wisdom literature. In an interview with Galen Williams in 2001, Shapiro
notes that Reznikoff was "important for me because I like the protagonist
in his poems. The man who is in all of his poems is a city man and he's
troubled and moving through the city as if it were a kind of labyrinth,
looking for the way. He's not heroic, he's not Byronic. He's used, abused,
and having trouble, and I identified with that."[68] And as Shapiro tells us
in a related essay, "A middle-aged man wanders about the city looking
for the Way. He seems harassed by the life he leads, but he takes joy in
much of what he sees – until he remembers that there is no real joy for
the man who cannot figure things out. He could be a Jew."[69]

Could be a Jew? The diasporic sensibility that such poets share moves
them ceaselessly between faith and doubt, tradition and modernity. But
here, Reznikoff himself should have the last word:

67. Harvey Shapiro, *A Momentary Glory*, 95.

68. "A Poetic Life: Harvey Shapiro with Galen Williams," *The Brooklyn Rail* (February
   2013), http://www.brooklynrail.org/2013/02/express/a-poetic-life-harvey-shapiro
   -with-galen-williams.

69. Harvey Shapiro, "I Write Out of an Uncreated Identity," in *The Writer in the Jewish
   Community: An Israeli-North American Dialogue*, ed. Richard Siegal and Tamar Sofer
   (Rutherford, NJ: Fairleigh Dickinson University Press, 1993), 23.

As I was wandering with my unhappy thoughts,
I looked and saw
that I had come into a sunny place
familiar and yet strange.
"Where am I?" I asked a stranger. "Paradise."
"Can this be Paradise?" I asked surprised,
 for there were motor-cars and factories.
"It is," he answered. "This is the sun that shone on Adam once;
 the very wind that blew upon him too."[70]

70. *Poems of Charles Reznikoff*, 232–33.

FOUR

Allen Grossman and the Poetry of Holiness

IN 2006, THE YEAR THAT ALLEN GROSSMAN RETIRED FROM TEACH-ing at Johns Hopkins, his daughter, Bathsheba Grossman, set up a website for her father. This website, which is still accessible, presents a biography of the poet, a bibliography of his work, and a selection of his poems.[1] The site is simply designed, and its sole decorative element is the Hebrew letter aleph at the top of each page. The homepage declares that "This is the official site of Allen Grossman, poet of love, holiness, and mortality." Considering the philosophical and religious ideas which inform his work, we shall soon see that this is a perfectly fitting description.[2] Drawing from his deep knowledge of Jewish tradition, Grossman fashions a postmodern poetry of holiness, a mode of sacred utterance that paradoxically maintains its religious status even when the notion of divinity is called into question or perceived as infinitely withdrawn. Grossman's understanding of poetry is not existential; it is, rather, fundamentally *social*, and this understanding accounts for his extraordinary achievement in both his poems and his

1. http://www.allengrossman.com/
2. "Allen Grossman's Theophoric Poetics," my chapter on Grossman in *Not One of Them in Place*, presents an extended analysis of the Jewish dimension of his work, including readings of a number of poems from the early and middle stages of his career. I also consider the single most important statement of his Jewish poetic vision, "Jewish Poetry Considered as a Theophoric Project."

essays on poetics. Acutely sensitive to the psychology of human needs and desires, he never ceases to listen for the reciprocity in the voicing of poetic utterance: how and why the poet sings to his or her audience, and how that audience responds.

At the start of *The Winter Conversations* (1981), the first of two dialogues that Grossman holds with Mark Halliday, Grossman asks a fundamental question: "What is poetry for?"[3] Posing the question in this way, Grossman immediately orients us to his vision of poetry, a vision that has somewhat less to do with poets (that is, poetic identity) than it has to do with people: people acknowledging each other's presence, people speaking to each other, people attending to each other. Grossman insists that "Poetry's function is performed properly, is performed safely, only when it is conceived of as an act of respect for another – only when it is conceived of, therefore, as *interactive*. When a poem is truly present in the world, it is present in the form of an interaction which is as profound and extensive as the social order itself."[4] The author of such poems writes them out of a sense of sacred vocation, and in creating these poetic interactions, reproduces "the profoundest human covenant, which is the covenant of language through which they give and obtain the world simultaneously, and only obtain the world when they give."[5] Indeed, for Grossman, "Poetry is not a proper instrument for the mere self-characterization of speakers."[6] The speaking self is entirely secondary, and in his *Summa Lyrica*, his "Primer of the Commonplaces in Speculative Poetics," Grossman performs a marvelous reversal, asserting that "Poems create poets.... One of the *consequences* of the existence of poetry is the existence of 'the poet'.... The poem is a thing made which makes its maker."[7] Personhood is constantly renewed and repaired by poetry, but becoming a poet is not really a matter of personhood per se. Rather, it is a status bestowed upon an individual when that individual

---

3. Allen Grossman, *The Sighted Singer: Two Works on Poetry for Readers and Writers* (Baltimore, MD: Johns Hopkins University Press, 1992), 5.
4. *The Sighted Singer*, 13.
5. Ibid., 284.
6. Ibid., 13.
7. Ibid., 260.

enters into the linguistic covenant. The poet "is the person who has enacted the deed of presence" through the making of a poem.[8]

Grossman's use of the term "covenant" reminds us of the original covenant made between God and the Chosen People, and though the covenant to which he refers is in some respects underwritten by the divine, it is important to note that it is ultimately a pact that binds humanity to itself through language, our fundamental means of communication. The poet understands, respects, and enacts this covenant, and that, in effect, is what makes this individual a poet. The implications of this formula are severe, entailing a strong critique of what we might call the (idolatrous) cult of the poetic personality. Grossman makes this quite clear in *The Winter Conversations*: "The goodness of the poem in my project lies in the degree to which it is un-owned by the author and a completely devoted possession of the reader.... I do not believe that one can obtain from poetry legitimation of the author's personal presence in the world, and at the same time do the business of the poetic art, which is to give the world to another, rather than to arrogate the world as an adjunct of the insufficiently validated selfhood of the poet."[9] The lofty, perhaps impossible idealism of Grossman's project – the giving over of the poem entirely to the reader, and the denial of the poem as any sort of self-legitimation on the part of the poet – should not be dismissed as a sort of utopian hyperbole. Rather, we must seriously engage with Grossman on this crucial point.

Two of Grossman's keywords come to mind in this regard: "manifestation" and "countenance." For Grossman, a poem is a manifestation, which is the word he prefers to "appearance." "There are no appearances," he tells us, "which are not appearances to someone...An appearance or manifestation is the likeness of a presence."[10] The poet is the individual who has learned "the constitutive rules of manifestation...and the central contingency of these rules is the collaborative nature of image construction, the social nature of presence."[11] So writing poetry, for Grossman, is not only an ineluctably social act, but also a collaborative act – even

8. Ibid.
9. Ibid., 109.
10. Ibid., 275
11. Ibid.

when the poet appears to be alone in the act of writing. When the poet writes, there is an Other always coming into presence; that Other is both in the poem and, paradoxically, is the poem, for it is the image or likeness of the other's presence. In Grossman's poetics, then, the poem, if it has truly achieved its manifest being, is always already a collaborative act.

And what is made manifest in and by the poem? Here, Grossman's other keyword, "countenance," comes into play. Grossman observes in *The Winter Conversations* that "a countenance is the manifest presence of the person."[12] In section 34 of the *Summa Lyrica*, one of the sections devoted to the status of the "Person" in poetry, he refines and develops this notion, drawing extensively on the thought of the philosopher Emmanuel Levinas in his work *Totality and Infinity*. Grossman quotes a number of passages from the section of Levinas' book called "Exteriority and the Face," including the following: "The face is present in its refusal to be contained. In this sense, it cannot be comprehended, that is encompassed. . . . The face, still a thing among things, breaks through the form that nevertheless delimits it. This means concretely: the face speaks to me and thereby invites me to a relation incommensurate with a power exercised, be it enjoyment or knowledge."[13] Levinas emphasizes that in our experience of the face of an Other, we cannot and do not exercise power. We are left open to the Other – and it is this openness, for Grossman, that is analogous to the openness created by language in the poem: "Speech, as it comes into poetry, is absorbed in, centrally preoccupied with, its status as a synecdoche of the countenance. In this sense, speech is the countenance which you *can* see that *means* (points toward) the countenance that you cannot see. It is the portrait of the inner and invisible (intuitional) person."[14] The poem makes manifest the human countenance in the wholeness of its lineaments, the countenance that is both external and internal. Given the horrors of the twentieth century, Grossman's great nightmare is the shattered face or countenance, which for him is made manifest in the tortured difficulty of much modern poetry. Thus, part of the poet's social responsibility lies in finding the speech that can restore the shattered countenance and reenact, in

12. Ibid., 95.
13. Emmanuel Levinas, quoted in *The Sighted Singer*, 307.
14. Ibid., 306.

a proper fashion, the deed of presence or manifestation. Indeed, as Grossman tells Mark Halliday, "The highest form which poetic ambition, in my mind, can take is to join together oracular profundity with the whole, intact, harmonious, and socially-addressed countenance."[15]

One beautifully wrought instance of this high ambition is "The Piano Player Explains Himself," the first poem in *The Ether Dome and Other Poems: New and Selected 1979–1991*. Deliberately positioned in this manner, "The Piano Player Explains Himself" may be read as an allegory of the poet's struggle to achieve "oracular profundity," while still meeting the obligation to preserve and restore "the whole, intact, harmonious, and socially-addressed countenance." In this respect, the poem fits perfectly with Walter Benjamin's observation that "an appreciation of the transience of things, and the concern to rescue them for eternity, is one of the strongest impulses in allegory."[16] The scene and figures of the poem point to the transience of human life, and the consequent need for social rituals to preserve the human countenance in memory. Opposed to this is the isolated poet-piano player, whose prophetic power, attuned to metaphysical truth, inevitably challenges social conventions. Here are the opening lines:

> When the corpse revived at the funeral,
> The outraged mourners killed it; and the soul
> Of the revenant passed into the body
> Of the poet because it had more to say.
> He sat down at the piano no one could play
> Called Messiah, or The Regulator of the World,
> Which had stood for fifty years, to my knowledge,
> Beneath a painting of a red-haired woman
> In a loose gown with one bared breast, and played
> A posthumous work of the composer S –
> About the impotence of God (I believe)
> Who has no power not to create everything.[17]

15. Ibid., 97–98.
16. Walter Benjamin, *The Origin of German Tragic Drama*, trans. John Osborne (London: Verso, 1998), 223.
17. Allen Grossman, *The Ether Dome and Other Poems: New and Selected 1979–1991* (New York: New Directions, 1991), 3.

Let us recall that for Grossman, the poet "is the person who has enacted the deed of presence" – a presence that endures even through death.[18] This is a concept that those who live according to the conventions of social life may find difficult to comprehend or accept; hence the violence of the mourners, who kill the revived corpse. Their outrage is due at least partly to their wish, in accordance to social convention, to have done with the dead man through the appropriate rituals. But prophecy (read: poetry) is always already dead, and always already resurrected. The spirit thus passes into the new poet, for the poet-prophet by definition is open to the spirit, and stands ready to receive it through the ineluctable reality of death. But that reality is also sanctioned by the social ritual of the funeral, and when the ritual is violated, as it is here, the mourners are outraged; they would kill the prophet again but cannot, because there is always "more to say."

Poetic prophecy always seeks its medium, its instrument, which is also its redemption; hence the poet plays a piano called "Messiah, or The Regulator of the World." Why this strange nomenclature? Seated beneath a portrait of the muse (who, with her bared breast, is both mother and lover), he performs a "posthumous work of the composer S – / About the impotence of God (I believe) / Who has no power not to create everything." The piece that he performs is "posthumous," and yet in its performance it lives again; its living presence is restored. It prophetically addresses God's boundless, and apparently, *unregulated* creativity, a notion similar to that found in the Lurianic Kabbalah, with its emphasis on God's powers failing to be contained within the *sefirot*, or divine vessels. Who, therefore, regulates the creative force of the divine? For Grossman, it is the messianic figure of the poet, announcing an order of being that includes but transcends the reality of death upon which the mourners insist.[19] "For a long hour," we are told,

18. *The Sighted Singer*, 260.
19. According to Grossman's widow, the writer Judith Grossman, calling the piano "Messiah" is also a reference to the Stradivarius violin by that name, which is in the collection of the Ashmolean Museum and very rarely played. Judith Grossman, email message to author, July 15, 2015. In the same email, Ms. Grossman informed me that the inscription on the piano ("When I was green and blossomed in the Spring / I was mute wood. Now I am dead I sing.") "comes from another museum whose name I

> The poet played The Regulator of the World
> As the spirit prompted, and entered upon
> The pathways of His power – while the mourners
> Stood with slow blood on their hands
> Astonished by the weird processional
> And the undertaker figured his bill.[20]

The long hour during which the poet plays is the hour of the poem itself, the hour in which the prophetic spirit regulates the "pathways of His power," serving the community by mediating between the orders of the human and the divine.[21] Like the people at the end of Coleridge's "Kubla Khan," terrified by the entranced poet whose vision recapitulates the importance of the community but also isolates him from the community, the mourners in Grossman's poem, with "slow blood on their hands," are "Astonished by the weird processional." Yet ordinary life must proceed, as "the undertaker figured his bill."

What is it, then, that the piano player *does* when he "enters into the pathways of His power"? How, to return again to Grossman's formulation, is the playing of the piano, the inscription of the poem, *interactive*, as Grossman tells us poetry should be? Let us recall that poems such as this one are intended to enact "the profoundest human covenant, which is the covenant of language through which they give and obtain the world simultaneously, and only obtain the world when they give." In the rest of "The Piano Player Explains Himself," we see this exchange, this giving and obtaining of the world, as the poem, the covenant of language, is affirmed in the figure of the poet – or perhaps more precisely, as the figure of the poet stands forth because the poem enacts the covenant of language:

forget, but Allen and I visited and saw an old keyboard instrument with the sense of that written on it in another language – Latin maybe? Many years ago." I have been unable to identify the instrument or the museum.

20. *The Ether Dome*, 3.

21. In his use of the phrase "pathways of His power," Grossman may be referring to the kabbalistic idea of the *tzinorot* ("channels") between the *sefirot*: "The interaction among the various *sefirot* takes place through a network of connecting *tzinorot* ('channels'), which carry the flow of divine energy throughout Creation." Moshe Miller, "Emanations Interact," http://www.chabad.org/kabbalah/article_cdo/aid /380812/jewish/Emanations-Interact.htm.

> – We have in mind an unplayed instrument
> Which stands apart in a memorial air
> Where the room darkens toward its inmost wall
> And a lady hangs in her autumnal hair
> At evening of the November rains; and winds
> Sublime out of the North, and North by West,
> Are sowing from the death-sack of the seed
> The burden of her cloudy hip. Behold,
> I send the demon I know to relieve your need,
> An imperfect player at the perfect instrument
> Who takes in hand The Regulator of the World
> To keep the splendor from destroying us.
> Lady! The last virtuoso of the composer S –
> Darkens your parlor with the music of the Law.
> When I was green and blossomed in the Spring
> I was mute wood. Now I am dead I sing.[22]

It is autumn, the season of nature's passage into death, and at first, it seems there is only potential: the unplayed instrument, the memorial air at the loss of prophecy, and the muse, who is now revealed as a goddess of nature as well. It is she who sows the seed from the "death-sack" at her "cloudy hip," and as in Shelley's "Ode to the West Wind," the wind and rain are harbingers of death and rebirth. Likewise, they are harbingers of poetic prophecy, for again, as in Shelley's poem, the poet is possessed by a demon (or *daimon*), a spirit who comes to "relieve your need, / An imperfect player at the perfect instrument / Who takes in hand The Regulator of the World / To keep the splendor from destroying us."

Grossman's use of pronouns here is worth noting. The "I" who sends the demon is the poet who *writes* the poem, but he is conjoined with the poet-piano player, who is a figure *in* the poem. In other words, the poet is both inside and outside his poem; in a transcendental register, he stand apart from the community, but he is also one with the community, as in the phrases "your need" (the piano player and the mourners) and "To keep the splendor from destroying us" (the same, and perhaps the poet

---

22. *The Ether Dome*, 3.

who writes the poem as well). The divine splendor or creativity, as pre-
viously observed, is unregulated, and the poet must perform "the music
of the Law" in order to maintain the boundary between the Creator
and Creation. In the last lines, another equally significant conjunction
of identity takes place, that of the poet and his instrument. The "I" who
speaks here is clearly the piano itself, "The Regulator of the World." Once
green, blossoming, but mute wood, it, like the poet, has passed through
death, and is now capable of making the music of the Law. The poet and
poetry are one, inseparable, and through the invocation of the muse, or
nature, they can at last declare their shared identity. In this respect, the
poet fulfills his oracular function while preserving "the whole, intact,
harmonious, and socially-addressed countenance."

As my reading of "The Piano Player Explains Himself" indicates,
Grossman borrows freely from Jewish religious ideas and combines
them with concepts derived from the Romantic tradition of the poet-
prophet. The result is a phantasmagoric vision or performance of poetry,
but one that is "performed safely" and "conceived of as an act of respect
for another." It is also not an accident that this poem, like many of
Grossman's most important lyrics, is concerned with the memorial
power of poetry, with the personhood and function of the poet in rela-
tion to the community or social ensemble, and with the reality of death
as an individual and as a collective experience. What I will now present
is a detailed interpretation of what I regard to be one of Grossman's
greatest achievements, the sequence of lyrics called "Poland of Death."
A sublime work in the tradition of Shelley, Yeats, and Wallace Stevens,
"Poland of Death" is also one of Grossman's deeply Jewish poems. Not
only does it draw from Jewish ritual and liturgy, and reflect a thorough
understanding of crucial Jewish theological ideas, it is also infused with
an uncanny sense of Jewish humor, reminiscent of Thomas Mann's
characterization of Kafka as "a religious humorist."[23] Granted, Kafka
and Shelley would appear to be an unlikely combination, even for a
contemporary poet, but such, as we shall see, is indeed the case: a sign

---

23. Thomas Mann, "Homage," in Franz Kafka, *The Castle*, trans. Edwin and Willa Muir
(New York: Schocken Books, 1974), x.

of Grossman's originality and his remarkable rethinking of literary and religious traditions.

Put simply, "Poland of Death" is a radical rethinking of the Kaddish, its function in Jewish liturgy and its significance in the expression of Jewish religious belief. The Kaddish is commonly regarded as a prayer of mourning, but it is actually a prayer sanctifying the Holy Name, at the heart of which is a communal response to that act of sanctification. As Hayim Halevy Donin explains, "The response is the heart of the Kaddish and should be said aloud. Kaddish is therefore not said when one is praying alone. Its very essence is as a public prayer."[24] Such being the case, the prayer's relationship to death and grief (an association which may be traced back at least to the thirteenth century) has always been open to interpretation. One explanation, which, as we shall see, relates to the events in "Poland of Death," has to do with the experience of bereavement: "In a time of tragedy and loss, one might become bitter toward the Lord and reject Him. At precisely such a time, we rise to praise Him and publicly to affirm our belief in His righteousness."[25] How the prayer came to be associated with mourning is also the question that Leon Wieseltier probes in his extended talmudic work *Kaddish*, one of the boldest attempts to combine traditional Jewish issues and textual procedures with a contemporary American sensibility. At one point, Wieseltier analyzes variations of a well-known midrash in which Rabbi Akiva saves a dead man from eternal punishment by leading the man's son back to Jewish observance, which culminates in the recitation of the Kaddish. Wieseltier comments: "The themes of the story? That the dead are in need of spiritual rescue; and that the agent of spiritual rescue is the son; and that the instrument of spiritual rescue is prayer, notably the kaddish."[26]

Likewise, in his essay "Holiness," Grossman observes that the Kaddish prayer "is an act of ridding the pollution of death from the world of the living. In this context, the pollution of death is understood to be the disease of a will that can no longer praise the Name, that can

---

24. Hayim Halevy Donin, *To Pray as a Jew* (New York: Basic Books, 1980), 217.
25. Ibid., 222.
26. Leon Wieseltier, *Kaddish* (New York: Vintage, 1998), 127.

no longer by words of sanctification on its own behalf return the world to its maker."[27] "Poland of Death" is a Kaddish for Louis, the father who begs his son to "Give me a word" but cannot accept it, and for Beatrice, the mother who bids him to "Sing me something about the / Forest primeval."[28] In death, at the beginning of the poem, neither parent can praise the Name. It is the specific task of the Jewish child to recite the Kaddish for his or her parents, to align their wills with that of God, as they were able to do for themselves while they lived. "Poland of Death" works its way toward what Grossman in "Holiness" calls "[t]he peace that is prayed for at the end of the Kaddish . . . the order of the world restored, as in the moment before creation, to its original unity, of which holiness is the sign."[29] But in order to reach this desired endpoint, the speaker of the poem must help his parents come to terms with their deaths. He must help them adjust to "Poland of Death," where Beatrice declares that "This necropolis is a *disgrace*," and where "Louis of Minneapolis" becomes "A big Rabbi of rats dressed in a suit / That fits."[30] And in doing so, as we shall see, he also achieves his poetic birthright. He may even become the prophetic figure whom Grossman calls in his essay on the theophoric nature of Jewish poetry, "the Jew's *great* poet . . . called monologically by Presence itself."[31]

Structurally and methodologically, "Poland of Death," like much of Grossman's mature poetry, is a visionary work in which symbolic figures and gestures are juxtaposed through a sort of "dream logic," moving in registers both narrative and dramatic toward the resolution of a problem that has been obscurely posed at the beginning of the poem. The problem in this case is the classic Jewish one of sanctification in the face of death, but the procedure of the poem is not primarily that of prayer, but of spectral projection and inner sight. In this respect, "Poland of Death" is an inheritor of the romantic and modernist traditions of the phantasmagoria, a term which, though it originally refers to eighteenth-century magic

27. *The Long Schoolroom*, 186.
28. *The Ether Dome*, 31, 30.
29. *The Long Schoolroom*, 186.
30. *The Ether Dome*, 33, 35, 36.
31. *The Long Schoolroom*, 163.

lantern shows, has come to signify, as Terry Castle puts it, "the alienating power of the imagination," or even "the mind itself" as "a kind of super-natural space, filled with intrusive spectral presences – incursions from past or future, ready to terrify, pursue, or disable the harried subject."[32] The experience of the phantasmagoria, either as spectral show or haunted interiority, would at first appear fairly remote from the Kaddish chanted by the dutiful Jewish son for his deceased parents: the former maintains the restless, individualized being of the dead, while the latter attempts to reconcile the dead with the God of Israel's overarching Being. Yet it is just this categorical – hence generic and discursive – instability which gives Grossman's poem its peculiar power.

"Poland of Death" unfolds as a series of uncanny encounters and dialogues, set, for the most part, in the realm of death, the necropolis named in the poem's title. This necropolis is unquestionably a place of fearful sights, obscure horrors projected outward, which may derive from the unconscious of Castle's "harried subject." In one of the speaker's meetings with his father, we are told that

> – He showed me
> The severed head of a mother in her tears
> Kissing and eating the severed head of a child;
> And one familiar spirit like a snarled hank
> of somebody's black hair. And he showed also
> A bloody angle of the wires where groans
> Of men and women drowned the roar of motors
> And mounted to a prophecy.[33]

I will return to the significance of these images, but for the present, I want to point out that they are part of a colloquy in which father and son try to understand the *place* of death (both as psychic space and existential meaning) in the structure of reality. The language of Grossman's image-casting and dialogues in the poem has little to do, apparently, with the language of the Kaddish, which never mentions death, but is rather a

32. Terry Castle, *The Female Thermometer: Eighteenth-Century Culture and the Invention of the Uncanny* (New York: Oxford University Press, 1995), 155, 167.
33. *The Ether Dome*, 31–32.

litany in Hebrew and Aramaic of the sanctified qualities of God's Name. Yet the intent of the poem and prayer is the same. As Wieseltier points out, "In the company of death, subjectivity is wild. So subjectivity must be tamed. The taming of subjectivity is the work of the kaddish. Three times daily, the inner perspective of the mourner is unmagnified, unsanctified. Psychology is belittled."[34] If the Kaddish is recited, as Grossman tells us, to sanctify the Name on the behalf of a will that can no longer perform such sanctification, then what unfolds in "Poland of Death" is a phantasmagoric dramatization of the psychic effort to align the will of the deceased with that of the Living God. Grossman has, in effect, turned the religious significance of the prayer into a visionary poem which unfolds as a drama in the realm of death itself. Through the objective power of narrative, the subjective psychology of the mourner, as in the case of the Kaddish itself, is "belittled."

But why is the phantasmagoric necropolis envisioned here called *Poland* of Death? For the relatively assimilated American Jews of Louis's and Beatrice's generation, Poland is preeminently the "Old World," the world from which *their* parents emigrated and to which they, ironically, must now return. "Since you dug me down in America," Louis tells his son, " I've been scratching a way with a nail, / And now I have come to Poland of death."[35] "'This is the worst place I've ever lived in,'" Beatrice resentfully informs her son. "'I want', she says, 'a clean house and a quiet town,'" as if Death were a noisy and dirty shtetl from which one should escape as soon as possible, rather than the American town to which she is accustomed.[36] Furthermore, in recent history, Poland had literally become a place of death, particularly for Jews. As the country where the Nazis established the largest extermination camps, Poland is associated not merely with death, but with a mass annihilation of Jews which no Kaddish, it would seem, could ever sanctify. Poland, in all its horror, is "[t]he severed head of a mother in her tears / Kissing and eating the severed head of a child"; it was in the Polish camps that one saw and heard "[a] bloody angle of the wires where groans / Of men

---

34. Wieseltier, 166.
35. *The Ether Dome*, 31.
36. Ibid., 34.

and women drowned the roar of motors / And mounted to a prophecy."
By contrast, America has meant *life* to the American Jews of the parents'
generation, individuated and free.

The return to "Poland" is a return to the Collective, not only on
the level of history, but also on what we may call the psycho-poetic
level – and for Grossman, "the Collective means death." As he explains
in the *Summa Lyrica*, "Traditionally, the life of the Collective and death
of the individual intersect.... Death is the condition of access to the
Collective, and the death of the individual is the condition of the life
of the Collective."[37] Thus in death, the poet's parents relinquish their
(American) individuality and enter the (Jewish) Collective, signified,
in the case of the father, by his becoming "a proud Jew now, dwelling
among the dead"[38]

Yet the Collective also "authorizes poetic speech"; likewise, "[t]he
speaker in the poem prays the common prayer."[39] Authorized by and
speaking on behalf of the Collective, the son offers the poem/prayer that
is intended to bring the parents into the Collective through the recogni-
tion of their death. Grossman writes of "the immortal self-consciousness
of the human collective" and asserts that "[t]the Collective, death, and
the divine are equivalent expressions."[40] But in "Poland of Death," this
is not only, or not merely, the human Collective to which the parents are
joined. It is the *Jewish* Collective, the Congregation of Israel, chosen by
God as holy and bound together by a culture of holiness, what Grossman
calls in "Holiness" "a system of transactions by which through the medi-
ation of holiness man and God can be included within the precinct of
the same term."[41] Louis and Beatrice, the Jewish parents of a Jewish son
who recites the Kaddish on their behalf, cannot simply enter the immor-
tality of Collective being. Their immortality depends on the alignment
of their wills with that of God: in death as in life, they partake in "the
Hebrew culture of holiness," and must as Jews acknowledge that there

37. *The Sighted Singer*, 240–41.
38. *The Ether Dome*, 36.
39. *The Sighted Singer* 241, 244.
40. Ibid., 240, 244.
41. *The Long Schoolroom*, 180.

is "no affirmation less than total even in the face of death. The refusal of the will to accept God's description of the one world is the refusal of being."[42] The poem/prayer of the son may be read as an attempt to prevent such a refusal, so that even in death, the participation of the parents in a state of divinely regulated being is insured.

But the poet must proceed somewhat differently in the case of each parent, since "It is the duty of every man, / And woman, to write the life of the mother. / But the life of the father is written by / The father alone."[43] Here, Grossman draws on the elaborate distinction between "mother tongue" and "father tongue" that makes up section 42 of his *Summa Lyrica*. The father tongue is the fictional or representational; the mother tongue is the natural, "not meaningful in itself but the ground on which meaning is inscribed."[44] "And yet poetic knowledge is knowledge of the mother tongue," Grossman insists.[45] "Unlike the father tongue which is primarily word, the mother tongue is the source of silence. It would be better to say that the mother tongue is necessity produced as utterance, the speech of the unwilled and the unwillable, the speech of the wordless, of presence."[46] To take on poetic knowledge, then, is to write the life of the mother, to speak her silence, which is the silence of nature.

This accounts for Beatrice's obsession with "the forest primeval." The phrase itself, of course, comes from the first line of Longfellow's *Evangeline* (1847): "This is the forest primeval. The murmuring pines and the hemlocks…"[47] *Evangeline* is a classic American work, a tale of love and loss in the New World that would have been studied by a schoolgirl of Beatrice's generation, and even then its opening phrase had already become a cliché. Yet like all clichés, it carries great resonance; thus the romantic sublime, as represented in the Prelude of Longfellow's poem, is recalled after a lifetime by the old woman Beatrice and associated with the power of death. Beatrice is blind in one eye, and as she moves

---

42. Ibid., 186.
43. *The Ether Dome*, 35.
44. *The Sighted Singer*, 356.
45. Ibid., 360.
46. Ibid., 362.
47. Henry Wadsworth Longfellow, *Evangeline* (New York: Avon Books, 1971), 23.

into death "her blind eye – the dead one – stares out / As if to say, 'This is the forest primeval. / This is death at last.'"[48] In death, we are told,

> Her tears mingle with the freshness of the streams,
> Wept for primeval forests in the darkness where
> All the prisoners rest together, out of the air,
> Wept from the left eye of our mother (the dead one),
>
> In its dream of other worlds in the Millennium.[49]

"Because she is mute, nature mourns," writes Walter Benjamin.[50] Beatrice is by no means mute, and mourns imperiously on her own terms, but she still identifies herself with nature, and her speech is the speech of unwilled and unwillable presence. That commanding presence summons even Death himself (for Death is a part of the natural order), and upon that summons, a strange scene unfolds:

> But he will not come. Her "offense" is great.
> Death says repeatedly, *"You do not love me, Bea!"*
> He also says to her, "I am your only son."
> "My brother!" I reply (astonished), "I understand you.
> But you must do this *for our sake*. Mother Beatrice,
> A woman of strong will, multiplies worlds."
> "*I believe*," Death says, "in the one world that is."[51]

As Grossman notes in *The Sighted Singer*, Death is "always summoned as a challenge or, even more specifically, as an affront to [our] conceptions of sociability."[52] As a strong, social individual, Beatrice resists and has no love for Death, but as the female principle of nature, she must lose her will in the greater Will, and enter what Death calls "the one world that is." A cosmic power that has its ultimate origin in God, Death speaks of the unity of all things. This is why the poet becomes the brother of Death and joins forces with him:

48. *The Ether Dome*, 32.
49. Ibid., 33.
50. Walter Benjamin, "On Language as Such and on the Language of Man," in *Reflections*, 329.
51. *The Ether Dome*, 33–34.
52. *The Sighted Singer*, 75.

> And I myself cry out, taking my brother's part
> "Keep it simple, please – so we can understand!"
> And hear our mother calling in strange tones
> Across black water, against the storm: "Adorn!
> Adorn the necropolis, and sweep the sill,"
> Calling to her stubborn son who hates her, her only one,
> And who will not kill her, or take her home, or mourn.[53]

As she calls out to clean and adorn the necropolis, the mother comes to terms with Death, knowing that she *is* dead and that the necropolis is now her home. She joins what Grossman calls "the Collective," all of humanity that have been gathered into death (hence the vision of a necropolis, a city of the dead, which dominates the poem), and as Grossman tells us in *The Sighted Singer*, "the life of the Collective and the death of the individual intersect."[54]

The father, by comparison, accommodates himself more successfully to the realm of death, but in death he too must be led to affirm the unity of being under the Divine Will. At the beginning of the poem, Louis scratches his way from his grave to the necropolis using a nail, which he will eventually bequeath to his son. The nail is an apt symbol of the father and the father tongue, meaning fictionalization, representation, education, tradition – the voluntary instead of the compelled, word instead of silence, art instead of nature. The nail is a means of construction, of holding made things together; it also resembles a stylus, an writing instrument. It could be said then that on one level, the father voluntarily writes himself into death. When the son first comes upon him in the necropolis, they face each other naked, presenting their bodies to each other, and it is on this occasion that the father shows the son the vision quoted above, which I have associated with the mass death of the Holocaust. What follows indicates that Louis is still not quite ready to accept his place:

> ... Then he gave me
> a sharp look and said, "Thank God I have no children,"
> And ran off with a cry down an alley of

---

53. *The Ether Dome*, 34.
54. *The Sighted Singer*, 240.

That place like one who remembered suddenly
The day of his own death – [55]

In death, Louis, like Beatrice, has trouble accepting the son as his own, for both parents know that it is only in colloquy with him, the speaker of their Kaddish, that their place in the necropolis, and in the divine order, will be secured. Conversely, it is this colloquy which allows the son to come to terms with, and separate himself, from his parents' deaths. But whereas Beatrice seeks "the forest primeval," Louis seeks "the word." Thus when the son comes upon him again, he has become not only a "big Rabbi of rats" but also the *maître à penser* of the necropolis," a "Doctor of Philosophy" for whom "[t]he celebrations of commencement were elaborate."[56] Asked by his son to "[s]ay something / I can understand," Louis responds with a prophetic pastiche out of Ezekiel, Revelation, and Blake, an outburst which the son cannot understand, and, in effect, ignores.[57] He answers his father by offering "a new song": "And the abyss / Supplied its word, 'Halleluya!' *Praise* / *The Lord.*"[58]

The son's praise of the Name, arising from the abyss that precedes Creation, takes us to the climax of Grossman's poem, the moment when the son, in order to convince his parents of their new place in Creation, sides with "the Hebrew culture of holiness," a culture that, as we have seen, is "peculiarly severe, admitting, as in the Kaddish, no affirmation less than total even in the face of death."[59] This is the lesson that the poet must teach his dead, this is the "new song":

"Father, not father, *O roi magicien!*
Mother, not mother, O name of Beatrice!
Does the cloth forget the weaver, does the field
Of millet in its season no longer remember the sower,
Or the birds that feed on it honor in later summer
The labor that laid it down? O Yes! And the pot
The woman's hand who made it has forgot.[60]

55. Ibid., 32.
56. Ibid., 35, 36.
57. Ibid., 36.
58. Ibid., 38.
59. *The Long Schoolroom*, 186.
60. *The Ether Dome*, 38.

The parents are no longer the parents; they forget themselves, just as the created objects forget the act of creation, forget the power of agency that has brought them forth. Beatrice and Louis are folded into the order of Creation, and in a sudden moment of horror, Louis is "driven out / (The Doctor in his garment of superior cloth) / Into the field behind the wall and shot!": a death not truly his own, but one that unites him with so many of his fellow Jews in "Poland of Death."[61] And with the definitive loss of the father, the son, "[t]he chronicler," receives the nail in turn, asking and answering the father's question: "What is the WORD? Halleluya. The Lord is ONE."[62] The word that the father has sought, which the son provides from the abyss, is the word of the Shema, the unitary creed that Jews are to declare with their dying breath: "Hear O Israel, the Lord is our God, the Lord is One."

One would think that "Poland of Death" would end at this point, but that is not the case. The poem has one more long section, an extended coda in which the parents are hardly mentioned at all. Practically a complete poem unto itself, this fifth and final section confirms, as I indicated above, that "Poland of Death" is not only a Kaddish: it is also a poem of election, a poem that seeks knowledge of, and identity with, what Grossman, in his essay on the theophoric nature of Jewish poetry, calls "the Jew's *great* poet" who "is called monologically by Presence itself," the appropriate chanter of a prayer that aligns Creation with its Creator.[63] Unlike muse-inspired non-Jewish poetry in the West, which, according to Grossman, is a discourse of loss and memory founded upon the myths of Philomela and of Orpheus, Jewish poetry is inspired by the Shekhinah, God's indwelling spirit gendered female, and is based on God's covenant with the Jews.[64] Writing under the sign of the Shekhinah, the poet of "Poland of Death" is ultimately intended "to construct the place where 'Light and Law are manifest', to which the nations may come because it is where they are ... where loss is given back as meaning and where the People and the peoples are equally at home."[65]

---

61. Ibid.
62. Ibid., 39.
63. *The Long Schoolroom*, 163.
64. See "Orpheus/Philomela: Subjection and Mastery in the Founding Stories of Poetic Production," in *The Long Schoolroom*, 18–38.
65. *The Long Schoolroom*, 166. For a comprehensive treatment of the Shekhinah in Jewish

Perhaps it is because "the People and the peoples are equally at home" that the poem itself presents the figure of the "great poet" in an extraordinary passage that successfully appropriates the tone and theme of Wallace Stevens, one of Grossman's most important precursors:

> – How hard, then, to know the greater poet! And the work
> of the greater poet? How shall I know what it is?
> And if I know what it is, how shall I make it known
> Scratching with this nail? How shall I make it known
> To you? And if I make it known to you, what then shall
> I do? How shall I endure my pain and your pain,
> Knowing the greater poet and the work? Is it like
> A tree that casts no shadow and bears no fruit,
> And yet is all shadow and all the fruit there is?
> Is it, perhaps, the fatal earth: a stone colossus
> Made by mind that sends for all the dead, and stands?[66]

In a certain respect, Grossman's "greater poet" is a metonymy for poetry writ large, a creative spirit which could be equated with God's creative spirit, the kabbalistic tree that is all shadow and bears all fruit. As Stevens says in his equally mystical "Final Soliloquy of the Interior Paramour," "We say God and the imagination are one."[67] Individual poets may embody, and, for a time, become one with this spirit; thus, as we have seen, Grossman asserts that "Poems make poets.... One of the *consequences* of the existence of poetry is the existence of 'the poet'... The poet is not the strongest or the most beautiful or the most tested man or woman of the time. He or she is the person who has enacted the deed of presence and therefore passed into manifestation."[68]

In the last section of "Poland of Death," Grossman introduces the

---

American poetry, see Selinger, 250–71. For additional analyses, see Maeera Y. Shreiber, "The End of Exile: Jewish Identity and Its Diasporic Poetics." *PMLA* 113, no. 2 (March 1998): 273–87, and *Singing In a Strange Land, passim.* My reading of the Shekhinah may be found in *Not One of Them in Place,* 11–12 and 72–74.

66. *The Ether Dome,* 40.
67. Wallace Stevens, *The Collected Poems of Wallace Stevens* (New York: Vintage Books, 1982), 524.
68. *The Sighted Singer,* 260.

figure of Irene, whose story is told in *White Sails*, a sequence of lyrics in his later book, *How to Do Things with Tears* (2001). Irene is "the SIGHTED SINGER, the American poet who has dreamed the dream of the poet's vocation"[69] – a figure who, mutatis mutandis, is the poet Grossman himself "[i]n another life."[70] Having received the symbolic nail from his father, the poet also buys from Irene, his other self, "an Edison phonograph together / With numerous rolls," among them the songs that constitute his mother's life, which he is charged to inscribe.[71] Because he has fulfilled the terms of his poetic election, having reconciled himself with both male and female principles, he is, in effect, prepared to pass into manifestation, to be made into that "greater poet."

Thus, in one of the last and weirdest turns in the poem, he sets himself up as "The Universal American Travelling Workshop" ("Makes, alters, and repairs everything") traveling "up and down the Transcaspian Line" to repair all that is broken "[i]n Baku, Kizil-Arvat, and Ashkhabad and Andjian" for "the Asiatic customers of Sears."[72] With this move, reminiscent of Kafka's "Nature Theater of Oklahoma" in *Amerika*, it is difficult to tell whether Grossman is poking gentle fun at American cultural imperialism, or simply giving us an instance of the universality of the poet's task. In any event, at the end of the poem,

> ... They are dancing in Baku at noon in the bazaar
> To the roll that repeats the circulation of the air,
> Souvenir of the Chicago Fair (1893) and called "The Mind
> As It Is Known" or "The Stone": witness to the mother's life
> That mends the soul.... [73]

The song now sung all along the Transcaspian line is the song of the mother, the mother tongue to which the poet is obliged to give words. That song is called "The Mind As It Is Known" because poetry for Grossman is above all "an instrument for thinking."[74] It is called "The

69. Allen Grossman, *How to Do Things with Tears* (New York: New Directions, 2001), xi.
70. *The Ether Dome*, 41.
71. Ibid.
72. Ibid.
73. Ibid., 42.
74. *The Sighted Singer*, 207.

Stone" because it corresponds to the stone "in the mouth of the great god, poet divine / And what the song will be nobody knows."[75] What follows is "Thunder in the air. / Sighs along the ground. A proverb (something about a fool) / In the right hand of the son. And in his left, a nail."[76] Part of poetry's sublimity lies in the fact that there is no telling what the song will be; that is, there is no telling when and how poetry will be made manifest again, appearing even through the figure of the proverbial fool, the archetypal poet-hero. But the fundamental human needs which it answers are always there to be satisfied. "The function of poetry," says Grossman, "is to obtain for everybody one kind of success at the limits of the autonomy of the will.... The limits of the autonomy of the will discovered in poetry are death and the barriers against access to other consciousnesses.... The kind of success which poetry facilitates is called 'immortality.'"[77] This function is abundantly fulfilled in "Poland of Death."

After *The Ether Dome* in 1991, with its extraordinary gathering of new poems, including "Poland of Death" (these new poems are in a section called "Pastorals of Our Other Hours in the Millennium"), Grossman goes on publish four more books of poetry: *The Philosopher's Window and Other Poems* (1995), *How to Do Things With Tears* (2001), *Sweet Youth* (2002; this book includes a generous selection of Grossman's very early poems), and finally *Descartes' Loneliness* (2007). In 2009, he was awarded the Bollingen Prize. Suffering from Alzheimer's during his last years, he died of complications of the disease in 2014. Given the overriding concerns of Grossman's poetry – Eros (including sexual love, but also, more broadly, the psycho-spiritual power that binds people together into social units), holiness (the transactions that take place between the divine and human), mortality (both the death of the individual and of successive generations), and the legislating, covenantal force of poetic language – it behooves us to ask how the poet pursues his great themes as he himself enters the final stages of his life. Thinking of both "The Piano Player Explains Himself" and "Poland of Death," we recall

75. *The Ether Dome*, 42.
76. Ibid.
77. *The Sighted Singer*, 209–10.

that Grossman's understanding of the social function of poetry emerges out of a fundamental dialectic of sociability and isolation, a dialectic which is itself determined by the twofold nature of poetic obligation: the restoration of the human countenance and the prophetic singularity of poetic inspiration. The fact of mortality heightens the tension in this dialectic, making it all the more urgent, especially for poets themselves. Inclined toward the isolation, the loneliness of prophetic utterance, or what Grossman calls "oracular profundity," poets in the prophetic tradition also understand that their responsibility is to find the language that enacts the deed of presence, making manifest the human countenance, however broken, for individuals and for the community. And in the poem lies the hope that the countenance can be restored and made whole.

Nowhere is this struggle more apparent than in his last book, *Descartes' Loneliness*. Grossman explains that the name of the philosopher Descartes "stands for all persons insofar as we – you and I, *each of us alone* – discover the world for the first time and, therefore, must think (*each of us must do so alone*, there is no other way) as if no one had ever thought before. It is this person who writes *poetry* and for whom it is written."[78] The problem that Grossman recognizes, and wrestles with in his last poems, is that the poet by inclination, and, I would guess, by necessity, must be isolated, must be alone, in order to enact the essentially social act of manifestation, of bringing the poem into presence. Hence what may well be Grossman's last formulation of poetic identity: "Poets are persons aware of aloneness and *competent to speak in the space of solitude* – who, by speaking alone, make possible for themselves and for others *the being of persons*, in which all the value of the human world is found."[79] And hence the wry beauty of the opening stanza of the poem "Descartes' Loneliness," with which the volume begins:

> Toward evening, the natural light becomes
> intelligent and answers, without demur:
> *"Be assured! You are not alone...."*

78. Allen Grossman, *Descartes' Loneliness* (New York: New Directions, 2007), 63.
79. Ibid., 63–64.

> But in fact, toward evening, I am not
> convinced there *is* any other except myself
> to whom existence *necessarily* pertains.
> I also interrogate myself to discover
> whether I *myself* possess any power
> by which I can bring it about that I
> who now am shall exist another moment.[80]

Grossman honors Descartes not in the confidence, not in the assurance of the isolated mind thinking itself, but rather in the doubt that arises from the Cartesian situation. "I am conscious of no such power," the speaker of the poem continues.

> And yet, if I myself cannot be
> the cause of that assurance, surely
> it is necessary to conclude that
> I am not alone in the world. There is
> some other who is the cause of that idea.[81]

The self-reflective poet in isolation, because he is unsure of his being and yet intuitively knows himself to be, is inevitably led to conclude that he exists along with others who likewise doubt and yet are assured of their being. We return to the idea, implicit here, that the poem, when it is uttered, is a collaboration, a manifestation of one in the presence of another.

Be that as it may, *Descartes' Loneliness*, as befits a last volume of poems, must confront the ultimate condition of isolation, that of death, when no more poems will be written, when sociability will end, and when the possibility of presence through poetic speech will be foreclosed. One such poem is "The Famished Dead," a reimagining of the *Nekuia*, the descent of Odysseus into the underworld in Book XI of the *Odyssey*. In Grossman's poem, the bloody pit to which the ghosts come to drink is his own heart. The poem also resembles Yeats' "All Souls' Night," in which the poet summons the dead using the fumes of muscatel: "His

---

80. Ibid., 3.
81. Ibid.

element is so fine / Being sharpened by his death, / To drink from the wine-breath / While our gross palates drink from the whole wine."[82] Here is the first stanza of Grossman's poem:

> To this bloody pit – my heart – they crowd.
> They drink my blood.
> The way they become visible – *aware* –
> and speak.
> "Open that bloody pit."
> "Look!" I reply,
> "I have other plans!"
> "In fact," Death says, "you've nothing else
> to do."
> They block the stair and quarrel
> among themselves. I tell them,
> "The rule is *one at a time*."
> But whenever *anybody* is let in
> the rest utter heartbroken cries.... [83]

Typical of late Grossman is the weird combination of terror and comedy, producing a sort of sublime slapstick that is his alone. Death and the poet present themselves as a comedy team, though the poet is hardly enthusiastic about his calling. Nevertheless, one at a time the dead come to speak – Louis, the poet's car dealer father; his grandfather Harry Berman, cracking Yiddish jokes about the Pope; Pat, Grossman's nursemaid; and, just as matter-of-fact, the Shekhinah, enthroned in the lower branches of the kabbalistic Tree of Life; and the Lord Himself at His table. Each of these figures appears in at least one of Grossman's earlier poems, and the point here is the recalling into presence of the poet's personal mythopoeic pantheon. These are the figures who will live on past the poet's death, called forth by his own heart's blood one last time.

---

82. W.B. Yeats, *The Poems: A New Edition*, ed. Richard J. Finneran (New York: Macmillan, 1983), 227.
83. *Descartes' Loneliness*, 32.

I will conclude this chapter with a one other brief poem from *Descartes' Loneliness* called, appropriately enough, "At Sunset":

> Now the sun sets and all the ways grow dark.
> Persistent warble of a bird at my window,
> in the dark. March 18, 2001 –
> my conviction of my own death ("Get ready!")
>
> Beginning with someone else's death, a word,
> and ending with the other death, my own,
> the first word of the next life is "death,"
> and the last word of this one is not yet
>
> thought upon. But elegy is the song.
> Teacher, do not set enigmatic tasks.[84]

In his discussion with Mark Halliday of a much earlier poem, "The Thrush Relinquished" (in which the poet declares "No poetry tonight. Death tonight."), Grossman observes that "The term that in this poem I offer is the term 'death', both empty and very full, the point at which the other disappears as the self disappears. The value of the person arises in the space of that disappearance, unqualified by the contingencies of reference, or even of hope as it is constrained by possibility."[85] I think that this applies to an even greater extent to "At Sunset," in which the self's conviction of its disappearance, a conviction that is located precisely in time – March 18, 2001 – is connected in turn to the death of an unspecified other, "someone else." When the self of the poet is gone, the other is gone, for the power of poetry which resides in and which makes the poet a poet, is gone too. With this awareness, the act of manifestation is performed one last time, as a Kaddish for the self and for the other. The Teacher does not set enigmatic tasks, and in this poem, the task is set and accomplished with great economy, grace, and panache. And who is that Teacher? Poetry. For Grossman is poetry's Poet.

---

84. Ibid., 58.
85. *The Sighted Singer*, 73, 75.

FIVE

Michael Heller:
Between the Sacred and the Profane

IN JUNE OF 1965, MICHAEL HELLER AND HIS FIRST WIFE BOARDED the Yugoslavian freighter *Novi Vinadolski*, en route to Malaga via Morocco. After traveling through Europe for some months, they settled in the small Spanish village of Nerja, on the Andalusian coast. They would live in Nerja until September of 1966. Heller's sojourn there was based on a deliberate decision: he wanted to leave his familiar surroundings behind so as to see if he could transform himself into a poet. Born in Brooklyn in 1937, raised in Miami Beach, and educated as an engineer at Rensselaer Polytechnic Institute, Heller had been working at Sperry Gyroscopes when he met two former students of Louis Zukofsky, including the poet Hugh Seidman, who remains a close friend of his to this day. Poetry seized Heller's imagination. He went to readings, frequented Manhattan's literary bars, and took a creative writing workshop with Kenneth Koch at the New School. It was after winning a prize there that he made his decision. While in Nerja, writing and studying, he was visited by the poet Hannah Weiner, who took away a sheaf of his poems. Six months later, two of them appeared in *The Paris Review*. In 1967, back in the States, Heller took a post at New York University's American Language Institute, where he would teach until his retirement. A body of work – poetry, criticism, memoir, fiction, an opera libretto – would steadily grow. His first full-length collection of poems, *Accidental Center*, appeared in 1972; *This Constellation Is a Name: Collected Poems 1965–2010*, was published forty years later, in 2012. His most recent volume of poems, *Dianoia*, came out in 2016, as did the first collection of essays on his work, *The Poetry and Poetics of Michael Heller: A Nomad Memory*.[1]

Heller is closely associated with the Objectivist tradition in modern American poetry, and most discussions of his work rightly begin with invocations to such figures as Louis Zukofsky, Charles Reznikoff, Carl Rakosi, and, most importantly for Heller, George Oppen. He was friends with all of these poets, and was especially close to Oppen. Heller's *Conviction's Net of Branches* (1985) is the first book-length study of the Objectivists; more recently, his studies of Oppen have been gathered in *Speaking the Estranged: Essays on the Work of George Oppen* (2008; 2012). Read just a little more deeply in Heller, and one quickly discovers the equally important figure of Walter Benjamin (Heller wrote the libretto of an opera about Benjamin, *Constellations of Waking*, with music by Ellen Fishman Johnson), and in Benjamin's company, writers and thinkers such as Gershom Scholem, Paul Celan, and Emmanuel Levinas. From both the American and European perspectives, then, the complex permutations of Jewish thought and culture in the passage from modernity to postmodernity loom large for this poet. Yet Heller is also deeply absorbed in Buddhism, and was for some years a student of the controversial founder of Naropa University, the Tibetan Buddhist sage Chögyam Trungpa Rinpoche.

Taking these influences and affinities all together then, Heller could well be described as a philosophical poet, a meditative lyricist for whom thought's engagement, through language, with history, culture, textuality, and the material world, defines and determines the poetic act. I take this description to be accurate enough, but it only tells part of the story. In his essay "Notes on Stevens," Heller writes of Wallace Stevens, our paradigmatically "philosophical" modern poet, that "the lyrical voice of a [Stevensesque] poet arises or is occasioned by the breakdown, for that poet, of the philosophical web or system or series of understandings in

---

1. *The Poetry and Poetics of Michael Heller: A Nomad Memory*, ed. Jon Curley and Burt Kimmelman (Madison, NJ: Fairleigh Dickinson University Press, 2016), includes a complete bibliography of secondary material on Heller. See also my section on Heller in *Not One of Them in Place*, 142–55.

which the poet lives. That a poet is pushed toward the lyrical when he (or she) discovers that he is hemmed in by authority, by discourse or rhetoric, in short, by the 'philosophical' as it hardens into concept or rule or 'truth.'"[2] In other words, what we take to be philosophical lyric in such a poet is actually a lyric *departure* or *escape* from the relentlessness of philosophical investigation, at least within a given "web or system." This tendency, this complex desire to know but not to settle into knowledge (*Knowledge*, ironically, is actually the title of Heller's second collection of poems) may well account for Heller's early adoption of Oppen as mentor and guide. From Oppen especially, he learned early on how to write a "free verse" poem (the term is wholly inadequate, but will have to suffice) in which every line moves to the rhythms of deliberation, the stresses of thought. Oppen's *The Materials* (1962) accompanied Heller on that sea voyage to Spain. In his essay "Encountering Oppen," he describes himself lying on his bunk worrying about the line that opens the poem "Leviathan": "Truth also is the pursuit of it."[3] The line, and the poem from which it comes, were both insight and command, revealing to the young man, as he notes years later, "how little words counted against the strange unknowableness of the world. How everything of true depth to the individual struck me as being *unnamed*, and thereby unsayable even as its shadow in the form of desire swept across one."[4] "I am no longer sure of the words," Oppen declares in "Leviathan," and Heller must have recognized that it is out of this very loss of certainty that the desire for form – the form of desire – arises and brings the poem into being.

Heller's devotion to "The Uncertainty of the Poet" (the name of a 1913 De Chirico painting which becomes the title for another important Heller essay) informs everything he writes. In that essay, he refers once more to Oppen: "If I understand Oppen correctly, the poet is caught between a philosophical sense of his or her craft and a religious sense of the mysteriousness of the world."[5] Again, consciousness of an in-between

2. Michael Heller, *Uncertain Poetries: Selected Essays on Poets, Poetry and Poetics* (Cambridge, UK: Salt Publishing, 2005), 63.
3. George Oppen, *New Collected Poems*, ed. Michael Davidson (New York: New Directions, 2002), 89.
4. *Uncertain Poetries*, 191–92.
5. Ibid., 13

status becomes a source of inspiration for a poet who becomes increasingly attracted to mystery in the religious sense but is never truly released from the scientific education and rationalist worldview which originally shaped his sensibility. Or only *partially* shaped his sensibility: Heller's great-grandfather David Heller was an important rabbi in the Polish city of Bialystock, and his grandfather Zalman, whose presence suffuses Heller's brilliant memoir *Living Root* (2000), also a rabbi and teacher, supposedly authored a lost talmudic commentary entitled *The Just Man and the Righteous Way*. Religious belief, and more importantly, religious ritual and religious commentary, play out endlessly in Heller's seemingly secular poetry. As he notes in *Living Root*, "Science had not rendered God dead. Rather, His death came from the believer's hand at His throat, by the unspiritual nature of desperate spiritual clinging. In this game, not with God but with ourselves, He had become a horizon, ever receding as we presumed to get closer."[6] The practical result for the poet, as is true for the earlier generation of Jewish Objectivists, is simply but profoundly expressed: "I, who am godless, took much from my father, including this legacy: to seek for the precise word, the secular word, which would deliver."[7]

It is worth noting how Heller's conclusion, especially his devotion to the "precise word," differs radically from postmodern linguistic skepticism, however much uncertainty in regard to the process of signification plays a part in both intellectual tendencies. Jacques Derrida, for instance, argues that "the signified concept is never present in itself... Every concept is necessarily and essentially inscribed in a chain or system, within which it refers to another and to other concepts, by the systematic play of differences."[8] Likewise, Fredric Jameson: "Meaning on the new view is generated by the movement from Signifier to Signifier: what we generally call the Signified – the meaning or conceptual content of an utterance – is now rather to be seen as a meaning-effect... when the links of the

---

6. Michael Heller, *Living Root: A Memoir* (Albany: State University of New York Press, 2000), 71.
7. Ibid., 6.
8. Jacques Derrida, "Differance," in *Speech and Phenomena and Other Essays on Husserl's Theory of Signs*, trans. David B. Allison (Evanston, IL: Northwestern University Press, 1973), 140.

signifying chain snap, then we have schizophrenia in the form of a rubble of distinct and unrelated signifiers."[9] And Jean Baudrillard proposes that when such a linguistic stance is assumed, "the whole system becomes weightless; it is no longer anything but a gigantic simulacrum: not unreal, but a simulacrum, never again exchanging for what is real, but exchanging in itself, in an uninterrupted circuit without reference or circumference."[10]

Taken together, these quotations adumbrate the linguistic and cultural trajectory of postmodernism, to which Heller as a philosophical poet responds. What we may call the Age of the Simulacrum is one in which meaning or the signified is never present in itself but moves endlessly across chains of signifiers, chains which continually break down into rubble or, weightless, endlessly exchange themselves without reference to reality. We have moved from signification to simulation, a condition which critics and theorists have generally accepted to be the case, and which contemporary poets have variously resisted, accommodated – or celebrated.

Along this range of responses, where is Heller to be found? In his essay "Aspects of Poetics," drawing on the mythopoesis of such poets as Walt Whitman and Robert Duncan, Heller posits "a self embodying or dancing with other selves, with texts and masks of selves and the attendant cosmological machinery of those dances. Such multitudes are embedded in the sympathetic magic of language, in the sense that the employment of a signifier creates or arouses the specter of the signified, thus always producing an environment of interpretation."[11] Heller's understanding of Whitman and Duncan, an understanding which extends, I believe, to his own work, is in distinct contrast to the cultural and semiotic situation described by Derrida, Jameson, and Baudrillard in the Age of the Simulacrum. For Heller, the signified of an utterance (and by extension, the self or subject making that utterance) is not dispersed along a chain of signifiers; it is not seen as constantly at risk of breakdown or of endless self-referentiality. Rather than the endless

9. Fredric Jameson, "Postmodernism, or the Cultural Logic of Late Capitalism," *New Left Review* 146 (July/August 1984): 72.
10. Jean Baudrillard, *Simulations*, trans. Phil Beitchman (New York: Semiotext(e), 1982), 10.
11. *Uncertain Poetries*, 232–33.

circling and unbounded weightlessness of simulation, we have a dance of selves, which, in the poem, becomes a signifying dance of texts implying the continued existence of "cosmological machinery." Heller rethinks the politics of the sign: through "the sympathetic magic of language," the poet's signifier "creates or arouses the specter of the signified."

As I understand this, we are not left with the rubble of unrelated signifiers because the schizophrenic rupture between the signified and the signifier is never complete. Yes, they may have come apart: Heller, a deep reader of Gershom Scholem, knows all too well that, as in the Lurianic Kabbalah, the vessels of creation (which are primal utterances) have broken and fallen. Given Heller's kabbalistic view of language, for him it is in the nature of poetry to repair or rebind the sign: the "specter of the signified," a phantom of meaning, is called back by the signifier. This calling back is choreographic, magical, and erotic: the signified is aroused by the signifier and the result is "an environment of interpretation," generative of meaning. Interpretation is an act of love, and it is the task of the philosophical (or kabbalistic) poet to engage in such acts of interpretation in every poem he writes.

This passionate attitude toward interpretation – deeply Jewish, but perhaps also central to the act of interpretation itself – results, as it were, in a state of semiotic arousal that reunites the specter of the signified with the signifier. It constitutes not only a repairing of the sign, but a kind of secular redemption or restoration of language – in kabbalistic terms, a sort of *tikkun*, or cosmic repair. But what could a secular version of *tikkun* possibly mean? In his essay "Remains of the Diaspora," Heller quotes Scholem from *On Jews and Judaism in Crisis*: "Perhaps a double way is possible, secular and holy, toward which we are evolving? Perhaps this holiness will be revealed at the heart of the secular, and the mystical is not recognized because it appears in forms which are new to the concepts of tradition."[12]

For Heller, secular poetry may be one of those new forms, and poetic language is central to what we may paradoxically call a secular Jewish metaphysics, just as scriptural language is central to a traditional Jewish metaphysics of observance and belief. In both cases, the word and the

12. Quoted in "Remains of the Diaspora," 177.

world are intimately bound up; the word always seeks entry into the world, with that same force of attraction and desire that bind signified to signifier. This is why Heller's understanding of language is ultimately kabbalistic. As Heller well knows, in the language mysticism of Kabbalah, divine language pre-exists Creation and participates in Creation, and in some texts, it is difficult to determine where Torah ends and God begins.[13] But Heller, as a secular Jewish poet, gives the traditional formulation a new twist. In a secular world, if language has lost its divine authority, then it now longs to enter into worldliness; hence the importance of the poet, whose work in language is at all points sensitized to and energized by this desire. As Heller writes in "Remains of the Diaspora," "the poet who is in touch – allied in some fashion – with Judaism's speculations on language has as his animating creative goad primarily his awareness of the 'between', of the space of the diaspora. This 'between' is, in a sense, foundational. It exists in the relational sphere between the law of religious observance and secular life."[14] Heller has long advocated a "diasporic poetics," a term he first applies to the Objectivists in an essay with that title. Writers in the Objectivist tradition – and at this point, I can assert with confidence that Heller is our greatest living practitioner of this mode – are always intensely aware of "the space of the diaspora." It is a space in which language becomes an externalized and articulated mode of thinking, a space in which thought comes into being through the utterance of the poem. Negotiating this space between language and the world (because both, kabbalistically speaking, are in a perpetually diasporic condition), Objectivist poets such as Heller set their work in opposition to the simulacrum. To put it bluntly, they keep it real.

This is not to say that Heller avoids or evades the linguistic skepticism that leads to the simulacrum. On the contrary, Heller sees it as a challenge that the responsible poet must accept. Yet Heller's skepticism is, as I have indicated, less postmodernist than late modernist, and in this respect, it proposes an argument against easy versions of poetic lineage

13. Cf. Gershom Scholem, "The Meaning of the Torah in Jewish Mysticism," *On the Kabbalah and Its Symbolism*, trans. Ralph Manheim (New York: Schocken Books, 1965) 32–86.
14. "Remains of the Diaspora," 171.

that trace their way toward our present moment. For Heller, as for other recent poets, "the lyric is neither a product of thought nor of intention but rather comes as a recognition of a gap or rupture in one's thought or intention."[15] Yet in a cautionary mode, Heller also insists that "[w]hen description and referentiality are consciously rejected by the maker of the text, the language field in which 'reality' is constructed is left open to the play of socio-political forces which trade not on referentiality but on the decontextualized imagery of the media, the inflections of sentimentality in advertising, the easy symbology of patriotism" – this from "Avant-Garde Propellants of the Machine Made of Words," a tour-de-force that includes a penetrating critique of the philosophical and conceptual premises and underpinnings of Language poetry and related textual practices.[16] Poetry therefore must at least attempt to maintain its referential stake in the language game, as is movingly proposed at the end of the poem "Winter Notes, East End," one of a number of poems in memory of Heller's friend Armand Schwerner, another poet whose work challenges quick assumptions about the canon of contemporary avant-garde writing – and about Jewish-American writing. Thinking of Schwerner, Heller finds himself

> Scouring words for the relieving aura,
> breathing deeply old vocabularies of the sea,
>
> of pine, ever-present tinge of salt.
> Panoply of stars, planets. But often
> one can't find what is being searched for,
> the galaxy seemingly drained of that covenant.
>
> Thus is it written out for syntax's rules,
> for the untranslatable memory of black holes,
>
> for voice, for love and against concept.[17]

15. *Uncertain Poetries*, 235.
16. Ibid., 221.
17. Michael Heller, *This Constellation Is a Name: Collected Poems 1965–2010* (Callicoon, NY: Nightboat Books, 2012), 379.

Heller seeks to restore the auratic quality of lyric poetry even when he knows that the postmodern condition produces a "galaxy seemingly drained of that covenant." Covenant refers, I think, to the *linguistic* covenant, the binding of signified and signifier that postmodernism deconstructs but still seems unable to overthrow, at least within the boundaries of lyric utterance. Likewise, the word "untranslatable" here is especially poignant, given how in *The Tablets*, Schwerner's masterpiece, the word appears over and over, signifying the impossibility of reaching back to the origins of written language, as inscribed on the clay tablets which the poem's mad hero, the "Scholar / Translator," is supposedly bringing to light out of the black holes of the archaic past. Nevertheless, the text gets "written out for syntax's rules"; the elegiac poem achieves its auratic status in spite of itself, "for voice, for love and against concept."[18]

But why "against concept"? As we observed previously, the lyric utterance for Heller flees from the philosophical before "it hardens into concept or rule or 'truth.'" The poem, as he notes in "Aspects of Poetics," emerges out of "a condition induced by knowledge of our unreliability, our deference, if you will, before the limitations and understanding of language and of otherness. Uncertainty, in effect, is already an aspect of an utterance, of saying and affirming. It advocates a kind of lightening up about our purported certainties and the hopes and fears in which most of those certainties are lodged."[19] This is why Heller's provocative poem "To Postmodernity," despite its ironic acknowledgment that "Some of the poets have discovered / that we are anxious to disconnect / the dots and words," still ends with an affirmation of that most important engagement with otherness, love:

> And yet love's obliquity
> is still a language,
> a tutoring mastery of desires
> and hurts, leaps and kneelings
> at the utterance of a name.[20]

18. For Heller's critical reading of Schwerner, see his essay "Armand Schwerner: The Semiotician of Self Work," *Uncertain Poetries*, 125–39
19. Ibid., 231.
20. *This Constellation*, 358.

"The power of poetry," Heller argues in the "Avant-Garde Propellants" essay, "is that it puts a word back into the voice of an Other, that it is a power for him or her and so confronts my particular empowerment of it. The word again becomes an object of thought."[21] The site of this thoughtful confrontation, or as he calls it in the line just quoted, this "tutoring mastery of desires," is the poem. There is a constellation, to use Heller's favorite Benjaminian term, made up of the poetic speaker, the Other, and language or utterance itself – and to appropriate the title of Heller's collected poems, *This Constellation Is a Name.*

Heller's poetry constitutes an extended witnessing that is simultaneously a working through, a construction of this constellation even as it is comes into sight. Of necessity, such a poetry must include the darkest moments of modern history. Consider these precise words from the aptly named "Constellations of Waking," composed "on the suicide of Walter Benjamin at the Franco-Spanish border, 1940":

> These constellations
> which are not composed of stars
> but the curls of shriveled leaves
> by which the tree expressed
> the notion of the storm. You
> lived in storm, your outer life:
>
> "adversities on all sides
> which sometimes came
> as wolves." Your father –
> Europe was your father
> who cast you on the path,
> hungry, into constellated cities:
>
> Berlin, Moscow, Paris
> Where would
> Minerva's owl alight,
>
> on what dark branch
> to display its polished
> talons?[22]

21. *Uncertain Poetries*, 215.
22. *This Constellation*, 280.

Benjamin's own description of his adversities as "wolves" (the quote comes from a 1923 letter to the theologian Florens Christian Rang)[23] is juxtaposed to a reference to the famous "owl of Minerva" passage in the *Preface* to Hegel's *Philosophy of Right*: "When philosophy paints its grey in grey, one form of life has become old, and by means of grey it cannot be rejuvenated, but only known. The owl of Minerva takes its flight only when the shades of night are gathering."[24] What to make of this menagerie? As Heller implies, Benjamin, by rights the philosophical heir of Hegel (and, of course, Marx), suffers and dies because the European intellectual tradition that fathered him is not merely helpless before the wolves of political adversity, but actively betrays him. Hence the threatening image of the owl with "its polished / talons," settling in the dark and closing down not merely a historical era, but the life of one of its most ardent followers.

"*Bandelette de Torah*" is another of Heller's profound meditations on the fate of the Jews and of Judaism in relation to the history in the West. I use a double term – the Jews *and* Judaism – because both the Jews (as a people or nation) and the Jewish religion (as a covenantal relationship to divinity, as a body of sacralizing rituals, or as a set of scriptural practices) are seen in the poem less as definable historical entities than as forms of a "hunger." As Heller sees it, this "hunger" is an endlessly transforming and transformative desire which seems to be both determined by history and continually transcending history, no matter how disastrous history becomes, particularly for the Jews. Furthermore, this yearning is specifically linguistic; it is a hunger "for the word between us, / between outside and in, between Europe / and America, between the Jew and his other, / the word and the non-word."[25] The crucial theme of diaspora, of wandering "between," becomes a matter of speaking between and of writing

23. In the original letter, Benjamin writes "I am less sure of my path than I would like and, on top of that, there are adversities in the circumstances of my life that sometimes beset me from all sides like wolves and I do not know how to keep them at bay." Walter Benjamin, *The Correspondence of Walter Benjamin 1910–1940*, ed. Gershom Scholem and Theodor W. Adorno, trans. Manfred R. Jacobson and Evelyn M. Jacobson (Chicago, IL: University of Chicago Press, 1994), 206.
24. G.W.F. Hegel, *Philosophy of Right*, trans. S.W. Dyde (London: G. Bell, 1896), Marxist Internet Archive: https://www.marxists.org/reference/archive/hegel/works/pr/index.htm.
25. *This Constellation*, 394.

between. Let us recall what Heller notes in "Remains of the Diaspora": "This 'between' is, in a sense, foundational. It exists in the relational sphere between the law of religious observance and secular life"[26]

How, the sympathetic reader is led to ask, can a conceptual space, a "between" as Heller presents it, be "foundational"? What does this poet of the diaspora have to stand on? A foundation, after all, is a base upon which one builds a structure, an edifice. In posing this question, I am reminded of an earlier poem of Heller's, the dark, Blakean meditation on the fallen city called "In the Built Place." In that poem, under the light of a street-lamp, "the clatter of failed myths, / of hierarchies dies" – though in the poem's last line, he does invoke "These flimsy beatitudes of order," partial and temporary constructions that do not leave us totally without structures of meaning by which to live.[27] Thus, it would appear that Heller himself justifies my asking how one can build upon a firm conceptual foundation – the *negative* concept of Jewish diasporic or wandering meaning – when it consists of an empty "between" that signifies nothing but the *loss* of myths, of hierarchies, and to a great extent, of structure itself. According to Heller, "the attempt to conceive of the diaspora as a new kind of homeland runs against the tensions of the self's poetic 'exodus'. It would be unfaithful, in other words, to turn diaspora into a new kind of Law."[28] So is the notion of diaspora, so important to the framing of modern secular Jewish identity, especially that of artists and intellectuals, itself a failed myth as well? Or if not a failed myth, then perhaps a perpetual state of negation, a refusal of positive ground? These questions are especially relevant to one particularly compelling "between" that Heller posits: the space that he indicates in his essay "between the law of religious observance and secular life." What Heller is doing, in effect, is calling for a reassessment of the conditions of belief in the context of secular Jewish life.

Let us look more closely now at *"Bandelette de Torah."* The French term indicates the band that ties the Torah scroll, and more generally, the covering or dress that is placed over the scroll while it is in the ark. In the synagogue, during readings of the Torah on the Sabbath or holy days,

26. "Remains of the Diaspora," 171.
27. *This Constellation,* 220, 221.
28. "Remains of the Diaspora," 178.

the scroll is ritually "undressed" to be read and then "dressed" again to be put back in its accustomed resting place. The covering to which the poem refers, on display in the Musée de Judaïsme in Paris, dates from 1761. (Paris evokes a number of Heller's poetic meditations on Jewish fate, as in the extraordinary poem simply titled "In Paris," "where hope was stifled once between *le mot juste* and *le mot juif.*"[29]) The secular Jewish poet contemplates the antique religious artifact, observing that "In the museum case, belief has been sealed / behind glass."[30] Belief itself becomes an antique; nevertheless, the hunger, particularly the hunger of faith, endures. The poet, drawn to the *bandelette de Torah*, enters into a poignant historical meditation:

> The hunger was once for textured cloth, brocade
> of thread, gold-webbed damask, tessellate fringe,
> for sewn-in weight of lead or brass, the chanter
> lifting all heaviness from the page, singing out
>
> lost richness. He followed the gold *yod* of divining,
> alchemic word intoning the throne's measure in
> discarded lexicons of *cubits* and *myriads*. The cloth
> lay over Europe's open scroll between Athens and Jerusalem,
>
> between library and dream.... [31]

From the poet's secular Jewish perspective, the imagined chanter, or *chazzan*, cantillating the words of the Torah, sings out a "lost richness." His "alchemic word" produces only "discarded lexicons"; the "*cubits*" and "*myriads*," metonyms for a superannuated biblical history, lose the transformative power they once presumably had for a believing Jewish congregation in the eighteenth century. The ornate cloth that is removed from the scroll before the chanting begins, becomes, in an equally ornate conceit, the fabric that metaphysically connects Athens and Jerusalem. Hellenism and Hebraism, the two traditional sources of Western wisdom, are historically conjoined but perpetually at odds as well, given the West's long history of ethnic and religious strife. Thus,

29. *This Constellation*, 351
30. Ibid., 394.
31. Ibid.

The hunger was for the lost word

that lay between Jerusalem and Athens. Later, terrors
came to be its portion, flames beyond remonstrance,
synagogue and worshiper in ash. Celan in the Seine
with its syllabary.... [32]

The figure of Paul Celan is even more powerfully metonymic, for
the poet's suicide (Celan, the Holocaust survivor, drowned himself in
the Seine in 1970) stands for the culmination of European antisemitism.
Celan's work (and let us keep in mind that he was a gifted translator as
well as a great poet) represents the modern, secular Jewish equivalent
of the cantor's "alchemic word" – but unlike the chanting of Scripture,
which, in the presence of the congregation, transforms text into the pal-
pable experience of belief, the modern Jewish poet, secular and diasporic
in his sensibility, produces a very different kind of linguistic experience,
an experience of doubt, ambiguity, absence and loss.

How does this experience unfold for the modern poet, and subse-
quently for his readers? In the case of Celan, Paris becomes his post-
Holocaust refuge; he moves there in 1948 and marries the French artist
Gisèle de Lestrange in 1952, and it is there that his work flourishes – dark,
elliptical, warring with divinity, but as he later declares, "ganz und gar
nicht hermetisch" [absolutely not hermetic].[33] Yet in the end, he cannot
fend off the horror of his past, suffering for years from depression before,
as Heller would have it, he drowns in "the Seine / with its syllabary." A
syllabary is a list or set of written symbols; the Seine's syllabary, if it may
be said to have one, would be the set of Roman letters, the alphabet in
which Celan writes his German poems in his adopted French homeland.
Yet insofar as Paris is also a home to the Jews, could not its syllabary also
contain Hebrew characters? These would be the characters that make

32. Ibid., 394–95.

33. See Michael Hamburger, introduction to *Poems of Paul Celan*, trans. Michael
   Hamburger (New York: Persea Books, 1988), 27. The question of hermeticism looms
   large in any discussion of Celan's work, as Hamburger's introduction indicates. It is
   worth considering that despite Heller's great admiration for Celan, his own stylistic
   response to diasporic ambiguity is entirely different. Indeed, it could be argued that
   Heller's style is anti-hermetic.

up the Hebrew words chanted by the eighteenth-century cantor; he and
Celan (who also knew Hebrew and Yiddish) are therefore both linked
and opposed to each other, with Heller's diasporic space "between" them.
Continuing to ponder the words of the Torah scroll, Heller brings his
poem to its conclusion:

> They lay across the lettered scroll, ink on paper
> enveloped in darkness, desperate to be inmixed
> with matter. The words were between us, poised
> to rise into constellated night as task unto the city,
>
> to enter *this* place unshielded between the One
> and nothingness, if only to exist as from an echo
> between hope and horror, between sacred sound
> and profane air. Between Athens and Jerusalem and America.[34]

As in the beginning of the poem, the operative word is "between."
The language of the Torah scroll, the language of Celan's poetry, and
by implication, the language of Heller's text itself – in short, to borrow
the title of another Heller poem from the same period, "the language
of the Jews" – all their languages – have the power to carry us across
various psychological, existential or even religious spaces. In Heller's
vision, language is the mediating power in the otherwise empty space
of the diaspora, which is why, to answer the question I posed earlier,
the secular Jewish myth of the diaspora is *not* a failed myth, however
difficult it may be to build upon it. The words, particularly the words
of the poem, move between One and nothingness, hope and horror,
sacred sound and profane air, Old World experience and American life,
which, as some have argued, is perhaps a life that for American Jews is
actually post-diaspora. But words can accomplish all this only if, in their
desperation, they are "inmixed with matter."

What does this mean? Let us step back a bit from the poem and my
explication du texte to recall Heller's understanding of the way in which
language becomes charged with meaning, not merely personal meaning
(though that is part of it), but with cultural significance. Poetic language

34. *This Constellation*, 395.

for Heller is central, or to use his term, "foundational," to what we may paradoxically call a secular Jewish metaphysics, just as scriptural language is foundational to a traditional Jewish metaphysics of observance and belief. In each case, the words are "desperate" to enter into "matter," a word that points to the materiality of being, but also to meaning, importance, i.e. what truly matters. As we have seen, Heller's understanding of language is ultimately kabbalistic – with the crucial difference that it is not underwritten by divinity. Language is now "desperate to be inmixed / with matter." According to Heller, this is why poets are so important to a post-religious world. Yet he also notes that "What makes poets and their poetry vulnerable is not so much newness or uniqueness but communicability, an opening to being verified or falsified by experience."[35] The secular poet cannot reclaim the traditional authority of Scripture, or what Heller describes in his poem as "Jerusalem's sky...written over in fiery labyrinth, in severe figures, / unerring texts."[36] Language is "vulnerable," "unshielded"; no modern book of poetry is dressed in a *bandelette de Torah*. But in Heller's case at least, it is just that vulnerability, its openness to experience, that is its greatest strength.

A poem in Heller's recent sequence "Afikomens" (dedicated to Harvey Shapiro) demonstrates this openness and vulnerability with exceptional poignancy, humor and tact. (An *afikomen* is the bit of matzah broken off at the beginning of the Passover seder, usually hidden for a child to find and ransom, since it is necessary to eat this bit as a "dessert" to end the seder.) The poem is called "Beyond Zero":

> According to Rosenzweig,
> God has removed himself
> to the point of nothingness.
> And according to me, mankind
> has been removing itself as well,
> unsure of its mode, unsure of its path –
> back to the trilobite or fated to remake the planet
> in the image of a grand, blinding supernova.

35. "Remains of the Diaspora," 181–82.
36. *This Constellation*, 394.

> But I do know the one I love in the singular
> has taken on an existence beyond the point
> of any *somethingness*, more like the taste
> before an aftertaste. I'm at least one step removed
> from that removed God. How to explain it?
> When I move my arm out to hold her hand
> or touch her on the shoulder,
> she has already moved with me.[37]

The wonderfully insouciant opening move, from the mock pedantry of "According to Rosenzweig" (that would be Franz Rosenzweig, the German-Jewish philosopher and author of *The Star of Redemption*) to the cheeky "And according to me," is yet another fine example of Heller's claim that the poet is "pushed toward the lyrical" when philosophical authority weighs too heavily upon him. Indeed, the tone throughout the first stanza achieves an unusual balance between philosophical weight and lyric lightness. God has removed himself, and we too are working, with whatever uncertainty, at removing ourselves, ending, perhaps, in a nuclear disaster "in the image of a grand, blinding supernova." Against this, the poet proposes love, "beyond the point / of any *somethingness*." As inexplicable as the *deus absconditus*, the mystery of love is such that it *anticipates* our knowing, anticipates even our expression of feeling. The mutual movement of the lovers is the truest expression of presence.

To be sure, presence is an ineluctable notion when one reads Heller, and a poetry of presence is one of his most important modes – his most directly Objectivist and, I would argue, his most Jewish. In "Commentary Is the Concept of Order for the Spiritual World," despite its title (drawn from the writings of Gershom Scholem), Heller's meditation leads him to consider the linguistic representation of the *material* world, touching on the spiritual world only by implication. The poem becomes one of

> ... those records   of an observing eye
> noting the lichen's patch   on the rock face,
> the waters slow   eroding of the boulder,
> (such witness   an ongoing work

---

37. *This Constellation*, 527.

of resistance),   wouldn't this proclaim
that *he is most apt   who brings with himself*
the maximum   of what is alien –
a sense of world-depths   that no longer crowd the mind,
thus a rich compost   of the literal
of what is said.

And then might not   our words loom
as hope against fear   for near ones,
for their gesturing   towards a future?[38]

Here, observation of and commentary upon natural objects and pro-
cesses become "an ongoing work / of resistance," and the poet himself is
he who *"is most apt   who brings with himself / the maximum   of what is
alien."* The italicized words come from Franz Rosenzweig's description of
the Free Jewish School that he envisioned for assimilated German Jews.
Thus, Heller implies an analogy between the Objectivist poet observing
the "alien" world of nature (in his famous poem "Psalm," Oppen writes
of the "alien small teeth" of the deer watching him) and the assimilated
Jew studying the "alien" world of traditional Jewish learning.[39] The poet,
then, engages "a rich compost   of the literal / of what is said," in turn
producing words that "loom / as hope against fear...gesturing towards
a future." Commentary, therefore, is a concept of order for both the
spiritual and the material worlds.

In Heller's poetry of the last few years, the movement between these
worlds (if not the spiritual and the material, then at least the interior and
the exterior) has modulated, and a somewhat different discourse, per-
haps more Symbolist than Objectivist, has come to the fore. Two power-
ful sequences of poems dominate the final sections of *This Constellation
Is a Name*. The first, *Beckmann Variations*, is a set of ekphrastic poems
based on the paintings of the German artist Max Beckmann (1884–1950),
whose work, Symbolist and Expressionist in its orientation, was lauded
during the Weimar period but condemned by the Nazis and displayed
in the famous *entartete Kunst* (degenerate art) exhibition in Munich in

38. Ibid., p. 466.
39. Oppen, 99.

1937, which led quickly to Beckmann's exile. The original publication of *Beckmann Variations* includes prose meditations based partly on Yeats's occult masterpiece *Per Amica Silentia Lunae* (1918), though these have not been republished in the *Collected Poems*. But as Heller explains in his Notes, "The more I studied Yeats, the more he seemed a likely guide or companion through which to view Beckmann's pictures. So while my speculations are primarily on Beckmann's art, they also invoke Yeats as a sort of Virgil figure to the moral, social and political infernos depicted in many of Beckmann's pictures."[40] It would appear that Heller has certainly turned a corner. Here are the final stanzas of the first Beckmann poem, "Space," based on the painting "Journey on the Fish" [Man and Woman]" (1934):

> ...And then, in the painting,
> we saw the man and woman bound by silken sashes
> to the backs of fish, the waves' surfaces to be breached.
>
> And who now could live only by a word or by an image;
> who could stand back, look and speak, only to fall silent?
> Who, in these times, did not sense death and non-being
> as a shadow, something brushed against the cranial wall?
>
> The bound lovers in their journey are plunged downward
> and must embrace fear, rapture, the throes of love, their lips
> clamped shut against the pressure. Great silvery fish sound
> the ocean's deeps and seed the darkness with their silence.
>
> *If you wish to get hold of the invisible*, wrote Beckmann,
> *you must penetrate as deeply as possible into the visible.*
>
> *Space is the infinite deity.*[41]

"And who now could live only by a word or by an image": for me, this is the key line in this surging passage, so revealing in terms of Heller's lineage and the growth of his poetics. For nearly the entirety of his career, Heller has been precisely the sort of poet who has lived by a word or an

---

40. *This Constellation*, 566.
41. Ibid., 479–80.

image: commentary has been one of his most important procedures, and the immediate presentation that remains crucial to any Objectivist-based poetry certainly has its roots in the image. Does Heller imply that, like Beckmann, he has reached some sort of epistemological boundary, "brushed against the cranial wall?" Has he, in his quest for the invisible, penetrated as deeply as possible into the visible?

We may find at least the hint of an answer in a passage from *Tibet: A Sequence*, which closes the *Collected Poems*. Loosely based on the work of Victor Segalen (1878–1919), the French poet and medical doctor who travelled extensively in Asia and studied Buddhist and Taoist thought, these poems, according to Heller, are not translations but "transpositions," connecting on a very deep level with Heller's own sustained studies of Buddhism. In "Ode to the Sky on the Esplanade of the New" (surely a quintessential Heller title), the poet declares:

> Most high, let us walk the ordered esplanade!
> Let us carry high the numerous and the just whirlwinds.
> Let us grasp the circle: let us catch the assailing blue.
> So high? Without hope: there are no rays.
> To aid here: the new embers of our appearance.
> Here the three mountains and the renewing of the hours.
> Recommencing: strong interior life.
> So we must let them blaze! Let us devour flesh and blood.
>
> It is necessary to arouse one's self, its fire crackling, to burn red.
> To penetrate one's heart with the deepest of gouges.
> To traverse on the vertical fires that the sky stirs,
> carrying ourselves to the level of the horizon filled with
>   winds.[42]

There are very few poets writing today who are taking linguistic – and existential – risks of the sort represented by these lines, as in Heller's call for "the renewing of the hours," for "Recommencing: strong interior life." There is something almost Shelleyan in those "new embers," the passionate recognition that "It is necessary to arouse one's self, its fire

---

42. Ibid., 538.

crackling, to burn red." A Buddhist "Ode to the West Wind"? Following Heller, we discover that we are "carrying ourselves to the level of the horizon filled with winds."

And yet the poet always leads us back down out of the transcendental heights, and when he does, his Judaism usually comes back into play. The opening poem in *Dianoia*, Heller's first book since the publication of his *Collected*, is called "Mappah." It is in the form of a series of prose sentences, each a separate stanza, with a tone that is, paradoxically, coolly aphoristic yet personal and intimate. It also combines Jewish ritual and Buddhist sagacity:[43]

> This brocaded cloth is nothing in itself, neither real nor unreal, woven with an edge that is no edge.
>
> No one can safely say where the sacred leaves off, where the profane begins.
>
> The teacher remarked that to regard the earth as the shrine-room floor is enlightenment.
>
> The sheath was slipped from the Torah to reveal the scrolls, the Torah laid upon its stand, the scrolls were opened for the day's reading.[44]

The term *mappah* is the Hebrew equivalent for *bandelette de Torah* – again, a cloth that binds and covers the Torah scroll when not in use. Here, it becomes the appropriate symbol for a poetry that is and is not a sacred object, that does and does not participate in a sacred discourse. As Heller puts it in a line that distills a career-long body of thought, "No one can safely say where the sacred leaves off, where the profane begins." The vicissitudes of the sacred in a culture that may be regarded as both

---

43. According to Stephen Fredman, "Buddhism, as a discipline of the middle way – of both this and that and neither this nor that – squares perfectly with Heller's sense of Jewish lostness, in that it prevents him from idolizing any form of thought, no matter how subtle or seductive. From this perspective, even lamentation over what has been lost in Jewish history must be relinquished." Stephen Fredman, "Judaism as Loss in the Poetry of Michael Heller," in *The Poetry and Poetics of Michael Heller*, 126.

44. Michael Heller, *Dianoia* (New York: Nightboat Books, 2016), 3.

post-religious *and* post-secular, a culture which, for Heller, still carries many of the trappings – the coverings – of traditional Jewish faith, is a subject to which the poet continually returns. We may say that he has spent his entire career negotiating the relations of the sacred and the profane, usually within a Jewish context. These negotiations produce a poetry that exemplifies the notion that Steven Wasserstrom calls *religion after religion*, and it is in this context that I want to consider this latest phase of his work.

Wasserstrom claims that in the work of such thinkers as Mircea Eliade, Henri Corbin, and Gershom Scholem, *religion after religion* constitutes a "stance toward religion [that] is itself religious, even as it is postreligious; it is itself a paradox, perhaps a *coincidentia oppositorum* [the coincidence or interpenetration of opposites, a crucial mystical notion popularized by Jung]" that epistemologically binds the mystic and the skeptic together.[45] The same applies to Heller, who intuits what Wasserstrom writes of the great Kabbalah scholar: that in Judaism, "The crisis of tradition is still tradition, both remaining within its spirit and yet leaving its current forms behind. If this relationship to tradition is paradoxical, Scholem did not shy away from this conclusion."[46] Nor, as we have seen, does Heller. For the poet, when it comes to the sacred and to the religious tradition which would embody it, it is clear that paradox and contradiction prevail. To quote Wasserstrom one more time, "The putative otherworldliness of a symbol-centered History of Religions is neither constructed by worldliness nor ignorant of worldly ways. Rather, it is a double worldliness – it is equivocal, dialectical, inside and outside history, and thus thickly ambivalent."[47] This strikes me as a nearly perfect description of Heller's recent work, for it is increasingly symbol-centered, pulled toward an otherworldliness yet still resolutely worldly. It has always been a highly self-conscious, dialectical poetry, a poetry intensely engaged with history but one that also maintains an ironic distance from it. In this respect, as well as in its formal dimensions, it too is "thickly

---

45. Steven M. Wasserstrom, *Religion After Religion: Gershom Scholem, Mircea Eliade, and Henry Corbin at Eranos* (Princeton, NJ: Princeton University Press, 1999), 79.
46. Ibid., 62.
47. Ibid., 110.

ambivalent." As Heller observes in "Mappah," "everything that is the case continues, and I am left with a suspicious sorrow that we grieve neither for truth nor falsity."[48] For Heller, it is the intrusion of the sacred into the profane, and vice versa, that casts both our worldly skepticism and our belief into doubt. We are suspended between the two; hence we grieve, but not for truth or falsity, since in our present condition, neither term really applies. Again from "Mappah," with its telling symbolism: "Let this be put another way: the cloth that shielded the Torah from light shielded light from the Torah."[49]

In "On the Poetics of the Jewish God," a dialogue that I recently conducted with Heller, he notes that "as one whose traceries are through language ... the idea of God (this nowhere/everywhere of his being) ... is that this God consists of *that which is markable*. That the appearance of the sacred is revealed by marks, by our marking and writing."[50] Heller then cites Oppen's poem "World, World," specifically the line "the mystery is that there is something to stand on," and from there makes the following remarkable connection:[51]

> the surface on which any of us write ... is not blank but the "something we stand on," the background space of possibility. The mark on the background is the beginning of inscription and also of the possibility of the sacred because the sacred must be visible in order to be sensed or seen, which is why, in my view, the supernatural is not necessarily a component of the sacred. Quite the opposite: I would define the sacred as that which has been made intelligible and in the process made the world intelligible. The "mystery" (not the supernatural) of the sacred – the arena beyond its literalness, the possibility that this arena is invisible, is to be read via the offices of language.[52]

48. *Dianoia*, 3.
49. Ibid., 4.
50. Norman Finkelstein and Michael Heller, "On the Poetics of the Jewish God," in *Imagining the Jewish God*, ed. Leonard Kaplan and Kenneth Koltun-Fromm (Lanham, MD: Lexington Books, 2016), 5.
51. Oppen, 159.
52. "On the Poetics of the Jewish God," 6.

In "Mappah," and throughout Heller's work, there is a constant restlessness, a perpetual instability, between the sacred and the profane, because as he puts it, the sacred is "that which has been made intelligible and in the process made the world intelligible." The poet's writing creates the sacred through a process of articulation that makes the world intelligible, a process which we would ordinarily associate with secularization. Poetry is engaged in continual discovery and renovation, a process, as Heller would have it, of "marking." In our dialogue, Heller quotes from Haim Nahman Bialik's great essay "Revealment and Concealment in Language." In the passage that Heller quotes, Bialik tells us that poets

> are forced to flee all that is fixed and inert in language, all that is opposed to their goal of the vital and mobile in language. On the contrary, using their unique keys, they are obliged themselves to introduce into language at every opportunity – never-ending motion, new combinations and associations.... By this process there takes place, in the material of language, exchanges of posts and locations: one mark, a change in the point of one iota, and the old word shines with a new light.[53]

And Bialik concludes, "The profane turns sacred, the sacred profane. Long established words are constantly being pulled out of their settings, as it were, and exchanging place with one another."[54] This, of course, is precisely what happens in "Mappah."

The second poem in *Dianoia* is "Abide with Me a Moment," an elegiac consideration of the writing of Allen Grossman. As we have seen, Grossman's thinking about the relation of modern poetry to the Jewish concept of the holy is fundamental to our understanding of these matters; indeed, I would say that at this point, his only rival is Heller himself; thus, it is worth noting how the work of the two poets variously embodies the contradictory notions of the sacred and the profane. "Abide with Me a Moment" is a meditation upon a number of Grossman's works, especially his collection *How To Do Things With Tears* (2001). What makes Heller's poem so moving is that the contradiction between the

---

53. Haim Nahman Bialik, "Revealment and Concealment in Language," trans. Jacob Sloan, in *Revealment and Concealment: Five Essays* (Jerusalem: Ibis Editions, 2000), 24–25.
54. Ibid., 25.

sacred and the profane is almost transcended, as if in communing with the spirit of Grossman, a momentary détente is established in the space briefly created by the passing of a fellow poet. The syntax of the poem, which is addressed to Grossman directly, is particularly complicated, making palpable the dialectical tensions which erupt when the modern, secular poet entertains traditional modes of Jewish belief. "This is a 'Jewish' poem alright," Heller assures us. Nevertheless, he is more resistant to prophetic flights than Grossman ever was, and this becomes clear when Heller, after invoking "Ezekiel's divine throne" as described in Gershom Scholem's book *The Mystical Shape of the Godhead*, goes on declare that

> ... I guess if one can call it
>
> a belief, then mine was, if nothing else,
> the Holy One had gone missing, and I was left
> to raise other thrones from the now abandoned
> languages of observation and objection.[55]

Heller's reference to his "now abandoned / languages of observation and objection" raises a number of questions. Observation, of course, is crucial for any poet writing in the Objectivist tradition. Objection probably means objection to traditional belief, insofar as Heller understands that the Holy One has "gone missing." But "objection" is only a couple of syllables away from "objectification," the *sine qua non* of the Objectivist program.

And here we come to the crucial difference between Heller and Grossman, a difference which sheds light on the problem of the sacred in Heller with which I am trying to come to terms. Grossman does not have much sympathy for the Objectivists. In his dialogue with Mark Halliday in *The Sighted Singer*, he levels a severe critique of the Objectivist program – which is to say, he objects to it:

> I see for poetry no possibility and, indeed, no need consistent
> with its nature or its purpose in the world to make any offering
> whatsoever toward a world which is not the person. The idea of

55. *Dianoia*, 5.

Objectivist verse seems to me simply a premature conclusion about the function or nature of a particular kind of poetry, which addresses the self without giving it its proper name – in effect, an evasion. The most remote thing that can come to mind is the inwardness and very being of another, and it is only that that the telescope properly focused can see. Poetry is the lens by which that thing is seen and in this age may be the only lens.[56]

Grossman's reference to the telescope is to his poem "In My Observatory Withdrawn," though it also proves, ironically, to be a revision of Louis Zukofsky's famous optical definition of the "Objective" in his founding essay "An Objective."[57] The point, basically, is that for a prophetic poet – especially a Jewish poet – such as Grossman, the vision of the poet must be on the inwardness and being of the human Other, and not the external world, however numinous. This may be a limited understanding of Objectivism (I think it is), but it delineates an important distinction.

Furthermore, unlike Heller, in Grossman's view the Holy One has never gone missing. We know that the Jewish God, sometime sublime, sometimes comical, plays a part in Grossman's poetry from the beginning to the end of his career. Grossman may not have been an "observant" Jew (so to speak), but as we have seen, he claims the mantle of a poet of holiness, and indeed, writes and rewrites what he calls "The Song of Lord" in the service of the human community again and again. At the beginning of *How to Do Things with Tears*, he goes so far as to declare that "The maxim of poetic thinking is: DO NOT BE CONTENT WITH AN IMAGINARY GOD."[58] And this is why, I think, that Heller, most subtle of dialectical poets, concludes his poem to Grossman by declaring their situation to be

---

56. *The Sighted Singer*, 63–64.
57. Zukofsky's essay begins "*An Objective – The lens bringing the rays from an object to a focus. That which is aimed at. (use extended to poetry) – Desire for what is objectively perfect, inextricably the direction of historic and contemporary particulars.*" (Italics in original.) Louis Zukofsky, "An Objective" in *Prepositions +: The Collected Critical Essays*, 12.
58. *How to Do Things with Tears*, xi.

as if the old story of the "Holy One"
were now the new one about language,
as if we sought too far back for a
tabula rasa on which Paradise and Eden

were inscribed, so that a poetry of tears
would still leave a portion of the earth

in worshipful form, the sacred as
insurance against unwarrantable flight.[59]

Given Heller's subtle ironies (note particularly his use of the conditional in this passage), Grossman's "poetry of tears / would still leave a portion of the earth / in worshipful form," while the *sacred*, and not the profane or the secular, would provide "insurance against unwarrantable flight." Thus the two poets, if not fully reconciled, are not altogether at odds regarding the sacred, and Heller too refuses to be content with an "IMAGINARY GOD," even if God has gone missing or is now folded into the new story about language. For Heller, writing a modern poetry of the earth, of the material, of our sense of immanence, of our being in the world, constitutes a modern sense of the sacred. And this is one of his greatest poetic insights.

59. *Dianoia*, 6.

SIX

Chana Bloch: Surfaces and Depths

THERE IS A POEM FROM LATE IN THE CAREER OF CHANA BLOCH that exemplifies a number of the themes I have so far addressed, while at the same time indicating Bloch's unique understanding of Jewish American history and culture. The poem is called "Hester Street, 1898," and here it is in full:

> No one told them to smile
> and they're too busy anyway
> with their wooden pushcarts:
> *Aprons! Prayerbooks! Pickles in brine!*
> They regard the camera with suspicion.
> Butting, shoving, elbow and shoulder,
> they tilt the street off-frame.
>
> That is the world they dreamt of
> when they slept in mud and misery?
> If you climb the skyscrapers up to the sky
> you can feel the moon on your cheek,
> cool and shivery, like calf's-foot jelly.
>
> Yesterday's laundry waves from the fire escape,
> catching a bit of breeze;
> a barbershop pole unwinds
> its carnival stripes. *Life is better already!*

Better and better.
This they believed, this they taught diligently
unto their children,
who taught it to me.

Whatever I give you, my sons,
I can't give you that.[1]

One could probably make the case that there is a sub-genre of contemporary American poetry dealing with cultural identity that could be called the "old photograph poem." In these poems, the poet, contemplating an old photo (either of family members or of people who could be family), measures the distance her particular ethnic group has come over a number of generations in America, what they have gained, what they have lost. Closely related, but more specific to Jewish American poetry, there is what may be called the "crisis of transmission" poem, in which the poet, in a personal epiphany, perceives a rupture in tradition, in the handing down of values or beliefs. The poem sometimes ends with an additional ironic turn, recognizing that this sense of rupture is *in itself* part of the tradition, which is therefore, paradoxically, carried on. Poems of this sort which I have already examined include Reznikoff's "I went to my grandfather's to say good-bye," Harvey Shapiro's "The Generations," and Osherow's "Ch'vil Schreibn a Poem auf Yiddish."[2] In the case of "Hester Street, 1898," looking at a photograph of the iconic pushcart vendors on the Jewish Lower East Side leads Bloch to imagine the crude energy of immigrant life (the butting and shoving among the vendors in the crowded street), and then to "frame" that life in additional verbal "photos" (the laundry hanging from fire escapes, the barber pole).

These images are entwined with the poet's imagination of the immigrants' *inner* life: their ambition, their optimism as they adjust to life in the New World, the idealism which they insist, above all else, on passing to their children. This is captured in the figure of climbing the

1. Chana Bloch, *Swimming in the Rain: New and Selected Poems 1980–2015* (Pittsburgh, PA: Autumn House Press, 2015), 15.
2. See also Heller's "The American Jewish Clock," "In a Dark Time, On His Grandfather," and "For Uncle Nat," *This Constellation*, 272–74, and my analysis of these poems as expressions of the crisis of cultural transmission in *Not One of Them in Place*, 150–53.

skyscrapers and feeling "the moon on your cheek, / cool and shivery, like calf's-foot jelly," with the skyscraper as a uniquely American image, and the simile of the moon like calf's-foot jelly as *haimish* a trope of Old World Jewish domesticity as one could imagine. Life is indeed better and better; having escaped the shtetl's "mud and misery," the immigrants are at last free to dream. When Bloch presents the handing on of the dream to the next generation, her language takes on an almost biblical tone – the Bible in English, that is, though Bloch, a translator as a well as a poet (she translated the Song of Songs, and the poetry of Yehuda Amichai and of Dahlia Ravikovitch), is fluent in Hebrew: "This they believed, this they taught diligently / unto their children / who taught it to me." Bloch almost certainly has in mind Deuteronomy 6:4–9, from which comes the *V'ahavta*, part of the *Shema*, the most basic prayer in Judaism ("You shall love the Lord your God with all your heart, with all your soul, and with all your might. Take to heart these instructions with which I charge you this day. Impress them upon your children...") . If this is the case, then the immigrants' injunction to their children, to think that life can only get better in the New World, is intended, perhaps unconsciously, to become a part of traditional Jewish belief.

Yet this vision of expanding belief and devotion, a continuation of tradition from parent to child, seems to abruptly dead end with the last two lines of the poem: "Whatever I give you, my sons, / I can't give you that." Why does the poet, this Jewish mother, say this to her sons? By the time Bloch writes this poem, her sons are grown men, with lives of their own. Presumably she has given them a great deal, yet there is a strong sense of loss and perhaps even of failure here. It would appear that, while this is not primarily a rupture in religious tradition, Bloch senses that some cultural element bordering on the spiritual – the *psychic* – has not been passed down. If it is the worldview of the first generation, with its powerful will to survive and make more of itself, that has not been handed down, does this in turn point to an exhaustion of that original energy, that earlier sense of opportunity opening for Jewish life in America? Has the achievement of the immigrants' dream left the poet's sons with a rich inheritance, but without the impetus to struggle and transform themselves in the way of their ancestors? And is this due to their having successfully assimilated, taking that "better" life for granted?

Bloch does not provide any answers to these questions, at least not in this one poem. But as we shall see, she returns to them frequently in her poetry, often presenting the perspective of a Jewish American woman who is herself the beneficiary of that immigrant energy, and who also often wonders about its loss as her generation passes into the American mainstream. For let us remember that it was Jewish women as well as men working among those pushcarts, calling *"Aprons! Prayerbooks! Pickles in brine!"*

Chana Bloch (1940–2017) was born in New York City, the child of Yiddish-speaking immigrants from Ukraine; her father, Benjamin Faerstein, was a dentist who learned English in night school, and her mother Rose was a homemaker.[3] As she writes in her contribution to *Jewish American Poetry: Poems, Commentary, and Reflections* (2000), an important anthology that includes a number of generations of Jewish American poets,

> At home my parents spoke English, not Yiddish – they wanted to be "American," whatever that meant – though they sent me to a Yiddish *folkshul* every day after school. Not a Hebrew school: Hebrew belonged to the men and boys. We lived in the South Bronx, in the shadow of the Jerome Avenue El, a neighborhood soon to become loud with gang wars, but at the time almost too quiet: My friends and I referred to it with disdain as the Bronx Bourgeoizoo. My parents had settled into a life of placid routine, and who could blame them? They'd endured their quota of violent uprootings. But the safety they plotted for me I experienced as a constraint. I was impatient to lose my innocence.[4]

This passage is revealing in a number of important ways. Most obviously, there is Bloch's sensitivity to gender difference: the young Chana (whose name at that time was Florence Ina Faerstein; she changed her name to

3. Basic biographical information on Bloch is drawn from the "About the Author" sections of her books, from her website (http://www.chanabloch.com/bio.html), from numerous interviews, and from her obituary in *The New York Times*, William Grimes, "Chana Bloch, Poet and Hebrew Translator, Is Dead at 77," June 9, 2017, https://www.nytimes.com/2017/06/09/books/chana-bloch-died-poet-and-translator.html.

4. Chana Bloch, "Commentary," in *Jewish American Poetry*, 37.

Chana when she was in her early twenties) understood that Hebrew was a male domain, while Yiddish, the Jewish vernacular and language of domesticity, was supposed to be sufficient for women. Yet Bloch was still *educated* in Yiddish: the *folkshul* to which her parents sent her in addition to public school undoubtedly reinforced and formalized the Yiddish she would have heard around her, despite her parents speaking English in order to be "American." Yiddish, rather than fading away, as it did for so many young Jews of her generation, remained a vital part of her linguistic, and eventually her literary, repertory, and she would go on to translate the poetry of the great Yiddish poet Jacob Glatstein, who encouraged her in the work. We also see an awareness of post-immigration life that we have already observed in "Hester Street, 1898": the idea that a better life in America finally frees immigrant Jews from the "violent uprootings" they faced in Europe, as they gradually enter into the relative security of a bourgeois "life of placid routine." Yet the desire on the part of their children to escape from this security and shelter, Bloch's impatience to "lose my innocence," marks an inevitable intergenerational conflict, which, considering Jewish American literature, becomes the subject of so much highly charged fiction in the second half of the twentieth century. Gender difference emerges even more strongly here. As Bloch wryly observes of her mid-century Jewish American upbringing, "Girls were second-class citizens; the Bat Mitzvah had not yet been invented. I was given to understand that my chief religious duty was to marry a nice Jewish boy."[5]

Bloch's path, however, proves somewhat different: she enters the world of letters and scholarship once reserved for men, studying both Hebrew and English literature, and becoming a distinguished poet, translator, and critic. The secular study of Jewish literature offers the means of losing her innocence: "Yiddish and Hebrew literature offered tastes, smells, pungencies of experience I found nowhere else...I was longing for what I called real life, the life of tragedy that lay beyond the pale of my uneventful girlhood."[6] Bloch received her undergraduate

5. Chana Bloch, "Questions of Faith," interview with Dianne Bilyak, *Poetry Society of America*, https://www.poetrysociety.org/psa/poetry/crossroads/interviews/page _7/.
6. "Commentary," 38, 39.

degree from Cornell in Semitic studies in 1961, and went on to Brandeis, earning master's degrees in both Near Eastern and Judaic studies in 1963, and in English literature in 1965. After teaching for several years at Hebrew University in Jerusalem, she moved to Berkeley and finished a doctorate in 1975, writing a dissertation on George Herbert, which was eventually published as *Spelling the Word: George Herbert and the Bible* (1985). By then she had married her first husband, Ariel Bloch, a linguist in Semitic languages at Berkeley, with whom she had two sons. Her long career at Mills College began in 1973; eventually she would help found and then direct the creative writing program there. Her first book of poems, *The Secrets of the Tribe*, appeared in 1980; it was followed by *The Past Keeps Changing* (1992), *Mrs. Dumpty* (1998), *Blood Honey* (2009), *Swimming in the Rain: New and Selected Poems 1980–2015* (2015), and the posthumous *The Moon Is Almost Full* (2017). Bloch calls *The Secrets of the Tribe* "my most consciously Jewish book," which also means her consideration of "the gradual erosion of the certainties that governed my childhood."[7] But Jewish themes, in poems about the Jewish past, in midrashic poems based on the Hebrew Scriptures, in poems involving Jewish holidays and rituals, and in poems confronting the Shoah, extend through nearly all her books. *Mrs. Dumpty* and *The Moon Is Almost Full*, though perhaps less explicitly Jewish, are works of remarkable courage: the former addresses the disintegration of Bloch's first marriage due to her husband's mental illness; the latter deals mainly with Bloch's cancer and her confrontation with "The Face of Death" – "till the last face-to-face / when I am taken with a kiss."[8]

In a review of *Swimming in the Rain*, Robert Hirschfield notes that "For years, Bloch said recently, she had tacked to her bulletin board a quote by the Objectivist George Oppen: 'Clarity, clarity, surely clarity is the most beautiful thing in the world… I have not and never did have any motive of poetry / But to achieve clarity.'"[9] These lines come from

---

7. "Commentary," 39.

8. Chana Bloch, *The Moon Is Almost Full* (Pittsburgh, PA: Autumn House Press, 2017), 24.

9. Robert Hirschfield, "It Is Either Serious or It Isn't," *Jewish Review of Books* (Fall 2015), http://chanabloch.com/review-pdf/JewishReviewBooksHirschfield.pdf.

Oppen's "Route,"[10] and in terms of poetic lineage, it would be rather neat if I could argue that Bloch, like Michael Heller, is a second-generation Objectivist with strong roots in that tradition. But this is not really the case, despite the quote on her bulletin board. When asked to describe her style, Bloch responds that "I value clarity, an old-fashioned virtue. I like poetry that appears to be clear on the surface, with complexity astir in the depths, rejecting the shallow notion that these are necessarily opposed. My poems are spare and precise, their often dark subject matter leavened with humor and irony. My language springs from the demotic idiom I grew up with in the Bronx, infused with the irony and wit of Jewish discourse as well as the seventeenth-century metaphysical poets I studied, wrote about, and taught."[11] This is a fair description, and we may add to it Norbert Hirschhorn's useful observation regarding the formal qualities of a typical Bloch poem: "sudden short lines, then line breaks to force a dramatic vocal reading; irregular stanza lengths; sharp epiphanies at the end."[12] I would also argue that Bloch, given her preference for poems with clear surfaces and complexities in the depths, would sympathize with Heller's vision, derived from Oppen, of the poet "caught between a philosophical sense of his or her craft and a religious sense of the mysteriousness of the world."[13] Like Heller and the original Objectivists, Bloch is a "Jewish humanist," for whom, as she observes, "the quarrel with tradition is one of the most distinctive features of Judaism, and one of the most compelling."[14] Indeed, this understanding

---

10. The passage in full reads "Clarity, clarity, surely clarity is the most beautiful thing in the world, / A limiting, limited clarity // I have not and never did have any motive of poetry / But to achieve clarity," Oppen, 193.

11. Chana Bloch, "The Real Truth," interview with *The International Literary Quarterly*, http://interlitq.org/Interviews/chana-bloch/job.php. Bloch's emphasis on a clear style, with complexity in the depths, seems to be a carefully thought-out position; she gives virtually the same response in another interview. See her interview by Zara Raab, *San Francisco Book Review*, July 11, 2011, http://zararaab.com/interview-with -chana-bloch-july-11–2011/.

12. Norbert Hirschhorn, review of *Swimming in the Rain*, *London Grip* (Autumn 2015) http://londongrip.co.uk/2015/08/london-grip-poetry-review-bloch/.

13. *Uncertain Poetries*, 13.

14. "Questions of Faith."

of Judaism is fundamental not only to Bloch or to Jewish poets in the Objectivist line, but to every poet discussed in this book.

That having been said, what exactly distinguishes Bloch from the Objectivists? The answer lies, I think, in the Objectivist engagement with linguistic skepticism, which one does not find in Bloch's work. As we have seen, this engagement results in what Heller names "diasporic poetics," which, given a specifically Jewish heritage and linguistic sensibility, involves a constant, often highly self-conscious, poetic negotiation between language and the world. In recent American poetry, this negotiation produces a sort of third way in terms of style: it entails neither the radical linguistic play and experimentation of Language poetry (which is related in many respects to a postmodern skepticism of linguistic representation and signification), nor does it gloss over the instability of the verbal sign and take for granted the coherence of the "lyric voice," which at least two generations of experimental poets have seen as problems of the so-called "workshop poem," the typical product of what Charles Bernstein labels "official verse culture" or what Ron Silliman calls the "School of Quietude."[15]

Bloch, however, despite the rich and productive quarrel that she and other recent Jewish American poets have with tradition, does not practice a "diasporic poetic." Rather, in some respects, her work, which tends to be anecdotal, written in the first person, emotionally expressive, and formally an instance of the modern free-verse lyric, could be seen as "workshop poetry" – and indeed, she spent much of her career teaching creative writing and directing a creative writing program during that

15. The debates to which I am referring are now nearly fifty years old, and have been variously chronicled, analyzed, and canonized by many critics and poets. One of the opening salvoes, which still nicely articulates what is at stake in these debates, is Ron Silliman, Carla Harryman, Lyn Hejinian, Steve Benson, Bob Perelman and Barrett Watten, "Aesthetic Tendency and the Politics of Poetry: A Manifesto," *Social Text* 19/20 (Autumn 1988): 261–75. Another important polemical essay dating from that period, which places the issues in the historical context of poetic modernism is Charles Bernstein, "The Academy in Peril: William Carlos Williams Meets the MLA," in *Content's Dream: Essays 1975–1984* (Los Angeles: Sun & Moon Press, 1985), 244–51. For a cogent and well-researched overview of the debates, see Gillian White, *Lyric Shame: The "Lyric" Subject of Contemporary American Poetry* (Cambridge, MA: Harvard University Press, 2014), 1–41.

period when such programs grew exponentially in American higher education.[16] "You have to find your own voice," she suggests in an interview, a standard notion in creative writing classes, and one that has become practically anathema among experimentalists.[17] Bloch also has little patience for categorizing poetry into schools and styles, despite (or perhaps because of) the fact that during much of her career, she lived and taught in the Bay Area, the scene of the most intense and often vituperative debates about style and the cultural role of poetry in the last fifty years. When Carol Dorf, interviewing Bloch, mentions that "In the Bay Area, for years we've had lyrical vs. experimental poets," Bloch's response is highly charged: "I hate those labels! *Lyrical! Confessional! Experimental!* Either a poem is good or it's not."[18]

While this attitude may be understandable in such an atmosphere, it also begs the question and tends to support the poetic mainstream, or as Alan Golding puts it, "an ideology of the unmediated or self-evident

16. Cf. Philip Terman's characterization of Bloch's work in his highly laudatory review of *Swimming in the Rain*: "Spare and musical, intimate while open to history, intelligent and emotionally rich in the details of divisions and connections, Bloch's poetry negotiates the complexities of her identity as a first-generation Jew, a woman, a child, a parent, a wife, a lover, and a citizen." "Spare and musical" are terms often applied to the modern free-verse lyric, while the emphasis on identity feeds directly into a first person expressive mode. Philip Terman, "The Poetry of a Jewish Humanist," *Tikkun* (Sumer 2015): 56–58. http://www.chanabloch.com/review-pdf /TikkunPoetryofaJewishHumanist.pdf.

17. Interview with Zara Raab. Jennifer Ashton neatly sums up the experimentalist (and particularly the Language poetry) critique of this notion: "The problem with writing programs that encourage students to 'find [their] voice' (a commonplace even now in the promotional material on many writing program websites) is apparently that the voices their students find are insufficiently their own." Ashton also quotes Language poet Bob Perelman from his book *The Marginalization of Poetry*: "the aesthetic necessity of 'finding your voice', masks the institutional circuits, the network of presses, reviews, jobs, readings, and awards that are the actual sounding board of voice." Jennifer Ashton, "Lyric, Gender, and Subjectivity in Modern and Contemporary Women's Poetry," in *The Cambridge History of American Women's Literature*, ed. Dale M. Bauer (Cambridge, UK: Cambridge University Press, 2012), 522.

18. Chana Bloch, "Chana Bloch: 'The Poem Begins to Shape You,'" interview with Carol Dorf, December 17, 2014, *Talking Writing*, http://talkingwriting.com/chana-bloch -poem-begins-shape-you.

that again suppresses the evaluative criteria involved in selection and removes the poetry from the circumstances or site of its production, collection and consumption: 'the work of the poets speaks best for itself.'"[19] Looking at representative poetry anthologies published since the nineteen-seventies in order to define the mainstream, Golding also notes how many editors (usually poets and creative writing teachers themselves) "buttress the cult of the individual 'voice' that came to define the centre of American poetry starting in the mid-1970s."[20] Claiming a "dislike of schools and dogma," these editors, when their anthologies are examined closely, have produced books with a "uniformity of background and of shared but *unstated* assumptions [that] work against the eclecticism and 'school-less-ness' that mainstream editors often assert."[21]

The poetic stance that Golding and other critics identify, and which we see Bloch articulating to some extent, in turn shapes the way she writes about her identity as a Jewish woman in relation to Jewish culture, tradition, history, and texts. But I do not want to argue that this stance limits Bloch in her exploration of issues of identity, which unfold in her work in a sophisticated, nuanced, and deeply moving fashion. Indeed, more generally in terms of style, I do not want to argue that Jewish American poets are necessarily going to be more or less successful in their exploration of Jewish themes if they practice either a "mainstream" or an "experimental" poetic, or even some alternative mode, such as Heller's "diasporic poetics" (however sympathetic I may be to that position). In *Not One of Them in Place*, when considering vexed questions of style and poetic ideology in modern and postmodern poetry, I develop the case that "Jewish American poetry may be understood as a peculiar fold in the larger debate" – which is to say, that if a contemporary American poet is writing about his or her Jewish identity, or about the Jewish world, the poetry that results will always be identifiable as an instance of, or

19. Alan Golding, "Recent American Poetry Anthologies and the Idea of the 'Mainstream,'" in *Poetry and Contemporary Culture: The Question of Value*, ed. Andrew Michael Roberts and Jonathan Allison (Edinburgh: Edinburgh University Press, 2002), 131–32.
20. Ibid., 130.
21. Ibid., 126.

perhaps a variation upon, one or another style or ideological stance in contemporary American poetry.[22]

Regarding women's poetry of the type that Bloch writes (expressive, written in the first person, anecdotal, etc.) in her closely argued and theoretically informed essay "Lyric, Gender, and Subjectivity in Modern and Contemporary Women's Poetry," Jennifer Ashton persuasively demonstrates that "lyric *is* an artifact of the present. It is also an artifact of the past that produced the present. What that means is that everyone has been doing and is continuing to do lyric, and more specifically, lyric self-expression – including the Language poets... The critique of lyric, and even the attempt to ignore it, becomes... a way of embracing rather than refusing or avoiding the idea of self-expression."[23] Ashton considers first-, second-, and third-wave feminism, which correlates roughly to the universalism and struggle for equality of the women modernists (Ashton cites Mina Loy), to the expression of a variety of female subject positions and identities among poets in the sixties through the eighties (for instance, Adrienne Rich or Gloria Anzaldúa), and to feminist versions of the radically decentered self seen in Language poetry, correlating to post-structuralism and *écriture féminine* (such as Susan Howe or Rachel Blau DuPlessis). What Ashton determines – and this is highly relevant to Bloch, who comes of age and begins writing her expressivist, identity-driven poetry during the second wave of feminism – is that in the face of a contemporary deconstructive critique of such poetry, "the effort to organize poetry by women under the auspices of 'innovative' and 'experimental' forms produces an essentialism of its own."[24] To be sure then, for a post-immigration Jewish American woman of Bloch's generation, the style – and the "voice" – through which she explores the vicissitudes of her life makes perfect sense.

But even a stylistic and historical analysis of this sort may not be sufficient to account for what Bloch is doing in some of her most intriguing poems. In a recent essay, Maeera Y. Shreiber argues that Bloch, in her desire to undo *difference* (which Shreiber traces back to the divine impulse

22. *Not One of Them in Place*, 6.
23. Ashton, 518.
24. Ibid., 530.

in Genesis that separates creation from the void, dark from light, the heavens from the firmament, man from woman, etc.), is actually an anti-lyrical poet. If the lyric poet follows God in creatively *separating* to order to bring forth form, "Bloch seeks to subvert, or reverse, this aesthetic paradigm in the interest of making poems that serve as occasions for returning to moments when the space between all but disappears – and there is no difference between realms of being and nonbeing."[25] Not only does this result in a troubling critique of Jewish Law (which depends on differences between the holy and the profane, the kosher and the non-kosher, and so on), but it also changes our perspective on Bloch's overall poetic project: "although her poems may look like lyrics – monologic performances of self-expression or reflection – they sometimes work to wholly different ends, inviting us to embrace the very condition against which many lyrics set themselves: an undefinable, ever-changing state of fluid precreation."[26] After considering a number of Bloch's poems, including "The Revised Version," in which Bloch playfully rewrites the first six verses of Genesis ("1:6 Night fell, the first of many"), Shreiber concludes that

> A cursory glance at the poems composing her oeuvre might suggest that Bloch is largely a maker of domestic lyrics, as many of them take hold of intimate memories, through which the poet explores the losses and loves that constitute a keenly felt life. In and of itself, this is a worthy contribution, as we treasure the vulnerabilities and knowings that these poems lay bare. However, read within the context of a poem such as "The Revised Version," which defies the dominant Western narrative by expanding the status of "good" to include all things – even the all-too-often-dreaded "Night" – these lyrics come into focus as vital additions to that body of writing called wisdom literature.[27]

If this is indeed the case, then Bloch is certainly something more than a poet of lyric self-expression, writing about identity through memory and anecdote. The reader will recall that at a number of earlier points

25. Maeera Y. Shreiber, "Embracing the Void: A Short Essay in Memory of Chana Bloch," *Shofar* 36, no. 2 (Summer 2018): 43.
26. Ibid., 43–44.
27. Ibid., 47–48. "The Revised Version," *Swimming in the Rain*, 30.

in this book, the poet whom I relate to the tradition of wisdom litera-
ture is Harvey Shapiro, who, like Bloch, specializes in anecdotal poems,
occasionally drawing on biblical material, which border on the parabolic.
Both poets also adopt a wry, worldly tone, and both delight in paradox,
which, arguably, is a mode of thinking and writing that undermines
difference and separateness, as Shreiber observes of Bloch.[28] Poetry in
the tradition of wisdom literature depends on its clarity to convey the
force of paradox and parable, which in turn leads its reader to wisdom.[29]
Let's consider how this unfolds in more of her poems.

In "Furniture," from Bloch's first collection, the poet reflects on reli-
gious belief, on becoming a writer, and more obliquely, on her relationship
to her mother, in an account of an episode that brings together her pres-
ent and her past. It is a fairly short poem, wry but subtly powerful, and
an early example of the clarity and depth that Bloch will come to favor:

> Last night we talked about God
> as metaphor, like
> the head of the table
> the leg of the chair
> God of the Universe
>
> "I haven't got a God to stand on,"
> I said. And flinched.
> No thunder.
>
> "Shame on you!
> God will punish you," my mother would say,
> if you write on Shabbos."
> When I wrote, I pulled down the shade.[30]

28. Paradox, of course, is a feature of seventeenth-century English metaphysical poetry,
and it should be recalled that Bloch was an expert in the work of George Herbert
and other poets of that period.

29. Shreiber also notices Bloch's emphasis on the surfaces and depths of her poems,
relating it to traditional Jewish hermeneutics: "Whenever asked about her poetic
predilections, Bloch inevitably expresses a preference for "clear" surfaces (in classical
Jewish Bible study we might say *peshat*, or direct meaning) with a good dose of *remez*
(implied meaning) that stirs underneath." Ibid., 44.

30. *Swimming in the Rain*, 60.

In the present, the grown-up poet feels free to discuss "God / as meta-phor," and even make a transgressive joke expressing her doubt. Yet she flinches, half expecting some childhood vision of divine punishment, and her involuntary reflex instantly produces a memory of her mother invoking that divine wrath when the young poet-to-be violates the Sabbath in order to write. The image of the girl pulling down the shade to hide from an omniscient God while she writes on Shabbos is funny, but it is also important to note that the voice of conscience which the girl internalizes is her mother's. In other words, it is the mother (and not the father, however much we think of the Jewish God as a patriarchal figure) who speaks for the Law, and insists that her daughter, longing to express herself, curtail her desire to write, and obey the commandment to remember the Sabbath and to keep it holy. Thus, the poem is about the coincidence of religious practice and maternal relations: the (masculine) God may be invoked, but it is the female parent who invokes Him. In the remainder of the poem, Bloch embellishes the memory:

> In those days there was thunder like furniture moved in heaven.
> God came down from the mountain.
> My heart ticked evenly as a clock at the head of the bed.
> On Friday the candles stood lit on the table,
> and four chairs, one at each side,
> squaring the round world.
>
> There were crumbs on the tablecloth
> and hot wax dripped from the candles
> so quietly
> we never heard them
> go out.[31]

What is striking here is the way Bloch intertwines the divine and the domestic, the cosmic and the ordinary: the thunder in heaven is like moving furniture, but conversely, the four chairs at the family dinner table on Friday square the round world, defining its boundary.[32] The last

---

31. Ibid.

32. Bloch, an expert in seventeenth-century Metaphysical poetry, may unconsciously be echoing the beginning of John Donne's "Holy Sonnet 7": "At the round earth's

stanza ends with a beautiful sense of silence, the stillness of the Sabbath, but the images of the crumbs, the hot wax dripping, and the candles going out also raise some troubling issues that are already implied earlier in the poem. From childhood on, faith has been on the wane for the poet; perhaps what is left is only crumbs as the Shabbos candles silently go out. God and His thunder are now only metaphors – but metaphors for what? The answer, I think, has to do with the young girl longing to write, who has become the adult poet, the creator of metaphors, and also has to do with the poem itself. These metaphors, however, remain centrally Jewish – the sublime grandeur of divine thunder, but the homey warmth of Friday night candles as well. Despite the daughter's rebellion, the mother's scolding may have had a lasting effect, for in the daughter's poem, Jewish thought and culture, if not normative Jewish belief, maintains its vitality.

Yet despite the possibility of such an affirmation, the poet harbors many doubts. Two other poems from *The Secrets of the Tribe* wrestle with questions of faith and tradition, especially in relation to Jewish American assimilation. "Exile" has an aggadic quality, in the sense of a tale or a bit of lore that seeks to answer a fundamental question of Jewish history, indeed, of Jewish being:

> What happened to the ten lost tribes
> is no great mystery.
> They found work, married, grew smaller,
> started to look like the natives
> in a landscape nobody chose.
> Soon you couldn't have picked them out of a crowd.
>
> And if they'd stayed where they were,
> what happiness would they have endured?
> We can't believe in it.
>
> The face of the cities scares us,
> day and night empty us till

imagin'd corners, blow / Your trumpets, angels…" This poem, like so many of Donne's religious works, reflects an intensely skeptical sensibility wrestling with the tenets of Christian faith. In her poem, Bloch too is confronting her religious doubts.

> we are no longer
> God's chosen.
>
> For a while we camp out under the strange trees.
> complaining, planning a return.
> But we have taken out papers and become citizens.[33]

Here, the "mystery" of the legendary ten lost tribes becomes a means to consider the historical phenomena of Jewish exile and assimilation, with the post-immigration Jewish American experience certainly implied. But beyond the "solution" to the mystery offered in the first stanza, is the equally important "We can't believe it" that follows. What would Jewish history have been like if the "lost tribes" hadn't been lost? Is there any point in even discussing it? The religious beliefs (of both Jews and non-Jews), historical speculations, and cultural theories pertaining to the legend of lost tribes makes it one of the most ideologically fraught of all those connected to the Jewish people.[34] Numerous groups and populations have been put forward as descendants of the tribes, some actually connected to the Jews historically or genetically, but most not. Overall, these are, according to historian Tudor Parfitt, "imaginary communities, either imagined into existence by themselves or by others."[35] Bloch's assertion of disbelief indicates how strongly the reality principle is at work in her understanding of Jewish history: accept the dispersal and exile, and acknowledge repeated patterns of assimilation.

But this is not an instance of diasporism, such as we have seen in Reznikoff's poetry, and in this poem, Bloch does not celebrate assimilation, or even take much comfort in Jews finding a refuge in exile. In the third stanza, each of the four lines is shorter than the one before it, as if the Jews, as they lose their status of Chosen People, dwindle into a crowd of natives, with nothing special about them. The final stanza is suffused with a sense of resignation: the Jews have become (American)

33. Ibid., 55.
34. See Zvi Ben-Dor Benite, *The Ten Lost Tribes: A World History* (Oxford: Oxford University Press, 2009), for a comprehensive survey and analysis of the legend.
35. Tudor Parfitt, *The Lost Tribes of Israel: The History of a Myth* (London: Weidenfeld & Nicolson, 2002), 246.

citizens, and plans for a return turn out only to be plans. The "we" of the poem have their new papers, but the tone is one of loss. For Bloch's collective "we," the concept of Jewish exceptionalism, of being chosen, however it may be defined, is cast into doubt.

That doubt is even more intense in "The Converts," which deals specifically with religious faith and the loss of tradition. It is Yom Kippur, and again Bloch employs that Jewish American "we," this time in the synagogue, where the poet, in the midst of the congregation, is counting down the hours till sunset and breaking the fast:

> On the holiest day we fast till sundown.
> I watch the sun stand still
> as the horizon edges toward it. Four hours to go.
> The rabbi's mouth opens and closes and opens.
> I think *fish*
> *and little steaming potatoes,*
> *parsley clinging to them like an ancient script.*
>
> Only the converts, six of them in the corner,
> in their prayer shawls and feathery beards,
> sing every syllable.
> What word
> are they savoring now?
> If they go on loving that way, we'll be here all night.
>
> Why did they follow us here, did they think
> we were happier?
> Did someone tell them we knew
> the lost words
> to open God's mouth?
>
> The converts sway in white silk,
> their necks bent forward in yearning
> like swans,
> and I covet
> what they think we've got.[36]

36. *Swimming in the Rain,* 59.

Anyone who has fasted on Yom Kippur (and, I would guess, on any other religiously obligated fast day) knows the feeling Bloch describes in the first two stanzas, including the fantasy of the upcoming meal – though in this case, the simile of the *"little steaming potatoes, / parsley clinging to them like an ancient script"* reminds us that the tradition encoded in the ancient script, including all its commandments, should be appreciated, if not actually savored, by the people to whom those commandments were given. But as the poet sees it, most modern Jews have lost that capacity for savoring the commandments, including the most severe. "Only the converts, six of them in the corner, / in their prayer shawls and feathery beards" appear completely engaged in the service, savoring the words but slowing down the davening of the increasingly impatient congregation (though of course, the fast will not end till after sunset regardless).

Bloch's ironic view of the proceedings is matched by her wonderful use of detail. The converts in their "white silk" (because they have apparently adopted the Orthodox practice of wearing a white kittel on the High Holidays) have "feathery beards": these are young men, perhaps growing their first beards as a sign of their conversion. The questions that Bloch poses about them in the fourth stanza reflect a complicated set of assumptions and doubts. If the converts were originally Christian, they have rejected the old theological canard that Christianity supersedes Judaism. On the contrary, they have embraced the philosemitic notion that the ancient Jewish faith, and specifically the Hebrew of scripture and liturgy, can provide "the lost words / to open God's mouth." Not only are Jews supposedly happier than gentiles (because of their spiritual condition?), but the means to this happiness, which comes in turn from a greater access to divine truth, has to do with the language in which they pray and study. This belief in the mystical power of the Hebrew language, while fundamental to Kabbalah, has also been held for centuries by non-Jews (including Hebraists and Christian Kabbalists), and it may well be that this popular notion is one reason why these six individuals have converted. As is often the case with Bloch, this results in a moment of wisdom arising out of bittersweet humor: on the one hand, there is something charming and slightly silly about the converts' enthusiasm, at least from the perspective of the hungry Jews who have been attending Yom Kippur services since they were children (and fasting since they were bar and bat mitzvah age). On the other hand, Bloch finds that there is something genuinely moving and beautiful about the converts, "their necks bent forward in yearning / like swans." What moves her is precisely that yearning for faith which has led them to convert, a yearning and an earnest hope for divine communion, or at least a spiritual *hunger*, that she and the rest of the congregation seem to lack. In a further twist, the converts believe that this faith is there already among the people they have joined; thus Bloch's final declaration that "I covet / what they think we've got." The word "covet" takes us to the tenth Commandment: "You shall not covet your neighbor's house, nor his wife, his man-servant, his maid-servant, nor his ox, nor his ass, nor anything that is your neighbor's" (Exodus 20:14). The poet is committing a serious sin – in synagogue, on the holiest day of the year, when it is believed that the Book of Life is about to be sealed. But apparently it cannot be helped: despite her irony, her feeling of loss, not just for herself, but for her community, is simply too intense.

The paradoxes of belief which arise out of the conflict between Jewish Law and human desire are fully displayed in "White Petticoats," from Bloch's second volume, *The Past Keeps Changing*. It begins with an instance of what Shreiber calls Bloch's "pointed critique of Jewish dicta," dicta that insist on the separation and difference which Bloch wishes to undo:[37]

> If the egg had one drop of blood in it
> the rabbis said "Throw it away!"
> As if they could legislate
> perfection. Dress the bride
> in white petticoats! Let there be
>
> no spot
> on your ceremony!
> As if we could keep our lives
> from spilling
> on our new clothes.[38]

37. "Embracing the Void," 43.
38. *Swimming in the Rain*, 83. Shreiber's example is "The Dark of Day" (*Swimming in the*

Not only do the rabbis insist on difference, and hope to "legislate / perfection," they are specifically concerned with female purity: the egg cannot have a blood spot (a sign that it may have been fertilized), and the bride is to wear white petticoats (a sign of her virginity). Religious ceremony under patriarchal control must be spotless, but as a feminist critic of halakhah, Bloch ironically observes that it cannot be: "As if we could keep our lives / from spilling / on our new clothes." She then provides a memory from her wedding night to prove it:

> That night we came home
> strangers, too tired to speak,
> fog in the high trees,
> and a trunk full of shiny boxes
> we didn't unwrap.
>
> There's a bravery in being naked.
> We left our clothes
> on the doorknob, the floor, the bed,
> and a rising moon opened its arms
> around the dark.[39]

The rabbinic attempt to legislate sexuality proves to be somewhat absurd in the face of the newlyweds' combined exhaustion and excitement. All the imagery in these last two stanzas gestures toward the undifferentiated dark to which, according to Shreiber, Bloch longs to return. The night is foggy; the individual wedding gifts in their shiny boxes are ignored; the new husband and wife scatter their clothes all over in their haste; and the moon embraces the dark. As Shreiber notes of this impetus in Bloch's work, "Determined to excavate a space that would not only accommodate but also honor dark truths," Bloch frequently challenges "this programmatic insistence on unassailable difference and the systemic insistence that (day) light always outranks the (night)

Rain, 179), another poem in which Bloch explicitly criticizes "the rabbis," who "taught us the mathematics of dividing / this from that."

39. Ibid.

dark."[40] Naked desire leads us back to primal union, a wholeness which seems as good as the orderliness of Creation.

It is sad but revealing that when "White Petticoats" was published in *The Past Keeps Changing*, it bore the simple dedication *"for Ariel"*; years later, when Bloch republished the poem in *Swimming in the Rain*, the dedication was removed. In between, separating, dividing, is the story of the marriage (perhaps the couple's beautiful translation of the Song of Songs is the monument to their love) and of its dissolution, as recounted in Bloch's *Mrs. Dumpty*. The last poem in that collection, "The Kiss," poignant but absolutely unflinching, is worth comparing to the rejection of rabbinic rules and the embrace of primal union in "White Petticoats":

> There was a ghost at our wedding,
> the caterer's son
> who drowned that day.
>
> Like every bride I was dressed
> in hope so sharp
> it tore open
> my tight-sewn fear.
>
> You kissed me under the wedding canopy,
> a kiss that lasted a few beats longer
> than the usual,
> and we all laughed.
>
> We were promising: the future
> would be like the present,
> even better, maybe.
> Then your heel came down
> on the glass.
>
> We poured champagne
> and opened the doors to the garden

40. "Embracing the Void," 46–47.

and danced
a little drunk, all of us,

as the caterer made the first cut,
one firm stroke, then
dipped his knifeblade
in the water.[41]

There is something almost gothic about the wedding in this poem, which, we must remind ourselves, is the same wedding to which "White Petticoats" refers. Haunted by the ghost of the caterer's drowned son, the event, as Bloch describes it, is fraught with foreboding, fatality, even hints of violence, in every one of its details. The long kiss that the groom gives the bride beneath the canopy seems awkward, too clingy, too much of an assertion of his love for her, and the laughter that follows may be a sign that everyone has sensed this. For Bloch, looking back, the kiss indicates the promise that "the future / would be like the present, / even better, maybe": and that "maybe," hanging at the end of the sentence and the line of verse, carries a great load of doubt. One thinks of the immigrants' hope in "Hester Street, 1898": *Life is better already! / Better and better.* But this is the child of immigrants, now taking a disheartened look at a Jewish American marriage that has since come apart. Her "maybe" is followed immediately by the new husband's heel coming "down / on the glass," the shattering ritual that reminds Jews of disaster even at the happiest and most hopeful of moments.[42] Indeed, hope itself in this poem is "so sharp / it tore open / my tight-sewn fear," a highly contradictory image of sexual assault and violation, and again, a distinct contrast to

41. *Swimming in the Rain*, 159.
42. Cf. Bloch's "Instructions for the Bridegroom," a very late poem in which the groom is reminded to "break a glass / to remember the Romans // demolished that Temple of yours." Bloch continues:

> Never forget
> you were put on earth to gather joy
>
> with melancholy hands.
> Now you may kiss the bride,
>
> your rose of Sharon, your darling
> among the shards.

the blissful flinging aside of clothes in "White Petticoats." Violence and division are there in the last stanza too, as the caterer, who presumably has just learned of his son's death, "made the first cut, / one firm stroke." Usually the bride and groom make the first cut of the wedding cake (and provocatively, the cake itself is never mentioned); here the caterer seems almost like a murderer or a biblical figure offering a sacrifice, as he dips "his knifeblade / in the water." What, we wonder, is being sacrificed here? The couple's future happiness, perhaps? Even the moment when champagne is poured and "the doors to the garden" are opened becomes a promise of Eden, now lost. Separation, division, loss of unity, sacrifice: the wedding ceremony has been conducted properly, but nothing is truly in order.

As I hope is apparent by now, Bloch's poems almost always draw us down into unanticipated depths through the surface clarity of her presentation and her seemingly casual, almost off-the-cuff tone. Conversational, low-key, intimate in the way that a friend might tell us her thoughts, her memories, and her daily experiences, Bloch's work, whether seen as modern wisdom literature, or, as I suggested in regard to "Exile," as ironic aggadah (especially in relation to what the poet perceives to be the overly restrictive nature of halakhah), rarely leaves the middle range of poetic discourse.[43] By this I mean that, although we have seen her connect her poetry to "the demotic idiom I grew up with in the Bronx," she usually maintains a relatively sophisticated but still unpretentious level of American speech, and almost never reaches for the heights. She

Love is always found "among the shards." The Rose of Sharon is, of course, the beloved of the Song of Songs (which Bloch translated with her first husband); the groom finds her not merely among the shards of the broken glass, but, I would speculate, among the shards of the fallen world, as in the Lurianic myth of creation and catastrophe. Chana Bloch, *The Moon Is Almost Full* (Pittsburgh, PA: Autumn House Press, 2017), 46.

43. In proposing the possibility of Bloch's poetry as modern aggadah, I am thinking of Walter Benjamin's subversive use of the term in "Some Reflections on Kafka" (originally written as part of a letter to Gershom Scholem). According to Benjamin, "Kafka's writings are by their nature parables. But it is their misery and their beauty that they had to become *more* than parables. They do not modestly lie at the feet of the doctrine, as the Haggadah lies at the feet of the Halakah. Though apparently reduced to submission, they unexpectedly raise a mighty paw against it." Walter Benjamin, *Illuminations*, trans. Harry Zohn (New York: Schocken Books, 1965), 144.

is not a poet of the sublime, not a visionary or prophetic poet. Even her poems about the Holocaust, a subject which frequently leads to a linguistic intensity and high emotional pitch in other Jewish American poets (we have observed this in both Rothenberg and Grossman), are tremendously affecting but still relatively restrained. In "Death March, 1945," she draws on her conversation with Rabbi Ben-Zion Gold, who tells her of his escape from on the Nazis while on a forced march to Dachau.[44] The poem consists mostly of Gold's own words, but in the last two stanzas, the poet speaks as well:

> "Where in that hell did you find the nerve to live?
> You knew what lay ahead if you were caught."
> I thought he'd say, "No choice. Jump or be killed,"
>
> but he wasn't giving lessons on being brave.
> "I was loved," he said, "when I was a child."
> I tell his story every chance I get.[45]

Not courage, but Gold's sense of self-worth, instilled by his parents' love, leads to his immensely strong will to survive. His quiet insistence on the importance of such love inspires the poet, so that, as she concludes, again with quiet insistence, "I tell his story every chance I get." The Rabbi's story becomes aggadah – lore – and Bloch, in writing her poem, devotedly continues the transmission of this lore and its kernel of wisdom.

There is one instance, however, where Bloch assumes something close to a prophetic tone and identity – and then, in effect, transfers this prophetic role to another poet. In her chapter in *Jewish American Poetry*, after discussing the painful but paradoxically "joyful, even exhilarating" experience of writing *Mrs. Dumpty*, Bloch presents a new poem called "Spell," "which brings together passages from Isaiah, Job, and the story of Elijah to articulate what I have learned about the difficult but rewarding work of writing."[46] But "Spell" was never included in any of Bloch's books

---

44. A timeline of the life of Ben-Zion Gold may be found at https://rabbibenziongold .com/timeline/.
45. *Swimming in the Rain*, 34.
46. "Commentary," 46.

of poetry. Instead, she drastically revised it, turning it into "Covenant," a poem in memory of Paul Celan, published in *Blood Honey*. Here are the two poems set side by side for comparison:

Spell

What I am given is too hot to
    touch.
Live coal, live

pain from the altar. I take it
in the tongs of language,
of metaphor, so it won't burn.

It does burn. I reach for it
anyway. Slowly. The poem
is a miracle

of perversity. It knows before I do
    how words
give what they take away. Slake
what they sharpen. Salt what they
save. I leave a place at the table

for the Prophet Elijah who rose
    in fire
in a cloud of words.[47]

Covenant
    in memory of Paul Celan

What he was given was too hot to
    touch.
Live coal, glowing from the altar.

He took it
in the tongs of metaphor
so it wouldn't burn.

But it did burn. He reached for it
anyway. Slowly, slowly.

His poems are a miracle
of perversity. They knew before
    he did
what words give

and words take away.
How they slake
and inflame. How they salt
every morsel they save.

He left a place at the table
for the silence
that pressed a burning coal
to his lips.[48]

If we consider some of the changes which Bloch has made in order to transform "Spell" into "Covenant," we can observe her technical skill, her thought regarding the poetic vocation, and most importantly, how these interact with her sense of Jewish identity. The change in the title

47. "Commentary," 46–47
48. *Swimming in the Rain*, 170.

and the shift from the first person, the "I" of the poet, to the third person, the "he" of Paul Celan, are the most obvious. I see these two changes as closely connected. In "Spell," Bloch assumes the role of a poet-prophet, which, as I indicated above, is very rare in her poetry. The source of most of her imagery is Isaiah 6, in which the prophet is vouchsafed a vision of God on His throne in the Temple, surrounded by seraphim. Believing himself to be unclean, Isaiah cries out:

> Woe is me! for I am undone; because I am a man of unclean lips, and I dwell in the midst of a people of unclean lips; for mine eyes have seen the King, the Lord of hosts.
> Then flew one of the seraphim unto me, having a live coal in his hand, which he had taken with the tongs from off the altar:
> And he laid it upon my mouth, and said Lo, this hath touched thy lips; and thine iniquity is taken away, and thy sin is purged.[49]

Isaiah then puts himself forward to speak God's word to the people, though the prophet is told in advance that they will not come to Him. In "Spell," Bloch presents her poetry as divinely inspired language, and becomes both the prophet *and* the seraph: like the seraph, she takes the live coal from the altar "in the tongs of language, / of metaphor, so it won't burn." But "It does burn," so like Isaiah, she feels the purging heat. In other words, she is both the source and the vehicle for prophetic utterance, an extraordinary claim even by the standards of poet-prophets throughout the Western poetic tradition.

Since antiquity, spells have been part of Jewish folk tradition; they are also found in the Talmud and in medieval kabbalistic texts. But though they may be part of Jewish cultural practice, they are not part of mainstream, normative, rationalistic modern Judaism, and one would be hard pressed to find magical ceremonies taking place in most American synagogues. Yet here is Bloch, the self-proclaimed "Jewish humanist," naming a poem involving divine vision "Spell." Is she *casting* a spell? Or, given the power of poetic language that she invokes ("It knows before I do how words / give what they take away..."), is she *under* a spell? My sense is the latter, which may be why she calls the poem (and note the

49. Isaiah 6:5–7 (KJV).

enjambment, to produce the maximum shock) "a miracle / of perversity." "Perversity" is a highly charged word. The poem is unacceptable; it goes against expected behavior; it transgresses by violating codes of propriety and of language, often in an intimate fashion. It transforms the poet from a subject to an object: *the poem speaks the poet*.

This accounts in part for the radical revision of the poem. Bloch escapes from the "spell" of poetic prophecy by projecting this role upon the figure of Celan, one of the very greatest Jewish poets of the twentieth century, and, given his experience of the Holocaust, one whom Bloch may believe to more rightly claim the mantle of prophet. Her revision is therefore a remarkable act of humility, and in modestly shifting the poem from the first person, she breaks the spell she has found herself under, while simultaneously honoring Celan. She also changes its name (in itself a biblical gesture) to "Covenant," a term much closer to normative Jewish religious belief. The covenant established between God and the Jewish people (as represented by a patriarch or prophet) promises that the people have been "chosen" by God, that they have been given the land of Israel, and perhaps most importantly in the context of Bloch's poem, that they will ultimately endure and prosper despite whatever hardships might be imposed upon them in the course of history. For Bloch, Celan is the Jewish poet-prophet who best represents a modern, post-Shoah understanding of the Covenant, a dark wisdom, especially given Celan's suicide in 1970.

As Pierre Joris, Celan's English translator, puts it, "Celan's life is insep- arable from the fate of the Jewish people in the twentieth century. The Shoah is thus core to the life and work, even if Celan did his best to make sure that neither would be overdetermined by or become reducible to those events. He is a survivor of *khurbn* (to use Jerome Rothenberg's 'ancient and dark word'), and his work is a constant bearing witness to those atrocities."[50] Bloch's "Covenant," therefore, is not merely an elegy for a great, tragic poet, but a reflection on the task of the poet when he or she writes out of and through the Shoah. This is why most, but not all, of the original prophetic imagery in "Spell" is transformed into "Covenant."

50. Pierre Joris, introduction to Paul Celan, *Breathturn into Timestead: The Collected Later Poetry*, trans. Pierre Joris (New York: Farrar, Straus, and Giroux, 2014), xxxi.

The latter poem, as we can see, is not only shifted into the third person, but is significantly stripped down. Extraneous phrases ("live / pain," "tongs of language") are eliminated. The revision is even more jagged, more enjambed – perhaps more like Celan's own verse. The explicit, perhaps somewhat sentimental reference to Elijah, "who rose in fire / in a cloud of words," is gone. In "Spell," Bloch leaves a place at the table for him, alluding to the Passover seder. In "Covenant," we are told instead that Celan "left a place at the table / for the silence / that pressed a burning coal / to his lips." If this is indeed a covenant, or a call to prophecy, then God has been replaced by "silence." To an even greater extent than Bloch's work, Celan's poems "are a miracle / of perversity," for they are prophetic expressions of radical negativity, expressions of an a-theology of the sort that he expresses so profoundly in his great poem, "Psalm":[51]

The "negative theology" of "Psalm" is succinctly present in the poem's first four lines:

> No one kneads us again out of earth and clay,
> no one incants our dust.
> No one.
>
> Blessèd art thou, No One.

To address a negated God – apophatically to engage absence – is to assert a continuing dialogue of the sort that is thought to be distinctive of Jewish devotion. Celan was aware that this active, intentional, encounter with absence has antecedents in both Jewish and Christian mysticism. However, Celan carries these tendencies toward negation and blasphemy even further than the traditional mystics; for him,

> A Nothing
> we were, are now, and ever
> shall be, blooming:
> the Nothing-, the
> No-One's-Rose.

51. Paul Celan, *Selected Poems and Prose of Paul Celan*, trans. John Felstiner (New York: Norton, 2001), 157

The result is a dialogue between the divine No One and the human Nothing, and the "no-One's-Rose" which represents this dialogue in the poem, this flower of language which blooms out of the silence separating divinity and humanity, is also simultaneously a presence and an absence, the most severe deconstruction of than sacred relationship or covenant.

"*Ganz und gar nicht hermetisch*" – absolutely not hermetic. This is the phrase that Celan famously inscribed in the copy of *Der Niemandrose* which he presented to Michael Hamburger.[52] Celan denied his hermeticism; despite the notorious difficulty of his poetry, he wanted it to be understood, and he wanted his readers to understand that it was comprehensible, despite its formidable syntax, pervasive neologisms, and innumerable allusions to history, religion, and his personal experience. Mystery on the surface, intelligibility in the depths. In this respect, we may think of a Jewish American poet such as Bloch as embracing an antithetical stance: clarity and intelligibility on the surface, mystery and complexity below. Like so many Jewish poets, Bloch understands the inescapability of this dialectic, not only in poetic language, but in the relationship of poetry to lived experience. As she writes in "Yom Asal, Yom Basal" (*One day honey, one day onion*, an Arabic saying), the first, wonderful lyric of *The Moon Is Almost Full*,

> In every maybe the fear of yes.
> In every promise a shattered glass.
>
> For every portion a cutting edge.
> For every rift a slippery bridge.
>
> In every hope some pickling salt.
> In every bungle a touch of guilt.
>
> Unto every plan God's ringing laughter.
> Unto every death a morning after.[53]

52. Hamburger, introduction to *Poems of Paul Celan*, 27.
53. *The Moon Is Almost Full*, 1.

SEVEN

"The darker wisdom of the Jews": Henry Weinfield's Dialectical Irony

HENRY WEINFIELD WAS BORN IN MONTREAL IN 1949. HIS PATERNAL grandfather, also named Henry, was born in Galicia, in the Austro-Hungarian Empire, in 1880, immigrated to Canada with his family in 1887, and became a distinguished jurist. His mother's family fled Nazi persecution in Germany and arrived in Canada in 1940. Weinfield moved to New York City with his mother and brother when he was fifteen; he received his B.A. from the City College of New York, his M.A. from the State University of New York at Binghamton, and his Ph.D. from the CUNY Graduate Center, where he studied with the great translator and poet Allen Mandelbaum (1926–2011), who had a profound influence on his work. I met Henry in 1973 in Binghamton; he was my first creative writing instructor, and he has been my friend and mentor for over forty years. This chapter is intended to be a critical study and not a memoir of our friendship, but I must make it clear that though our work is in some respects quite dissimilar, Weinfield has shaped my poetic sensibility and critical intelligence in more ways than I could possibly express. Although his work is not well known, I consider him one of our most important poets, as well as a critic and translator of great distinction. As I write in a review of his volume *The Sorrows of Eros* (1999), "Can poetry, 'Hallowed and hollowed out of emptiness' [the line comes from the title poem], still participate in the philosophical quest for a ground of being? The fact that Weinfield even poses such questions indicates how distinct his sensibility is from most poets today."[1] I hold to this opinion today, and would add, sixteen years later, that Weinfield's recent poetry, given its unequalled verbal clarity and formal power, makes him all the more significant.

There is little in Henry Weinfield's early poetry to indicate his Jewish heritage, or that Jewish matters will come to play an increasingly significant role over the course of his poetic career. "Adam and Eve," from Weinfield's second book, *In the Sweetness of the New Time* (1980), has a title that might promise some involvement with B'reishit, and as it turns out, it seriously engages the story of the Garden. But that engagement is strangely mediated. Here are the opening stanzas:

> Because it is perfect, it encompasses us. Then why
> do we think always of what lies beyond its boundaries?
> And having become conscious that what they evoke
> is ourselves, we begin to yearn for something
> which is always a dim intuition: its location
> unknown to us – far beyond the reaches of experience.
>
> Far beyond the reaches of experience, we imagine
> ourselves there, having invented the power to imagine.
> And with no other images, how should we imagine ourselves
> but as we are? We think of ourselves as being
> there, and it is perfect because it encompasses us.
>
> *The World was all before them, where to choose*
> *Their place of rest, and Providence their guide.*[2]

The italicized lines come from the end of *Paradise Lost*, which may be understood, if one adopts a rabbinic perspective, as Milton's sustained midrash on Genesis. But what to make of the strangely abstract, albeit beautifully crafted lines that lead up to the quote? Consciousness, boundaries, self-invention: this is Hegel, specifically Hegel's *Phenomenology of Spirit*, reborn as verse. Self-consciousness, in the Hegelian sense, suffuses

1. Norman Finkelstein, "Orphic Explanations," *Denver Quarterly* 35.2 (Summer 2000): 73–80.
2. Henry Weinfield, *Without Mythologies: New & Selected Poems & Translations* (Loveland, OH: Dos Madres Press, 2008), 67.

Weinfield's early poems, for they turn out to be nothing less than a brilliant synthesis of some of the most sophisticated concepts in the western philosophical tradition with the equally venerable tradition of English lyric poetry. From the beginning, Weinfield's breathtaking formal abilities are matched by his intellectual scope. A poet of the highest ambitions, in a postmodern age when such ambitions are regarded with skepticism (or simply ignored), Weinfield must employ his ironic self-consciousness, together with his mordant wit, to rescue the lyric from the debased cultural conditions into which he believes it has sunk. But at what cost? Here is section two of "The Unicorn Tapestries," which the poet describes as "a sort of Hegelian descant on the Unicorn Tapestries in the Cloisters Museum in New York City"[3]:

> Seeking itself through its activity
> To subsume nature into subjectivity,
> Freedom must itself endure captivity
>
> And dissolution through its sufferings.
> It must be torn asunder by the slings
> And arrows of outrageous priests and kings,
> Whose creed is *No idea but in things,*
>
> Because its truth is antithetical
> To nature. It must be deemed heretical
> And crowned with thorns, enclosed behind a wall
>
> Of terror, falsehood, and perversity.
> All this must freedom of necessity
> Endure, for thus it comes itself to be.[4]

There is something uncanny here about the way in which the density of allusion counterbalances the lightness and ease of the versification. An entire essay could be devoted to explaining how Weinfield deploys literary and philosophical references across his lines, sustaining and enhancing them through the rhyme scheme. For our purposes, I shall

3. Ibid., 175.
4. Ibid., 70.

only make a few observations. Freedom and necessity are fundamental terms in the Hegelian dialectic; later, Engels, in his *Anti-Dühring*, states that "freedom is the recognition of necessity."[5] The Marxist humanism of Weinfield's stance, as we shall see, remains a constant in his poetry through all its subsequent transformations. The Hegelian concept of negation as it manifests itself in the realms of both consciousness and history is materialized in the Marxian dialectic of the proletariat's struggle against the bourgeoisie. Consciousness makes itself in its struggle against the material necessity of nature; likewise the proletariat makes itself in its struggle against the bourgeoisie – but in both instances, it is negated "Because its truth is antithetical..." In Weinfield's poem, however, "freedom," the subject of these verses, is specifically negated, or "torn asunder by the slings / And arrows of outrageous priests and kings, / Whose creed is *No ideas but in things*." The reference to *Hamlet* ("Whether 'tis nobler in the mind to suffer / The slings and arrows of outrageous fortune / Or to take arms against a sea of troubles, / And by opposing end them") is especially ironic, since it is not indifferent "fortune" that would destroy freedom, but the oppressive human figures of "outrageous priests and kings."

But even more ironic is their creed, *"No ideas but in things,"* which readers of modern poetry will recognize as the Objectivist motto of William Carlos Williams. Williams, it is safe to say, is viewed by many poets and critics as a *hero* by the time Weinfield writes this poem: hardly an oppressor, he is a crucial member of the modernist avant-garde, a brilliant advocate of free verse and of a poetics of concrete sense perception that is intended to oppose sentimentality, abstraction, and vague poeticizing. But as Weinfield admits in his note to the poem, he has always regarded Williams' belief "as antithetical to my own perspective."[6] In the poem itself, by attributing Williams' "creed" to the priests and kings (and the word in this Marxist context implies an ideology or *false consciousness*), Weinfield sets himself in opposition to a century of poetic discourse. As he puts it in a related discussion of Williams, George

5. Frederick Engels, *Anti-Dühring*, trans. Emile Burns (Moscow: Progress Publishers, 1947), Marxist Internet Archive: https://www.marxists.org/archive/marx/works/1877/anti-duhring/ch09.htm.

6. *Without Mythologies*, 175.

Oppen, and the limits of the Objectivist perspective, the Objectivist creed as it is commonly understood stands for "a crude and narrow empiricism and ... a shop-worn group of ideas: that the world is *objectively* accessible to us, that the task of the poet is to derive 'clear pictures' of the world and communicate those pictures in clear language, and that this is what constitutes honesty and sincerity in poetry."[7]

Indeed, in "The Unicorn Tapestries," "freedom" is not simply in opposition to this hegemonic aesthetic of modernism, but "heretical / And crowned with thorns." This last allusion to Jesus indicates that "freedom" is bound to be *crucified*, must of necessity be sacrificed in its struggle to realize itself. The priests and kings of modernist poetry (however inadvertently) are, in effect, in league with ruling class ideology, and imprison poetic freedom "behind a wall // Of terror, falsehood, and perversity." It requires an act of revolutionary martyrdom, which is poetically equivalent to the self-subsuming formal turns in poems like "Adam and Eve" and "The Unicorn Tapestries" (and let us recall that in the medieval period, the unicorn was regarded as a type of Christ), in order to free the poetic consciousness from the prison of the here and now, the ideological status quo.

The Hegelian Marxism thematized in some of Weinfield's most challenging early poems is congruent with what we might term its dialectical formalism and lofty, abstract diction. Weinfield is a political and philosophical poet in the manner of, say, Dante or Shelley, and like these poets, his work becomes especially charged in that elevated space where politics and religion overlap. In the early poems, more often than not, that religion is Christianity, which periodically finds its way into his later work as well. Yet by the time Weinfield writes *Sonnets Elegiac and Satirical* (1980), this begins to change. His poems had always been strung dialectically between the poles of elegy and satire; as this becomes explicit ("the selfsame figure and the selfsame word / Can serve in satires or in elegies"),[8] the tone of the poems shift, and a different religious and cultural model comes to the fore:

---

7. Henry Weinfield, *The Music of Thought in the Poetry of George Oppen and William Bronk* (Iowa City: University of Iowa Press, 2009), 27.
8. *Without Mythologies*, 93.

An Irish boy was piping to a crowd,
As we were passing through a park arcade:
His face was so imperious and so proud,
As if he were the music that he played.
We had been talking of the Jews. You said
That those who were delivered to their doom
Restored the land for which their prophets prayed,
Where they were promised they would find a home.
I said that home is just a metaphor
For everything that we must leave behind:
There aren't any nations anymore
By which futurity can be defined.
Home is the hymn the angels play on high –
Upon the bagpipes of the Irish boy.⁹

"We had been talking of the Jews." A conversational middle register (I am reminded of Yeats in a poem like "Adam's Curse") mediates between the satirical and elegiac worldviews expressed here and throughout the sequence; and it is no accident that a Jewish note enters the political discourse at just this point. In this wonderful poem, Weinfield urbanely reintroduces himself as the secular Jew par excellence. The sonnet presents itself as a miniature dialogue (as other poems in the sequence indicate, probably a dialogue between the poet and his lover); for the poet, as opposed to his interlocutor, the conventional Zionist narrative of sacrifice and nationalist redemption does not cohere. Nationalist cultural identity may produce art, as in the case of the Irish boy's proud piping, but this is not the kind of art to which the poet aspires. Rather, in his case, Jewish experience is metonymic of modernity itself, an extended sequence of shocks from the formation of Enlightenment nation-states to the disaster of the Shoah. The Jews remain both homeless and most at home under modern conditions (which is why "home is just a metaphor / For everything that we must leave behind"); they are among the greatest contributors to and defenders of modernity, and its most hapless victims. Diasporism defines their thinking, their art, indeed, their very

9. Ibid., 96.

being. But diasporism extends, in this case, beyond the particular exile of the Jews to a universal exile, expressed as a transcendental yearning: "Home is the hymn the angels play on high – / Upon the bagpipes of the Irish boy." The hymn that the angels play can never be heard here on earth (or from a secular perspective, can never be heard at all); it can only make itself known through the music of the Irish boy's bagpipes. Then again, the sonnet itself, metaphysically speaking, offers us some sense of that transcendence. It is from these dialectical insights that Weinfield writes his Jewish poetry.

Thus, what Weinfield calls "the darker wisdom of the Jews," posed against the classical Greek "lamp that lit the Occident," produces yet another ironic hybridity, another dialectical balancing act between faith and skepticism:

> The early Christians were so confident
> That they could reconcile opposing views,
> They turned the lamp that lit the Occident
> Upon the darker wisdom of the Jews.
> Their concept was that God could interfuse
> The entire universe with His sole plan;
> Omniscient and omnipotent, could choose
> Miraculously to become a man.
> But men are murders, and all their art
> The skin-stretched lampshade of idolatry.
> – This bitter knowledge set the Jews apart
> Through all their wanderings through history:
> Their God was imageless; He had no name;
> And though they prayed to Him, he never came.[10]

Despite the political achievements of Zionism, the prophetic and messianic dimensions of Judaism are still predicated upon an infinite waiting game. The prophets may speak out against human injustice and suffer divine silence, but in the end they must acknowledge God's infinite distance, belief in which "set the Jews apart / Through all their wanderings through history." It is also a belief, of course, that always distinguishes

10.   Ibid., 95.

them from more "confident" Christians, whose God, given his divine plan, requires a kind of sacrificial violence that is ultimately related to Christian persecution of the Jews, and to the Nazis' "skin-stretched lamp-shade of idolatry." The Jews, on the other hand, have always understood that "men are murderers"; their faith, such as it is, is premised upon a divine horizon that is infinitely receding, upon a God who literally cannot be imagined or even named. Weinfield, obviously, fully identifies with this Jewish wisdom, and claims it for his own.

When God shows up in Weinfield's poems (and He does, with some frequency), He is so remote (or ineffectual) that He's not really there at all. Indeed, as Weinfield puts it in his discussion of George Oppen's great poem "Psalm," "Oppen's God has the decency not to exist," and the same could be said of Weinfield's. Weinfield calls Oppen's "Psalm" "a genuine poem of praise for our time," and as we shall see, much the same can be said of a number of Weinfield's recent works.[11] But as opposed to Oppen's poetry, where divinity is sometimes a palpable absence but is usually reduced to an unsettling experience of the "metaphysical," God as a rather hapless trope proves quite useful to Weinfield. When, for example, Weinfield takes on his otherwise beloved Dante in the poem "An Essay on Violence," God and the angelic hosts inevitably appear to assist him in making his point about human depravity:

> Whoever is the messenger of God
> Need not forbear to shed a little blood:
> The greater good requires violence.
>
> "The highest wisdom and the primal love,"
> Wrote Dante, are the attributes that drove
> Our Maker to make Hell's eternal violence.
>
> I beg to differ with the Florentine:
> Your violence is yours and mine is mine.
> It was not God conceived of violence.
>
> God, if He but existed, would be good!
> Would rid the world of evil, if He could,
> The imagination of its violence.

11. *The Music of Thought*, 190.

> He and His utmost seraphim on high
> Are utterly unable, though they try,
> To solve the antinomies of violence.[12]

The pathos of these lines is a matter of both tone and formal invention. Formally, the poem consists of twenty tercets rhymed a/a/x, with the third line always ending with the word "violence." As in the sonnet sequence (and thenceforth in so much of his poetry), Weinfield's tone is balanced between satire and elegy, between anger and loss. Dante, the greatest Christian poet, who justifies divine violence and God's creation of Hell, is answered by Weinfield's secular humanism, which has its origins in Jewish skepticism, that darker wisdom. Like the figure of God "and His utmost seraphim on high" in the poem, it cuts deeply but remains rueful in the face of the inescapable, endlessly repetitive, and entirely human "antinomies of violence." Hence the ending of the poem:

> We are the ones from whom that seed is sown
> And have to bear its burden on our own
> And all alone face up to violence.
>
> Read in these repetitions the lament
> Reverberating through past ages spent
> That we should do or suffer violence.[13]

Weinfield's humanism, however vexed, remains highly serviceable, even to the point of being placed at the service of a God who isn't there. "Men hate themselves and blame themselves on God," goes the refrain in "Fables from the Dark Ages," from which perspective the poet revises the stories of the Creation, of Prometheus, and of Job. Here is the first and shortest of the three fables, which takes the form of a sonnet:

> Out of the void, anterior to the world,
> There grew a Tree, whose tendrils were entwined
> Around the idea of love, whose branches curled
> Around the idea of uncreated mind.

12. *Without Mythologies*, 103–4.
13. Ibid., 104.

> The Tree of Life was blossoming with fruit,
> And God said *Eat thereof and be a god*;
> But Adam cut the Tree down to the root
> And trampled all that blossomed in the mud.
> At which God wept and all the Angels grieved
> To see their labor wantonly destroyed;
> But Adam was a serpent, so he weaved
> By devious turns his path back to the void.
> – Which even Milton never understood:
>   Men hate themselves and blame themselves on God.[14]

Normative Jewish and Christian accounts of the myth, including, at least to some extent, Milton's in *Paradise Lost*, blame the serpent for tempting Eve, who in turn seduces Adam into sin. Human weakness succumbs to satanic evil, and so we fall. The Gnostics reverse the equation: God (or the Demiurge) has trapped us in a fallen, created state, and it is the serpent, as a bringer of gnosis, who points the way toward spiritual truth. Weinfield is impatient with both accounts: for him, Adam *is* the serpent, and God and the Angels, rather than serving as stern agents of justice, are helpless in the face of human depravity. They cannot in any way save the beautiful Creation which they have brought forth through love and "uncreated mind," and their offer of godhood is utterly spurned by humanity, which destroys the Tree of Life, seeking the uncreated void. In short, the fable of the Garden and the Fall is just that, a fable, a fiction premised wholly on the ironically contradictory nature of the human soul, and the moral of the fable is to be read dialectically: it arises both to *explain* and to *explain away* (ideologically) human evil and self-hatred. Humanity has invented God and blames Him for all its faults, and being a fiction, there is nothing He can do about it. This is indeed a fable from the Dark Ages, for as in the epigraph to Weinfield's poem, which comes from William Bronk's "About Dynamism, Desire, and Various Fictions," "It is dark now as it always was." Again, in his note on the poem, the poet puts it best: "the 'dark ages' are the times in which the fables referred to in the poem were originally told, the times in which they were retold

14. Ibid., 117.

by the poets named in the poem [Milton, that is, in the section of the poem we are considering], and finally the present time."[15]

And yet, even though we may say, along with Weinfield and Bronk, that it is no more or less dark now than it has ever been, there is also a sense, as one continues reading in Weinfield, that the darkness is taking on a particularly insidious form, especially when it comes to contemporary Jewish culture and politics. The informing dialectic of satire and elegy, and what that implies not only for Weinfield's poetic sensibility overall, but also for his specifically Jewish vision, leads him to take remarkable risks – though these are not the sorts of risks that we ordinarily associate with contemporary poetry. As we have seen, Weinfield eschews free verse and any sort of avant-gardism, writing instead in traditional rhyme and meter. Just as importantly, he employs an unusually forthright but still highly nuanced discourse, a middle register that has a sophisticated conversational tone but still reaches toward the sublime. The overall clarity of Weinfield's discourse poses an unusual problem for the literary critic used to engaging "difficult" modernist and postmodernist poetry. Such poetry, with its strategic use of fragmented syntax, frequent code switching, recondite allusion, elaborate visual effects, and prevailing insistence on linguistic indeterminacy, usually demands the articulation of a theoretical framework and a sort of hermeneutic "translation" if the critic is to undertake an exploration of the poem's "meaning." In contrast, Weinfield's poetry, despite what I understand to be its pervasive irony, seems to express its meaning more directly. Poetic form in this case does not "defamiliarize" the production of meaning in the same way as poetry in the modernist tradition. Indeed, if defamiliarization occurs, at least for readers accustomed to modernist techniques, it is because such readers are not used to seeing "old-fashioned" rhyme and meter deployed with such straightforward expression, and with such apparent ease. Confronted with this radical alternative to what is usually taken to be "innovative" poetry, Weinfield's critic is not called upon to "translate," explain, or paraphrase his poems, rendering them into a comprehensible or accessible readerly discourse. Rather, the critic must move more directly to an engagement with the

15. Ibid., 178.

poet's ideas, and their often complex expression through the mediating forms of the verse. Depending upon the horizon of reader expectations, form can be every bit as defamiliarizing in Weinfield's poetry as in more obviously experimental modernist and postmodernist work.

Given the components of his mature style, Weinfield is able to speak out clearly, in a number of his most important poems, "without mythologies." This phrase, which serves as both the title of his volume of new and selected poems (2008) and as the title of one of a group of poems called, after Byron, *Hebrew Melodies*, is of crucial importance in understanding much of Weinfield's recent work. It is a phrase that takes in both the style and content of the poems, and in effect explains how the poet understands his task:

> Without mythologies the leaves are blown
> Hither and yon, seeds sown and flowers grown:
> They do it on their own without mythologies.
>
> Without mythologies they wax and wane,
> Neither complain nor hasten to explain,
> Since everything is plain without mythologies.
>
> Without mythologies when day is done
> Under the sun, songs sung and races run,
> A new one is begun without mythologies.[16]

What does it mean to perceive the world, to think about it, and above all, to write poetry "without mythologies"? Is it even possible to do so? According to Weinfield, there can be "songs sung" without mythologies, so given the anti-mythological thrust of the work, the term "mythology" needs to be unpacked. The earliest antecedent for the poem is the skepticism of Ecclesiastes: this is the source of the phrase "under the sun" (Ecclesiastes 1:9), as well as of the cyclical vision of natural and human life that serves as the philosophical foundation of the poem. For the Preacher of Ecclesiastes, "there is no new thing under sun"; what myths humanity invents are ultimately vain and self-serving, and we should seek continually to dispense with them. Then again, in

16. Ibid., 5.

the modernist tradition, one thinks of the significance of mythology to such figures as Yeats (an especially important influence on Weinfield's early poetry), Pound, and Eliot. Mythology serves to variously structure and give powerful thematic resonance to their poetry; Eliot, in his essay "*Ulysses*, Order, and Myth" (1923) goes so far as to argue that the "mythic method" developed by Yeats and employed to the fullest extent in Joyce's *Ulysses*, "is simply a way of controlling, of ordering, of giving a shape and a significance to the immense panorama of futility and anarchy which is contemporary history."[17] Weinfield would certainly take issue with Eliot's reactionary view of "contemporary history"; if "everything is plain without mythologies," then the adaptation of various myth systems by the modernists has the potential to obfuscate our understanding of history despite the great poetry that may result. The following poetic generation, including the (mainly Jewish) Objectivists such as Weinfield's friend and mentor George Oppen, turns away from that aspect of modernism: "*No Myths* might be the Objectivist motto," famously asserts Hugh Kenner.[18] Again, Weinfield would take issue with the nominalism and empiricism implied in Kenner's view of the Objectivists, but the point is that Weinfield's suspicion of mythology derives from a complicated set of issues that are central to the poetic tradition from which he in part emerges.

But there are other ways to understand "mythology" that are equally relevant. In the Preface to his classic work *Mythologies*, Roland Barthes notes how "the starting point of these reflections was usually a feeling of impatience at the sight of the 'naturalness' with which newspapers, art and common sense constantly dress up a reality which, even though it is the one we live in, is undoubtedly determined by history.... I wanted to track down, in the decorative display of *what-goes-without saying*, the ideological abuse which, in my view, is hidden there."[19] We have already

17. T.S. Eliot, "*Ulysses*, Order, and Myth" in *Selected Prose of T.S. Eliot*, ed. Frank Kermode (New York: Harcourt Brace Jovanovich / Farrar, Straus and Giroux, 1975), 177.

18. Hugh Kenner, *A Homemade World: The American Modernist Writers* (New York: Knopf, 1975), 187. For my discussion of these ideas in relation to the Objectivist poets and their Jewish identity, see *Not One of Them in Place*, 150.

19. Roland Barthes, *Mythologies*, trans. Annette Lavers (New York: Farrar, Straus and Giroux, 1972), 11.

seen that ideological critique plays an important part in Weinfield's poetry – and how could it not, given the kind of irony (or darker wisdom) toward which the work often tends? Barthes' analyses of modern mythologies are based on what he argues is the ideological confusion of nature and history. As Weinfield puts it, seeds are sown and flowers grow without mythologies. But is human culture ever created without mythologies? Weinfield ironically implies that this could be the case, but in his poem, the notion that there are "songs sung" without mythologies is itself mythological; nor, unfortunately, is "everything" ever truly "plain" – however we may wish it to be. In effect, we are now at a point in history where it is possible to dispense with mythologies, and yet we are unable to do so. Rather, we still find ourselves caught up in the mythologies of religion, of race, of nation, still caught in the situation so well described by Louis Althusser in his "Ideology and Ideological State Apparatuses": "It is indeed a peculiarity of ideology that it imposes (without appearing to do so, since these are 'obviousnesses') obviousnesses as obviousnesses, which we cannot *fail to recognize* and before which we have the inevitable and natural reaction of crying out (aloud or in the 'still, small voice of conscience'): 'That's obvious! That's right! That's true!'"[20]

But while the poet, like all of us, may not be able to completely disentangle himself from the mythological or ideological belief structures which magically transform history into nature and make historically derived social conditions into seemingly obvious, natural facts, there are some mythologies which he is fully capable of dismantling. In particular, these involve some of the most intransigent – and tragic – political problems facing the Jewish people in recent times, as the poem "The Crisis in the Middle East" makes abundantly clear.

The poem was written during the Second Palestinian Intifada, and has as its epigraph a quotation from an opinion piece by the Israeli novelist and peace activist Amos Oz, "Two Stubborn Men, and Many Dead,"

---

20. Louis Althusser, "Ideology and Ideological State Apparatuses," in *Lenin and Philosophy and Other Essays,* trans. Ben Brewster (New York: Monthly Review Press, 1971), Marxist Internet Archive: https://www.marxists.org/reference/archive/althusser/1970/ideology.htm.

which appeared in *The New York Times* on March 12, 2002. That month, known in Israel as "Black March," had the highest rate of Palestinian terrorist attacks on Israel: "In addition to numerous shooting and grenade attacks, that month saw 15 suicide bombings carried out in Israel, an average of one bombing every two days. The high rate of attacks caused widespread fear throughout Israel and serious disruption of daily life throughout the country."[21] In his editorial, Oz accuses Ariel Sharon and Yasser Arafat of denying and resisting what he believes to be the inevitable resolution of the conflict, two states living side by side in peace. For Oz, the two leaders are "each a prisoner of the other, each at the mercy of the other. Each ready to act every day exactly as the enemy foresees, to throw more fuel on the flames, to spill yet more blood."[22] Because of this, Oz, in the passage that Weinfield uses for his epigraph, calls them "Siamese twins" whom he then names "Sharafat," and observes that "fear and stagnation stifle them both."[23] Here is the poem in its entirety:

> I am the Chosen People, as you see.
> Nothing is yours and everything is mine.
> From Abraham I had this legacy.
> I tilled the land and it belongs to me,
> And I have pitched my tents in Palestine.
>
> I said to Pharaoh, "Let my people go!"
> He didn't listen, so I gave a sign
> And brought ten plagues upon him, as you know.
> As for your people, who cares what they do!
> And I have pitched my tents in Palestine.

21. *Wikipedia*, s.v. "Second Intifada," last modified June 3, 2016, https://en.wikipedia.org/w/index.php?title=Second_Intifada&oldid=723464082

22. Amos Oz, "Two Stubborn Men, and Many Dead," *The New York Times*, March 12, 2002. Oz continued to support a two-state solution, through all the vicissitudes of the last fifteen years. He defended Israel's actions in the Second Lebanon War (2006), and to a certain extent, Israel's actions in Gaza in 2014. See Amos Oz, "Hezbollah Attacks Unite Israelis," *Los Angeles Times*, July 19, 2006, and Philip Gourevitch, "An Honest Voice in Israel," *The New Yorker*, August 2, 2014, http://www.newyorker.com/news/news-desk/honest-voice-israel.

23. *Without Mythologies*, 22.

It's written in the Bible (or Koran)
That only those who worship the divine
As I do, go to heaven. Any man
Who doesn't, obviously never can,
And I have pitched my tents in Palestine.

Martyrs are called upon to sacrifice –
Suicide bombers (children will do fine).
Seventy-two virgins, each with coal-black eyes,
Will greet them as they enter paradise,
And I have pitched my tents in Palestine.

These people are all terrorists, I've found.
Don't even talk to them. Just hold the line.
I raze their parents' houses to the ground –
This policy has always proven sound,
And I have pitched my tents in Palestine.

Some call me Arafat and some Sharon,
And "Sharafat" is how these names combine.
Such are the seeds of hatred that I've sown,
No one will know the difference when I'm gone,
And I have pitched my tents in Palestine.[24]

As in the case of "An Essay on Violence," the use of a repeated rhyme and refrain is crucial to the mordant power of the verse. Here, the five-line stanza is rhymed a/b/a/a/b, with the first "b" line always rhyming with the refrain, "And I have pitched my tents in Palestine." The effect, again, is that of hopeless repetition of senseless violence, violence arising from an ancient religious and nationalist mythology that seems wholly incongruous with a modern, enlightened perspective, a perspective which can only be inferred from the text itself.[25] Rather, the voice of

24. *Without Mythologies*, 22–23.
25. Weinfield's understanding of violence, both in this poem and in "An Essay on Violence," is deeply influenced by the ideas of the literary theorist René Girard. For Girard, "sacrificial violence" is fundamental to the social order; as he postulates, "*Religion* in its broadest sense, then, must be another term for that obscurity that surrounds man's efforts to defend himself by curative or preventative means against his own violence.

the text is that of "Sharafat," and like conjoined or "Siamese" twins, this entity may seem to speak from two diametrically opposed political and religious perspectives, but it is ultimately one, conveying the same deluded notion. Extremist interpretations of both Jewish and Islamic scripture and belief result in an endless cycle of reciprocal violence, encouraged by narrow-minded and opportunistic leaders on both sides. "Such are the seeds of hatred that I've sown, / No one will know the difference when I'm gone": "Sharafat" is seen as a doomed, self-destructive monster. Like Yeats' "The Second Coming" and Shelley's "Ozymandias," which are also set in the desert and meditate upon the vanity of power, Weinfield's poem gradually moves toward the long historical vista, when the particulars of the conflict are erased and all that is left is ruin. The ideological claims of both Israelis and Palestinians are seen for what they are, lamentable delusions that cannot endure, despite the arguments of a "Chosen People."

This fundamental but highly ambiguous concept, so important to Jewish identity, is addressed even more directly in one of Weinfield's greatest poems, "Praise and Lamentation." At one hundred thirteen lines, mostly in heroic couplets, the poem is too long to quote in its entirety, so it is important to note that it unfolds almost like a persuasive and argumentative essay, with flashes of dark wit and irony. The tone and voice suggest an urbane but straightforward sensibility speaking in the conversational register that Weinfield has so beautifully refined in his mature work. Yet it is also touchingly sincere, and, in keeping with its simple title, lyrical in its expression of lamentation and praise.

It is that enigmatic quality that pervades the judicial system when the system replaces sacrifice. This obscurity coincides with the transcendental effectiveness of a violence that is holy, legal and legitimate successfully opposed to a violence that is unjust, illegal, and illegitimate." What all too often ensues, in any given society, is a "*sacrificial crisis*, that is, the disappearance of the sacrificial rites, [which] coincides with the disappearance of the difference between impure violence and purifying violence." See René Girard, *Violence and the Sacred*, trans. Patrick Gregory (Baltimore, MD: Johns Hopkins University Press, 1972), 23, 49. For Girard, one sure sign of the sacrificial crisis is the appearance in myth of *twins*, which comes to be seen as a "monstrous double." This surely speaks to the figure of Sharafat in Weinfield's poem. See Girard, 61–63, 164–66.

The praise, in this case, is for "an Israeli soldier named Nisan," whose situation is described in the opening stanza:

> I praise an Israeli soldier named Nisan:
> "They think that I'm a monster with a gun,
> Who prays each day, eats kosher, yes, and kills
> Arabs," he says. Sardonically, he smiles:
> "I never pray; I don't believe in it"
> (There's something oddly comforting in that);
> "I drink milk and eat cheese even with meat."
> He lives in a village bordering Lebanon,
> Which *Hezbollah* is always firing on;
> He's nineteen and he hasn't slept for days.
> Another reason to accord him praise
> Is that he hasn't any politics
> To speak of: all he wants is to go home!
> His people really are in quite a fix,
> So he's stuck standing guard in Bethlehem!
> These are my people, and I'm proud of them.[26]

The poet praises Nisan for his secularism – he doesn't pray, he doesn't keep kosher, and he is refreshingly apolitical, despite his sense of duty to his people. But he is not one of the "Chosen People," neither holding a special covenant with God, nor selected to suffer at the hands of others specifically because of that covenant. In other words, he is precisely the sort of Jew which the State of Israel came into being to produce – an ordinary person, at home in his country, his culture, and himself. It appears, though, that it is this very ordinariness that must be defended against enemies of the State, who would seek to destroy it and eradicate not only Nisan's lifestyle, but his very life.

But this, however, is only half the story. The poem proceeds as follows:

> These are my people and I'm proud of them,
> But now we too must learn to bear the shame

26. Ibid., 27.

> That other peoples, nations (*goyim*) do,
> For we are now among the nations too,
> And have ourselves begun to victimize
> Others (it's one of history's sadder ironies).
> Oh, it was easier in our own eyes,
> When violence was visited on us,
> To be a victim and be virtuous,
> But now it seems to end in violence;
> And though we say that it's in self-defense
> We know that it's a half-truth – hence a lie.[27]

Surrounded by enemies sworn to its destruction, Israel cannot truly offer its citizens a normal life – or rather, for Israelis, a normal life comes with a terrible political and psychological price, a fortress mentality and the need for a defensive posture that depends upon repressive military measures. Because they are no longer willing to be the world's victims, the Jews who returned to Palestine and their descendants must dispense with their previously cherished belief in their special virtues, based in the past, at least in part, on their victimhood. But they also refuse to admit that returning to the Land meant displacing the Arabs who were already living there. The ideology that thus develops would be no different from that of any embattled nation-state, except that this is the Jews of whom we speak – the Jews, whom the world acknowledges to have invented the notion of a fair, rigorous and systematic moral code (or to put it in Freudian terms, the superego) and a refined sense of justice which they were able to *teach* to all the nations, since the Chosen People are also the People of the Book:

> We who wrote Jonah and the Book of Ruth
> Had pity once on strangers, for in truth
> We had been strangers in an alien land.
> We who wrote Job, Ecclesiastes, and
> The Book of Samuel once understood
> That since we're really only flesh and blood,

27. Ibid.

> Apotheosis isn't in our line:
> We're human, all too human, not divine.[28]

Again we see "the darker wisdom of the Jews," a wisdom dependent upon the Jewish recognition of universal justice, fair treatment of the stranger, and above all, the shared humanity of all the nations, including the Jews themselves. Because this awareness is traditionally predicated upon the infinite distance between God and humanity, and because "Apotheosis isn't in our line," the contradiction of chosenness, the contradiction between universalism and particularism, becomes painfully acute, especially to the Jews themselves:

> The Chosen People are the ones who knew
> That no one's ever chosen; this being so,
> They learned to live within a paradox
> Inscribed in secret in their sacred books,
> Books that the centuries bequeathed to us.
> That's why their writings are anonymous,
> And why as wanderers without a home
> They learned to wait for what would never come.[29]

To be chosen, then, is to understand that "no one's ever chosen," the paradoxical point at which universalism and particularism are always held in tension, which Weinfield ironically presents as "[i]nscribed in secret" in the Jews' "sacred books." And at this climactic point in the poem, Weinfield turns his dialectical irony on himself, implicitly identifying himself with the anonymous writers of those books, and with the homeless generations of his wandering people:

> Easy to valorize, from where I stand,
> The People of the Book and not the Land,
> Here in the comfort of America,
> Not the worst corner of Diaspora,
> A promised land flowing with milk and honey –
> At least for those who have been blessed with money.

28. Ibid., 28.
29. Ibid., 28–29.

Easy to fail to recognize that these
Fanatic settlers are refugees
From Yemen, Egypt, Turkey, and the dark
Precincts of Williamsburg or Borough Park
(At any rate, from somewhere in New York),
Shaped, like the rest of us, by circumstance,
Contingency, exigency, or chance,
And, like the rest of us, committed to
A way of life, things that they think are so.
Their history is not your history;
And why should you imagine you are free
Of prejudice, much less that you were sent
To be a spokesman for enlightenment?
No one is chosen, as I said before
(It's very hard to hear this); what is more,
Nobody really chooses on his own.[30]

It should come as no surprise, given the way I have framed Weinfield's poetic, that I read these lines as some of the most penetrating, but also some of the most mordantly humorous that he has ever written. The assimilated, secular Jewish-American poet, securely ensconced in his relatively privileged corner of the diaspora (and note the devastating rhyme of "milk and honey," the biblical description of Zion, with "blessed with money"), has sufficient self-awareness to understand that the Jewish settlers are "[s]haped, like the rest of us, by circumstance." And though he cannot resist taking a jab at American Jews, mostly Orthodox, from "the dark / Precincts of Williamsburg or Borough Park" who make *aliyah* and end up as fanatic settlers in the West Bank, he also recognizes that he cannot be a self-appointed "spokesman for enlightenment" – whereupon he reiterates that "[n]o one is chosen" but adds, dialectically, that "[n]obody really chooses on his own."

Thus, what Weinfield identifies as "[c]ontingency, exigency, or chance," as opposed to a divinely appointed destiny, is ultimately seen as that which shapes our ends. As he brings his poem to an end, he

---

30. Ibid., 29.

makes the further distinction that whereas choice may operate in one area of human life – that of art – it operates far less in most others:

> To be, essentially, is to be thrown
> Into a world of possibilities
> Impossible to grasp, do what you please:
> A partial world in which we play a part,
> Not one that we have made as one makes art –
> And we are part and partial, never whole.[31]

The play on "part" and "partial" leads the poet, in his last lines, back to the figure of Nisan, who, like all of us, is called upon to play his part in a partial or perpetually incomplete and unfulfilled existence, thus confronting his fate as a "partisan":

> So here we are, and likely to remain,
> In the proverbial *condition humaine*,
> Arab and Jew, you, me, and everyone,
> A nineteen-year old soldier named Nisan,
> Stuck in the past, in bondage, partisan.[32]

The penultimate word of the poem, "bondage," is likewise fraught. It is as if the Jews had never left Egypt: they may think themselves free, and fight fiercely to retain their freedom, but like everyone, they are "[s]tuck in the past." Such is "the proverbial *condition humaine*."

Although Weinfield's understanding of the human condition – partial, imperfect, and above all, contradictory – frequently leads to a skeptical, if not sadly pessimistic and lamentable perspective, he still offers us moments of respite. These moments, tinged with melancholy, are often related to matters of faith. One such moment, still fraught with contradiction yet also charged with a feeling of lyrical repose, is articulated in "August: The Lake at Notre Dame":

> Mid-to-late summer on a sunny day:
> The air is clear; there's no humidity.

31. Ibid.
32. Ibid., 30.

A bright-blue sky, expansive and serene,
Bends over tree-tops, blending with their green.

Swans with their cygnets, soon to be full grown
And, in their turn, rear cygnets of their own,
Circle the surface, mirrored in the wake
Of sunlight glimmering on the glassy lake.

Who could be sullen in the afternoon
– In the sweet air that's gladdened by the sun,
Or fail in gratitude when song-birds sing,
A Great Blue Heron suddenly takes wing?

Our lady stands upon her golden dome
– In this place, which in some sense is our home,
With outstretched arm and blessings to confer
Even on those who don't believe in her;

And from the depths of her untroubled eye
Her gaze goes out into the bright-blue sky,
Where in the distance wisps of cloud are swirled –
As if there were no troubles in the world.[33]

There is much to be said about this seemingly simple lyric. On the biographical level, we need to recall that Weinfield, a secular Jew, has spent most of his academic career at the University of Notre Dame, teaching in the Program of Liberal Studies, which is based on a Great Books curriculum from a Catholic perspective. Issues of faith and doubt are regularly raised in the courses he teaches, as articulated not only in literature, but in works of philosophy and theology as well. We have observed that in his early poems (written prior to his move to Notre Dame), Christianity and Christian imagery are important references, whereas his "turn" to Jewish themes intensifies as he finds himself in a predominantly Catholic intellectual environment. To be sure then, the figure of "Our lady" – that is, the statue of Mary on top of the landmark

33. Ibid., 31.

golden dome of the University's Main Building – needs to be carefully examined. But a number of other allusions are equally important.

The poem's epigraph is from Dante, *Inferno* 7.122: "ne l'aere dolce che dal sol s'allegra." Weinfield also gives us the translation, "in the sweet air that's gladdened by the sun," as rendered by his mentor, the poet and translator Allen Mandelbaum, under whom Weinfield wrote his dissertation on Thomas Gray at the CUNY Graduate Center.[34] The line from Dante is reiterated in the poem itself, and Weinfield's use of the Mandelbaum translation is of particular significance. As a distinguished translator of Dante, as well as Homer, Virgil, and Ovid, Mandelbaum represents the height of the classical tradition in the Christian West. Mandelbaum was raised as an Orthodox Jew (both his father and grand-father were rabbis) and attended Yeshiva University for his B.A and M.A.; he also taught there after receiving his Ph.D. from Columbia. Trained in traditional Jewish scholarship, he is the author of *Chelmaxioms*, one of the most important (though sadly neglected) works of Jewish-American poetry.[35] *Chelmaxioms* shares with Weinfield's poetry a profoundly diasporic sensibility, and I would argue that Mandelbaum, through that single line of Dante, hovers over the poem, signifying that for Weinfield and other secular Jews, the classical and Christian literary tradition "in some sense is our home," even as Notre Dame in some sense is home for the poet.

The line which Weinfield quotes from Canto 7 of the *Inferno* refers to the sullen, who are eternally punished by being submerged in the Styx, depicted as a swamp of slimy water. As Virgil tells Dante,

> "...know for certain
>   that underneath the water there are souls
>   who sigh and make this plain of water bubble,
>   as your eye, looking anywhere, can tell.
>   Wedged in the slime, they say: 'We had been sullen

---

34. A revised version of this dissertation became Weinfield's first critical book, *The Poet Without a Name: Gray's Elegy and the Problem of History* (Carbondale: Southern Illinois University Press, 1991).

35. Allen Mandelbaum, *Chelmaxioms* (Boston, MA: David R. Godine, 1977). My reading of the poem appears in *The Ritual of New Creation*, 81–90.

in the sweet air that's gladdened by the sun;
we bore the mist of sluggishness in us;
    now we are bitter in the blackened mud.'
This hymn they have to gurgle in their gullets,
because they cannot speak it in full words."[36]

The swamp in which the sullen are immersed is in contrast with the beautiful lake at Notre Dame, around which the poet walks, exclaiming, "Who can be sullen in the afternoon / – In the sweet air that's gladdened by the sun." The idyllic scene with its clear air, low humidity (a blessing in August in the Midwest) and "bright-blue sky, expansive and serene," captures the perfection of the season and the deep sense of gratification it has to offer, a sense of gratification made all the more poignant by the presence of the swans "with their cygnets, soon to be full grown."

The graceful swans and their young, envisioned at the height of the summer season, symbolize the reproductive cycle of nature and the harmonious beauty of the natural world. These swans have appeared before in Weinfield's poetry: in part v of his sequence "The Sorrows of Eros," he describes the various birds he would see in "his perambulations round the lake" in allegorical terms, noting that "Swans in their silence, simple and complex, / Beauty's enigma curled on slender necks, / Circled the surface, mirrored in the deep."[37] Weinfield's swans in both of his poems also allude to swans in poems by two crucial Symbolist precursors: Yeats, in "The Wild Swans at Coole," and Mallarmé, in his untitled sonnet which begins (in Weinfield's translation), "The virginal, vibrant, and beautiful dawn." Weinfield's poem takes place in summer, Yeats' poem in autumn, and Mallarmé's in winter; the season in each case intensifies the poem's complex meaning, revealing in turn the particular thematic space that Weinfield's poem occupies within this ongoing tradition.

Thus, in "The Wild Swans at Coole," the autumnal beauty of Coole Park (the estate of Yeats' friend, colleague, and patron, Lady Augusta Gregory) signifies a profound sense of loss. The year is drawing to a close, and the aristocratic culture, with its orderly rituals and rooted

36. Dante Aligheri, *The Divine Comedy of Dante Aligheri: Inferno*, trans. Allen Mandelbaum (New York: Bantam Books, 1982), 109.
37. *Without Mythologies*, 133.

social hierarchy, is likewise passing away. Of the original thirty pairs of birds, one is missing a mate (swans mate for life), and there will be fewer cygnets; furthermore, the poet, who identifies himself and the traditional sociopolitical order with the swans, imagines them departing from Coole forever:

> I have looked upon those brilliant creatures,
> And now my heart is sore.
> All's changed since I, hearing at twilight,
> The first time on this shore,
> The bell-beat of their wings above my head,
> Trod with a lighter tread.
>
> Unwearied still, lover by lover,
> They paddle in the cold
> Companionable streams or climb the air;
> Their hearts have not grown old;
> Passion or conquest, wander where they will,
> Attend upon them still.
>
> But now they drift on the still water,
> Mysterious, beautiful;
> Among what rushes will they build,
> By what lake's edge or pool
> Delight men's eyes when I awake some day
> To find they have flown away?[38]

The stately cadences of the verse *contain* (that is to say, hold in place) an unsettling contradiction that the poet cannot fully articulate. On one level, the cycle of nature is eternal; the swans' passion, mystery, and beauty will always be there, and the poem implies that it is the hope of the poet that the poem will enter into and share that condition.[39] This is a hope not only of Yeats, but of Weinfield in his poem as well. But

---

38. Yeats, 131–32.
39. This hope becomes explicit in later poems such as "Sailing to Byzantium," when he implores the "sages standing in God's holy fire" to "gather me / Into the artifice of eternity." Yeats, 193.

Yeats is also intensely conscious that he is aging, that the aristocratic order he so loves is passing, and that natural loss comes to the swans too, however they may symbolize an eternal cycle. The poem ends with a question: will beauty remain when the swans depart? Can one maintain faith in the eternal virtues we believe to be represented in nature, and in the supernatural order which nature mirrors? Can art – can poetry – preserve that faith?

These sorts of questions are posed with even greater intensity by Mallarmé's sonnet (which actually predates Yeats' poem). In Weinfield's translation, it reads as follows:

> The virginal, vibrant, and beautiful dawn,
> Will a beat of its drunken wing not suffice
> To rend this hard lake haunted beneath the ice
> By the transparent glacier of flights never flown?
>
> A swan of former times remembers it's the one
> Magnificent but hopelessly struggling to resist
> For never having sung of a land in which to exist
> When the boredom of the sterile winter has shone.
>
> Though its quivering neck will shake free of the agonies
> Inflicted on the bird by the space it denies,
> The horror of the earth will remain where it lies.
>
> Phantom whose pure brightness assigns it this domain,
> It stiffens in the cold dream of disdain
> That clothes the useless exile of the Swan.[40]

Epitomizing his Symbolist technique, the sonnet is one of Mallarmé's most famous poems, and one of his most difficult, syntactically, to unpack. This linguistic complexity is in itself an important difference from the clarity and directness of Weinfield's poem. My sense is that while Mallarmé's poem is suffused with tension derived from immense metaphysical and psychic struggle, Weinfield's poem offers a feeling of

---

40. Stéphane Mallarmé, *Collected Poems*, trans. Henry Weinfield (Berkeley: University of California Press, 1994), 67.

calm, acceptance, and perhaps even resolution after such struggle has passed. ("The Wild Swans at Coole" would fall somewhere in between on this scale.) Weinfield offers an extensive commentary on the sonnet, much of which has great bearing on his own attitude toward nature, belief, transcendence and art as expressed in "August: The Lake at Notre Dame." There are actually two swans in the sonnet: the mortal creature frozen in the glacial lake, suffering "the boredom of the sterile winter," and the Swan, the constellation, which is on one level a transcendental projection or ideal of the earthly swan's beauty. "Can the privileged moment of inspiration triumph over the vast expanse of undifferentiated time into which it must ultimately be swallowed up and reabsorbed?" – for Weinfield, this is the question that Mallarmé poses in his poem.[41] That privileged moment is represented by the swan caught in the ice, which according to Weinfield "yearns for an absolute realm" which the "horror of the earth" denies.[42] In Weinfield's reading, "even insofar as the swan, the moment of inspiration, can be constellated as pure form, as the uppercase Swan, it can only assume what is essentially a new exile... The Swan is trapped in the stars in the same way the swan is trapped in the ice; what is congealed in the achieved form of the poem is the same desire for transcendence – that is, for life – that led to the poem in the first place."[43]

Given the eternal – and eternally thwarted – yearning for transcendence, as variously symbolized by the swans that we have seen in two precursor poems, how are we to understand the concept in "August: The Lake at Notre Dame"? In one respect, the answer is simple, and again reflects Weinfield's "dark wisdom": do not actively seek for transcendence at all; rest content in the here-and-now. Then again, this is impossible, as Weinfield well knows – this poem, like nearly all his poems, is suffused with transcendental desire. Still, as opposed to "the boredom of the sterile winter" and the swan-poet struggling to achieve the ideal, we have the human poet in summer, observing the contented lot of the natural swans and their cygnets. The poet, who refuses, as we previously observed, to succumb to sullenness, also seems relatively free of the discontent that comes from transcendental desire, and the lyric

41. Weinfield, in Mallarmé, 214.
42. Ibid.
43. Ibid., 215.

impulse to which he gives expression has little of Mallarmé's wintery struggle or Yeats' autumnal regret. But though there is a greater sense of acceptance in Weinfield's poem, we must also recall that his swans "Circle the surface, mirrored in the wake / Of sunlight glimmering on the glassy lake." If we are content, it is because we, like the swans, choose to remain on the surface of things, without plumbing the depths.

Furthermore, transcendental yearning, which poignantly arises in the midst of transitory natural beauty, still imposes itself, however gently, upon the poet in the figure of Mary "upon her golden dome." Mary stands "with outstretched arm and blessings to confer / Even on those who don't believe in her": that presumably includes the poet, who nevertheless treats her with great respect, and only the lightest touch of irony. The Christian worldview that she signifies extends the natural harmony of the scene at the lake to a metaphysical order that secular non-believers, at least for a moment in the poem, almost wish they could accept. In the last stanza, we are told that "from the depths of her untroubled eye / Her gaze goes out into the bright-blue sky": it looks toward a transcendental horizon, much as in the poems by Mallarmé and Yeats. Yet it is a scene of greater acceptance, a scene that posits calm, peace, and the magical possibility of transcendence, "As if there were no troubles in the world." *As if*: the scene at the lake, with Mary presiding, is posed in the last line of the poem in the conditional; it is, in effect, a beautiful fiction, like certain aspects of Christianity itself – or so, I would venture to guess, Weinfield implies, with a decidedly Jewish expression of doubt. We long for transcendence, and can never fully convince ourselves not to seek for it. Yet against the certain knowledge that the world is full of trouble, the beautiful summer moment is *heavenly*: the poem opens a space in which we may imagine paradise, and in its momentary being, it "in some sense is our home."[44]

44. Compounding the irony is the fact that the line itself, "In this place, which in some sense is our home," also echoes section 24 of *Of Being Numerous*, the magisterial political meditation of another of Weinfield's mentors, George Oppen:

> In this nation
> Which is in some sense
> Our home. Covenant!
> The covenant is

But only "in some sense" – for as we have seen, the predominant vision in Weinfield's work is one of existential homelessness, which is not a Christian perspective at all. I want to close this chapter with a consideration of a poem that brings homelessness, specifically Jewish homelessness, to a level of unmatched lyric intensity, another of Weinfield's "Hebrew Melodies," "My Father Was a Wandering Aramaean":

> "...you shall make this response before the Lord your God: 'A wandering Aramaean was my father; he went down into Egypt and lived there as an alien, few in number, and there he became a great nation, mighty and populous.'" (Deuteronomy 26: 5)

My father was a wandering Aramaean,
Bordering upon the Gentile and the Jew.
The promised land was never his to stay in,
He had no church or synagogue to pray in –
Music was the religion that he knew.

My father was a wandering Aramaean,
Enlightened by the darkness that he found.
He never lifted a triumphal paean:
No one is chosen – Hebrew, Greek, or pagan –
The self-same cloud encompasses us round.

My father was a wandering Aramaean,
Not reconciled or reconcilable.
Whether in Egypt or the deep Judaean
Plain, or Sheol where the shades complain,
The rigor of his refusals rings out still.[45]

There shall be peoples.

See Oppen, 176. Oppen's populism (as he called it) is tempered by a skepticism born of years of left-wing political experience, and his hopefulness, his doubt, and his transcendental yearning are all passed on to Weinfield in that one qualifying phrase, "in some sense." Oppen, raised in a wealthy, entirely assimilated home, struggled in his later years to understand his Jewish identity (see, for instance, his poems "Exodus" and "Semite). His "covenant" is in some respects a secular, universalist revision of the biblical covenant that God establishes with the Chosen People.

45. *Without Mythologies*, 4.

As in a number of Weinfield's other important lyrics, a single rhyme sound (in this case, the feminine rhyme on "Aramaean") controls the sonic structure of the poem: each of the three five-line stanzas has the same first line and is rhymed x/a/x/x/a. The rhymes on "Aramaean" resonate with a bittersweet melancholy. Resigned and mournful, the music of the poem, with its long vowel sounds and slow, measured cadence, subtly imbues us with an understanding of the historical vicissitudes that have shaped Jewish life for thousands of years, but which also make this, paradoxically, an intensely personal poem.

In the Foreward to *A Wandering Aramaean*, his book of Passover poems and translations in which the poem is reprinted, Weinfield notes that "My Father Was a Wandering Aramaean" "came directly from the verse in Deuteronomy that forms the poem's epigraph," though it only dawned upon him as a poem that had to be written when he was at a friend's Passover seder. He continues:

> The line, "My father was a wandering Aramaean," has a double meaning in the poem, and it was probably this that was initially so compelling. If "father" is a metaphor (as it is in the biblical text), then "Aramaean" has a literal meaning; if "father" is taken literally, however, then "Aramaean" becomes a metaphor. The poem is, among other things, an elegy for my own father. Part of the joy of writing it came from the problem of finding rhymes for "Aramaean" – not easy, because of the word's "feminine" ending (i.e., the fact that the accent falls on the penultimate syllable).[46]

Arguably, much of the Passover celebration and seder ritual are contingent on one fundamental biblical commandment: Remember. Jews are commanded to remember how the Lord freed them from bondage; they remember the Exodus; and they remember all that God did for them in bringing them to the Promised Land. The appearance of the verse from Deuteronomy in the Passover Haggadah begins an interpretive recitation of the Hebrews' experience in Egypt, including their enslavement and subsequent liberation. The Jews of the Bible are

46. Henry Weinfield, *A Wandering Aramaean: Passover Poems and Translations* (Loveland, OH: Dos Madres Press, 2012), xiii.

not usually referred to as "Aramaeans," who may indeed, as Weinfield would have it, be understood as "[b]ordering between the Gentile and the Jew." Weinfield's own father, Mortimer Weinfield (1912–1987) was an assimilated, highly cultured, music-loving Montreal attorney, and thus, from a traditional Jewish standpoint, bordering somewhat differently between gentile and Jew. We are dealing here, then, with the modern question of Jewish Enlightenment, which entails a loss of religious faith and observance and its replacement (or at least, displacement) by Western culture. This secularization and aesthetization of faith accounts for Weinfield's declaring that his father "had no church or synagogue to pray in – / Music was the religion that he knew." His father, in short, was a modern secular Jew.

But the dialectic of Enlightenment (to borrow the phrase of Adorno and Horkheimer) inevitably leads to an understanding of darkness – the darkness of modern Jewish history. This darkness is inextricably entwined with the post-Enlightenment bourgeois Jewish love of Western culture, however much antisemites, claiming to the true representatives of Western culture, expressed (and still express) disdain for intellectual, art-loving, assimilated Jews. The knowledge of the modern "Aramaean," therefore, is precisely what Weinfield has repeatedly insisted upon: "*No one is chosen* – Hebrew, Greek, or pagan – / The self-same cloud encompasses us round."

And so we return once more to the darker wisdom of the Jews in its modern, secular articulation. What makes secular Jews like Weinfield and the father he mourns "chosen" is the knowledge that chosenness is a myth, making them "[n]ot reconciled or reconcilable." Wandering will never cease, and we must find rest only in that restlessness. The poem's magnificent ending has a defiant negativity, but its alliterative last line – "The rigor of his refusals rings out still" – dialectically transforms itself into an altogether positive quality. It is a kind of virtue that can be given voice only when intelligence and passion are joined in equal measure, as they always are in Henry Weinfield's poems.

EIGHT

Rachel Tzvia Back:
Between Israel and the Diaspora

IN A RECENT STATEMENT FOR AN ANTHOLOGY OF WOMEN'S POETRY about migration and diaspora, Rachel Tzvia Back presents herself and her work in these terms:

> In an early and essential interview, American poet Susan Howe articulated a poetics of location thus: "Trust the place to form the voice"; so it is, so I have. Though I was born and raised in upstate NY, the place that forms my voice are the hills and history, the stones and spirits, the personal and the political of Israel.
>
> I have lived in Israel all my adult life and some of my childhood years, and the ancient rhythms of Hebrew are the rhythms of my life. And still, my language of poetic composition has always been, and will always be, English. Thus, in the Galilean hills that are my home, where Hebrew and Arabic are the spoken languages, my English language poetry wanders ever as an outsider. In significant ways, and certainly in connection to my poetry, I reside fully in the paradox of being ever a foreigner at home.[1]

Here, the poet frames for us what will be, in essence, the theme of this chapter. Back is a crucial figure for contemporary Jewish poetry in

---

1. Rachel Tzvia Back, "Trusting the Place," in *Women: Poetry: Migration*, ed. Jane Joritz-Nakagawa (Palmyra, NY: Theenk Books, 2017).

English, and this is especially the case given the linguistic vicissitudes of the poetry we have considered so far in this book. What are the implications of "the paradox of being ever a foreigner at home," when "foreigner" means a writer of American English, and "home" means Israel, the place to which modern Jewry turns and returns – or chooses not to? What we will consider, then, is a poet with a diasporic sensibility, writing in a major language of the diaspora, while choosing to live in the Jewish homeland.[2]

Coming from a family with deep roots in Galilee (she can trace her ancestry there back six generations), yet born and raised in Buffalo, New York, Back decided to move permanently to Israel in 1981, when she was twenty-one years old. She married and had three children. For many years, she has lived in a village in Galilee and has taught at Oranim Academic College, offering courses in American literature in English to Jewish, Muslim, and Christian students.[3] Back is a translator and critic as well as a poet, and nearly all her work has a significant political dimension. She edited the English edition of *With an Iron Pen: Twenty Years of Hebrew Protest Poetry*.[4] She has also published the first major collection in English of the Israeli poet Tuvia Ruebner, as well as two volumes of translations of Lea Goldberg.[5] Bringing less-known Israeli writers to English readers, therefore, is one important aspect of her overall literary agenda. Just as revealing, she has written one of the best studies of

2. But not actually writing poetry there: Back tells me that she almost never writes poetry while in Israel; she generally goes to writer's retreats elsewhere to work.

3. For Back's deeply moving and thoughtful meditation on her teaching, see Rachel Tzvia Back, *"This Bequest of Wings": On Teaching Poetry in a Region of Conflict*, The Judith Lee Stronach Memorial Lectures on the Teaching of Poetry (Berkeley: Bancroft Library, University of California, 2016).

4. *With an Iron Pen: Twenty Years of Hebrew Protest Poetry*, ed. Rachel Tzvia Back (Albany: State University of New York Press, 2009).

5. Tuvia Ruebner, *In the Illuminated Dark: Selected Poems of Tuvia Ruebner*, trans. Rachel Tzvia Back (Cincinnati, OH: Hebrew Union College Press / University of Pittsburgh Press, 2014); Lea Goldberg, *Selected Poetry and Drama*, trans. Rachel Tzvia Back (poetry) and T. Carmi (drama) (New Milford, CT: The Toby Press, 2005); Lea Goldberg, *On the Surface of Silence: The Last Poems of Lea Goldberg*, trans. Rachel Tzvia Back (Cincinnati, OH; Pittsburgh: Hebrew Union College Press / University of Pittsburgh Press, 2017).

Susan Howe, the Bollingen Prize-winning experimental poet who epito-
mizes contemporary American poetry's links to the nineteenth-century
transcendentalist tradition, especially Emily Dickinson, an important
influence on Back's poetry as well.[6] In short, the paradox of her "English
language poetry [that] wanders ever as an outsider" continues to com-
plicate itself the further we delve into Back's oeuvre.

When language – when poetry – conceives of itself as a perpetual
outsider, as perpetually wandering, we find ourselves once again in
that place which is not a place of diaspora. We have already seen how
outsider writing and the concept of "wandering meaning" applies to res-
olutely, self-consciously diasporic American poets like Charles Reznikoff,
Michael Heller, and Henry Weinfield. As an Israeli, Back obviously is a
different case. Nevertheless, it now appears that diasporic writing is, to an
even greater extent than we originally thought, an *existential* condition, as
much as it may be a psychological, sociological, linguistic, or geopolitical
one. In his essay "Remains of the Diaspora," to which we have referred a
number of times, Heller writes "If the diaspora is geographic and physical,
it is also psychic and emotional, rife with constantly agitated language
and even more agitated silence.... Texts and textuality, allegiances and
disavowals. Pressures. Every thought, every word should be useful, ripe
with both fullness and negations... The ground of the diaspora that is not
a diaspora is the place where this happens to words, where the pressure
on language is at its utmost."[7] Heller's antitheses, his "allegiances and
disavowals," his "fullness and negations," especially insofar as he relates
them to the "place" of language, strikes me as richly suggestive of Back's
situation. It is most obvious in her political poetry, where a marginal,
outsider discourse, a discourse fully open to the Other, opposes and
disavows the official discourse of the State, and of a militant, nationalist
ideology. But even when her poems turn to more personal, intimate
concerns, there is a pervasive sense, conveyed at least as much by form as
by overt content, that the utterance is standing apart from itself, and that
its very intimacy is predicated upon a fundamental psychic elusiveness

6. Rachel Tzvia Back, *Led by Language: The Poetry and Poetics of Susan Howe* (Tuscaloosa:
University of Alabama Press, 2002).
7. "Remains of the Diaspora," 170.

bordering upon refusal. Meaning, even as it suggests its presence, is always *elsewhere*: as Dickinson would put it, "Tell all the truth but tell it slant – / Success in Circuit lies." Back's poetry is constantly moving in "Circuit." Or as Back herself insists, there is "that *something* in a poetic text which may elude intellectual understanding even as it impacts directly and compellingly on the reader's heart and spirit."[8] The way the poem eludes explicit meaning, wanders away from itself, defines its nomadic being, its homelessness.

We see this already in Back's first book, *Azimuth* (2001), which is in some respects her most elusive. Personal references, family narratives, and allusions to the Israeli-Palestinian conflict in the last decades of the twentieth century are woven through the book, which consists largely of openwork serial poems continually making and unmaking themselves. Back often depends on verbal slippage, ellipsis, fragmentation, and indeterminate or only partially identified figures and events, procedures which she will continue to use and refine in her later volumes. The epigraph of *Azimuth*, which gives the etymology of the word, notes that it comes "from Arabic *as-sumut* the azimuth, plural of *as-samt*, the way – commonly relating to the course one pursues in journeying. An Arab of the desert, of the tribe of Keys says: *Thou shalt traverse (addressing a woman) a land without a description, journey without a sign of the way and without any track, such being the meaning of as-samt*."[9] The epigraph goes on to note the actual definition of the word ("a point of the compass as measured clockwise from the north point 0° through 360°"), and the irony of reading a compass and plotting the way, as opposed to wandering *"without a sign of the way,"* permeates the book. That the idea of journeying without any sense of direction arises in *"addressing a woman"* is also significant, since Back's understanding of open form and wandering meaning, while not exclusively related to gender, has a distinctly feminine cast. In this respect, she is part of an experimental

8. Rachel Tzvia Back, "'A Species of Magic': The Role of Poetry in Protest and Truth-telling (An Israeli Poet's Perspective)," *World Literature Today* (May–August 2014), https://www.worldliteraturetoday.org/2014/may/species-magic-role-poetry-protest-and-truth-telling-israeli-poets-perspective.

9. Rachel Tzvia Back, *Azimuth* (Riverdale-On-Hudson, NY: Sheep Meadow Press, 2001), n.p.

feminist tradition that extends at least as far back as Dickinson (surely a poet who felt herself to be in exile in her very home), and includes Susan Howe as one of its most important recent practitioners. In her discussion of the "difficulty" of Howe's poetry, Back tells us that "It is crucial to stress that Howe's rejection of authoritative reading is a rejection also of an authoritative patriarchy, and Howe's radical language experiments constitute a feminist commitment to dismantling 'the grammar of control and the syntax of command.'"[10] The same is true, I would argue, for the formal procedures in Back's own poetry.

The title sequence of *Azimuth*, which uses the points of the compass as a structuring device, and is based partly upon Back's military experience, is a clear instance of her feminist commitment to experimental form. An unidentified "he" "faced east / bowed five times, / fingered the beads / and flew." An unidentified "she" is depicted *"Barefoot / on brown weeds //* and hung the white / wings on the line // to sway."[11] Yet almost immediately after, we are told "He never flew. // She was not barefoot. // Believe none of it." And from there,

> The maps, folded and refolded,
> frayed, entire ranges lost
> at the creases.
> The compass needle
> in its own green light
> pulled toward passing metals:
> trains, tanks, satellites.[12]

We find ourselves in the midst of desert warfare; violence, loss, doubt, and misdirection are depicted through fragmentary images and oblique narrative references. Maps and compasses prove futile and testimony is cast in doubt, as Back plays bitterly with the wording of Maimonides' Thirteen Principles of the Jewish faith: "I believe with perfect faith / that

10. *Led by Language*, 5. The phrase "the grammar of control and the syntax of command" is quoted from Charles Bernstein, *A Poetics* (Cambridge, MA: Harvard University Press, 1992), 202.
11. *Azimuth*, 61, 63.
12. Ibid., 64.

I will find the strength to believe / that what happened really happened."[13] Again the poem turns back on itself:

> I believe with imperfect faith
>
> in faith imprecise
> as these instruments
> fragments of the flight here.
> I understood only the codes:
>
> caves
>
> constellations
>
> our loss ringing in the dark.[14]

The references to instruments and codes have a distinctly military quality to them, yet the poet too must become as precise an instrument as she can be, and must decipher the codes that will make her work intelligible, however uncharted and lost it may appear to be. As Back insists in a recent essay, "Accuracy (that strives toward truthfulness): This first attribute takes us back to the aforementioned abuse and mis- use of language; unlike political speech, poetry cannot afford to misuse language, for in misusing language, it negates itself and its very reason for existence. Poetry as a language art exists on its accuracy; less than accurate is unacceptable to the poet."[15] Back sounds remarkably like an Objectivist here, and indeed, she holds fast to these principles even when the truth seems difficult to ascertain.[16] The "Azimuth" sequence ends precariously balanced between faith in the poet's ability to give us the truth and the sad knowledge that we are frequently lost in the "country of words":

---

13. Ibid., 69.
14. Ibid., 70.
15. "A Species of Magic."
16. Recall, for example, Reznikoff's insistence that the poet "is restricted almost to the testimony of a witness in a court of law" and that "Poetry should be precise about the thing and reticent about the feeling." Charles Reznikoff, "A Talk with L.S. Dembo," in *Charles Reznikoff: Man and Poet* 98–99, 97.

We have returned
to nowhere

in this country of words

Still, I must tell you

the compass rose
will yet invent

a new direction:

strange blossom.

Believe what you will.[17]

Although the poet, in her last line, challenges the reader to believe, the "nowhere" of language is still the only country where "the compass rose / will yet invent // a new direction." Diaspora is still, perhaps, the only place of new possibility, the one place where we may imagine that "a new direction" may blossom.

Language is "nowhere" because it offers possibilities of being that "somewhere," some fixed or given place, would deny. Language, where meaning may be lost, trackless, opens utopian spaces, since "utopia" means "nowhere" and exists in the conditional. Granted, Back insists on the accuracy of poetic language, and likewise insists on "the personal accountability of the poet": "As a poet, wielding the written word, I am responsible for what the word may do. If the word – the verse, the image, the poetic line – falsifies, fails at telling the truth, I am at fault, I alone have failed."[18] As I understand it, accountability binds the poet and the language of her poem to a condition of truth, to what is, but that condition is also what may be, what is imagined or envisioned beyond the immediacies of a given time and place. If this is the case, how will the poet address specifically political exigencies that impose themselves urgently, brutally, upon her, as she tries to maintain her poetic accountability?

17. *Azimuth*, 73–74.
18. "A Species of Magic."

This question hovers even more strongly over Back's next full-length collection, *On Ruins & Return* (2007), which contains the entirety of her sequence *The Buffalo Poems* (1999–2005). The origin of this sequence is a vision which Back had in June, 1999. As she tells us in the introduction, she was driving through the "scarred and blackened" Jerusalem Hills, on her way home. Pregnant with her daughter (her two older children are boys), she experiences a bout of nausea, stops the car, and crouches by the roadside. Raising her eyes, she sees a buffalo – that is, an American bison – "Still, erect, frozen. Silent. Its thick furred hair motionless in the windless air. Its hump its own solitary mountain, carried from far-away places. Its head half-lowered, in profile – a dark brown buffalo, wandered into these Jerusalem hills."[19] This vision of the buffalo, itself a highly overdetermined symbol, inaugurates a sequence of poems dealing with the Second Intifada, which begins in September, 2000 and leads to the death of numerous civilians, including many Palestinian and Israeli children. As Back puts it, "The ledgers are quickly filled with the names of children. My three grow strong, as though they are safe. Hearts close, and then seal shut. I remember the buffalo, and a heart waiting (to be opened). From that moment, it stays with me, wanders through my days, carrying the weight of the violence on its broad back, in its vast and silent eye – and it allows me to write // what I could not have otherwise."[20]

In his extremely insightful review of *On Ruins & Return*, Andrew Mossin interprets Back's buffalo; his observations deserve to be quoted at length:

> The buffalo – at once metaphoric, historically actual, mytho-poetic, extinct – exists in this landscape as both birth-rite of a landscape that now exists only in the poet's memory (Back grew up in Buffalo, New York) and as fictive medium through which Back translates the grief-stricken actuality of present-day Israel, her adopted homeland.... The buffalo as hunted-down, slaughtered beast of the American West, appears in Back's reconstruction as a figure enmeshed in multiple topographies at once: as

19. Rachel Tzvia Back, *On Ruins & Return* (Exeter, UK: Shearsman Books, 2007), 10.
20. Ibid., 12.

symbol of the western plains where buffalo once dominated the
landscape; as instrumental referent to the poet's own journeying
away from homeland to homeland, adopted land to adopted land;
as emblematic figure of historic suffering, spanning that distance
between the genocidal killings by western settlers of Native
Americans in the 19th century and present-day Jerusalem...[21]

As Mossin indicates, the buffalo in Back's poems mediates between
past and present, and between America and Israel, with violence and
oppression presented as tragic constants regardless of historical specifics.
Then again, Back is intensely aware of those specifics, as the violence of
the American past is juxtaposed to that of the Israeli / Palestinian present.
To be sure, Back's sequence is both personal testimonial and objective
documentary, but it is also investigative, whether dealing with historical
or current events. In her book on Susan Howe, Back notes that "Howe
refuses to simplify the complex issues involved in history's silencing
tactics or to obliterate or undervalue the great effort of retrieving lost
voices. Thus Howe's poetry – dense, difficult, resistant to easy penetra-
tion – formally enacts the arduous process of tracking back through thick
and overgrown landscapes in search of history's missing."[22] *On Ruins &*
Return owes a good deal to Howe's procedures, and though Back does
not venture as far into the past as Howe, the retrieval of suppressed voices,
victimized and subject not only to physical violence, but the violence of
ideological writing and rewriting, is fundamental to her poetic task.[23]

The violence that marks almost every poem in Back's sequence – the
hunting of the buffalo to near extinction in American West, the genocide

21. Andrew Mossin, "Against Witness as Such," *Jacket* 35 (early 2008), http://
jacketmagazine.com/35/r-back-rb-mossin.shtml.

22. *Led by Language*, 11. The concept of poetry as investigation, which Back adopts
in relation to Howe, but again, is relevant to Back's own poetry, comes from Paul
Naylor, *Poetic Investigations: Singing the Holes in History* (Evanston, IL: Northwestern
University Press, 1999), which includes a chapter on Howe.

23. In the Epilogue to *Led by Language*, Back recounts her studies with Howe at Temple
University in 1989: "I had a weekly tutorial with her, during which she read my poetry
and encouraged me to 'open up' to the possibilities embedded within the language,
and within myself." Written ten years later, *The Buffalo Poems* – and like Back, Howe
spent part of her childhood in Buffalo – is partly the result of that encouragement.

of Native Americans (due not only to racist warfare and political betrayal but to the destruction of the natural resources on which they depended), the ongoing, brutal Israeli occupation of Palestinian territories, the terrorism of Palestinians against Israelis, and the Israeli retaliation – all causes a deep feeling of *homelessness* in the work. How, the poet seems to ask, despite her deep attachments, can either of these countries be called home? One poem early in the sequence utilizes two columns of text, one describing the slaughter of the buffalo, the other listing some of the dead on both sides of the Battle of Adobe Walls (1874), which began when Comanche and allied tribes attacked a trading post and town that they understood to be furthering the destruction of the buffalo on which these tribes depended. The poem ends with a letter from a "westward traveler" who sees nothing but dead buffalo wherever he goes: *"Forgive me, I was mistaken // In this forsaken country where I searched / for myself / I will never be found."*[24] This lost self in a forsaken country is an American wandering in the nineteenth-century west, but it could also be the poet herself in an Israeli desert landscape. However she may seem at home in her adopted country, the daily violence and the intractable, increasingly polarized political circumstances that she must confront produce an existential condition of shock, groundlessness, and loss.

Loss and grief grow increasingly intense as the sequence unfolds. One of the most poignant – and uncanny – poems is based on an episode at "Kfar Darom Settlement, Gaza – Nov. 2000: A Palestinian bomb is detonated on a road as a school bus drives by. The two adults on the bus are killed, 5 children are wounded. Three children from one family all lose their limbs."[25] Here are the poem's opening stanzas:

> The children were missing limbs
> In the southern sand region they
> were missing
> a leg a foot an arm
> I sent my northern children out looking

24. *On Ruins & Return*, 24.
25. Ibid., 37.

The moon was full the paths were white
night
was smooth just the ripple
of my children's high voices
skipping stone in the dry wadis:
>
> Hunter horn berry and bird,
> Hunter horn berry and fish.
> Hunter clover nut and bird,
> Whisper a secret, make a wish.

Drawing on "a very brief definition I found many years ago in a dictionary of literary terms," Back calls poetry "A species of magic... Poetry as a language art is only part grammar and syntax – that is, it is only partially meaning and content. It is also music, incantation, rhythm, sensations. Let's not forget that the first poets, the Israelite King David and the Greek Orpheus alike, were first of all master musicians."[26] In accord with this observation, Back's poem draws on the music and magic of the old English ballad tradition, transplanting it to modern Gaza. The ballad as a traditional form, with its haunting rhymes and typically violent subject matter, resonates with the tragedy of this episode. The poem moves back and forth between the children's magical quest and the incantatory refrain of the ballad quatrains. Formally, the poem is unusual for Back, given the extensive use of rhyme. The voice of the mother sending her children forth to find the missing limbs is reminiscent of the Fairy Queen and other powerful, frightening maternal archetypes, and as Back knows well, to quote Susan Howe, "There are traces of blood in a fairy tale."[27] The imagery is also somewhat reminiscent of the Egyptian myth of Isis, seeking organic wholeness and fertility by gathering the limbs of her husband Osiris, who has been dismembered by his evil, usurping brother, Set. Yet in keeping with the wandering meaning of her diasporic poetics, Back also brings in the central figure of the buffalo:

26. "A Species of Magic."
27. Susan Howe, *Singularities* (Hanover, NH: Wesleyan University Press / University Press of New England, 1990), 44.

> Hunter horn berry and bird,
>>Tell me, child, what have you heard?
>>The sky at sunset is redder than red
>>And buffalo-robes will be your bed.
>In the southern sand region
>under starched white sheets
>the children reached
>for missing legs that ached
>and called to them
>to leave the fevered body behind
>>Hide and seek in buffalo-clover
>>You'll wake up, child, when the hunt is
>>>over.
>>Hunter horn berry and bird,
>>Tell me no more of what you have heard.[28]

At the end of the poem, the spell, as it were, is broken: "my beautiful children came back / flushed / empty handed."[29] There is no magic strong enough to restore the children's maimed bodies; the mother, who seems hardly able to accept that bitter truth, can only bring the poem to a close.

On Ruins & Return ends with a section called "What is Still Possible (6 Love Poems)," followed by one last poem, "Bringing the Buffalo Back Home (October 2005, Adirondacks NY)." Gentle, melancholy, still suffused with loss but willing to entertain the possibility of hope, these poems, almost all in terse, abbreviated couplets, measure and judge the redemptive potential of love. But love is always a risk; there is always a price to be paid:

> with every kiss your
> tongue
>
> touching mine
> you swallow

---

28. *On Ruins & Return*, 36–37.
29. Ibid, 37.

another word
steal

what was mine
until

I am
wordless

would
there be love

in a wordless
world[30]

Is love worth it if the poet loses her words with every kiss? Can she live at all in a wordless world? Thinking of the title of this section of the book, is love even possible? There are no definite answers to such questions; at best, the poet tells her lover, it is "as if your word / love // could hold me / whole // in the world."[31] As if.

"I will always / come home," the poet assures him in the last couplet of the sequence, and assuming "home" in this context is Israel, then the poet's ritual journey to the Adirondacks in the final poem is but one more chapter in her perpetual diasporic wandering. Ending her book, Back ritualistically returns the buffalo, her symbol of spiritual and geopolitical displacement, to America, its original home. America, of course, is Back's original home too, for it is the home of the language of her poetry, which, as we have seen, may be the truest home of all. The buffalo, let us recall, functions in one respect as figure of *permission*, a trope that enables Back to write about both the American and the Israeli / Palestinian disasters that she could not confront otherwise. "Sacred and scarred," the buffalo first appears "among the parched and burnt / in a bloody valley"; she "broke open lies... / spoke a quiet / hope kept / me company / until // one day / she was gone –"[32] "No," Back realizes, "she brought herself / back home," and in a powerful moment

30. Ibid., 86.
31. Ibid., 87.
32. Ibid., 93, 94.

of self-realization, acknowledges "where her exile / my anger // took hold / Home // already then a place / haunted // by what / is untold."[33] The concepts of exile and home continually circulate in an endless play of opposites, powered by the outrage, the righteous, prophetic anger of the poet facing that long history of violence which the buffalo, in both America and Israel, has come to represent for her. This is why home is always already a place haunted by what is untold. In the telling, in the poem, the ghosts, again distilled in the figure of the buffalo, may finally be put to rest.

But there seems to be little rest for the poet. Back's next volume of poetry, *A Messenger Comes*, is her most personal, her most sorrowful, her most lyrical, and her most sheerly beautiful. It is an elegiac work, a book-length Kaddish, structured by the death of her father, and the terribly tragic, premature death of her older sister. And it is her most religious book, given the extensive references to Jewish ritual, midrashic treatments of Scripture, and reworkings of kabbalistic myth. It merits a sustained, comprehensive examination, but here I will limit my reading to a few passages which create a liminal space between home and home-lessness, related in turn to Back's diasporic imagination and the pervasive sense in her poetry that meaning – that life itself – is always *elsewhere*.

A Messenger Comes begins with a series of poems called "A Broken Beginning," which directly engages the Lurianic myth of Creation as *tzimtzum* (the contraction or withdrawal of God to make space for Creation) and *shevirat ha-kelim* (the shattering or breaking of the vessels, since the sefirot emanating from the Godhead could not contain the divine light and shattered, leading to the fallen condition of the world). Loss accompanies, indeed, may be said to be synonymous, with Creation, and the myth is often associated with the Jews' historical condition of galut (exile), as first interpreted by Gershom Scholem: "This 'breaking' introduces a dramatic aspect into the process of Creation, and it can explain the Galut... In other words, all being is in Galut."[34] Here is Back's equally diasporic and gnostic version:

33. Ibid., 97, 98.
34. Gershom Scholem, *The Messianic Idea in Judaism and Other Essays on Jewish Spirituality* (New York: Schocken Books, 1971), 45. For an important critique of Scholem's view,

In the beginning
it was sudden –
the world

that wasn't
yet
all at once

emerging
out of formless void –
space

of the infinite
broken
into pieces – God

retreating
to make way
for perfect human

imperfection:
Adam and Eve
dreaming

in the beginning
of a world that wasn't
and wasn't yet

broken either[35]

Back's vision of "God / retreating," leading to "perfect human // imper-
fection," indicates that from the beginning, nothing is in its place and
yet all is somehow as it is supposed to be. The second poem tells us that
when God was hovering over the waters, "his heart / was breaking," that
"he knew / this was / unavoidable." Creation comes from a "separated

see Moshe Idel, *Messianic Mystics* (New Haven, CT: Yale University Press, 1998),
179–80.

35. Rachel Tzvia Back, *A Messenger Comes* (San Diego, CA: Singing Horse Press, 2012),
13.

/ self," and at the moment of Creation, "his heart // shattered / into pieces."[36] The moment of greatest fullness, of greatest blessing, became a moment of loss, when "God's own / constellations of starry // sorrow / took hold."[37] If this is the divine condition, what then may we expect of mere human beings when confronted by the inevitability of loss?

Throughout *A Messenger Comes*, this notion of cosmic sorrow is specifically related to the capacity of human speech to express grief and engage in the verbal act of mourning. The last poem in *A Broken Beginning* gives us the stars "in their abundance / *winged / and now worded*": they speak themselves, and are moved to tell of "their own / long ago / lost // still luminous / selves."[38] In this respect, we are like the stars, seeking to tell the tale of our lost, luminous selves. "Lamentation," the central sequence of the volume, which recounts the last illness and anticipates the death of Back's father, Nate (Nissan) Back (1925–2009), begins with the same concern with which the previous section ended: "In worded a world / how broken / from beginning." The irregular syntax enacts this broken condition; from the beginning, to "word," to artic-ulate, our worldly being, is to pronounce it as broken. Thus, "we exist / in a shattered vessel / shards at our bare feet."[39] In one of the most remarkable poems in the sequence, Back works with the kabbalistic idea that in a fallen world, language itself is broken, since it is language through which Creation comes into being. In terms of structural lin-guistics, signification is an arbitrary process, and there is always a gap between signified and signifier, but Kabbalah can be even more radical. As Scholem explains, according to the sixteenth-century Safed Kabbalist, Moses Cordovero,

> ...the Torah in its innermost essence is composed of divine letters, which themselves are configurations of divine light. Only in the course of a process of materialization do these letters combine in various ways. First they form names, that is, names of God, later appellatives and predicates suggesting the divine,

36. Ibid., 14.
37. Ibid., 16.
38. Ibid., 31.
39. Ibid., 35.

and still later they combine in a new way, to form words relating to earthly events and material objects. Our present world took on its crude material character in consequence of the fall of man, and the Torah underwent a parallel change. The spiritual letters became material when the material character of the world made this change necessary.[40]

Back's poem may be said to reenact this linguistic fall, leading to a sense of both cosmic and personal loss at the imminent death of her father. In "*our* alphabet" (*our* meaning Hebrew, which Jewish tradition regards as God's language of creation), "*aleph-bet* / *aleph* // prepares itself / for radical / unraveling." The unraveling of the alphabet parallels an unraveling of Creation, and an analogous unraveling of the speaker's emotions. This transpires in the rest of the poem, which plays with English words beginning with the sounds of *aleph* and *bet*, a and b:

> *aleph* at
>> abyss edge
>> acerbic sky above and
>> air or ache all
>> abeyant but un
>> abating
>
> *bet*   because
>> ballast or balm
>> bond to
>> before behind be
>>> always
>
> *aleph*
>> again un
>> availed avale our
>> *Av* awhile then
>> away and absent
>
> *Aba*[41]

40. *On the Kabbalah and its Symbolism*, 71.
41. *A Messenger Comes*, 39.

The interplay between Hebrew and English here gives us an unusually clear perspective on how Back occupies an in-between space linguistically, culturally, and poetically. The aleph is the original letter; a kabbalistic legend tells of how God, in the beginning, chose the aleph to precede creation (which begins with bet, as in *Bereishit*), so it does indeed represent the edge of the abyss.[42] But this abyss also symbolizes the void of loss when the father is gone, leading to an ache that is "abeyant but un / abating." Can there be any "ballast" to secure the poet in the face of that loss, can there be any "balm" when the bond between parent and child is finally severed? To hope for such would be unavailing; it is "our *Av* awhile then / away and absent // *Aba*." *Av*, which literally means "father," is the eleventh month of the Hebrew calendar, associated with various historical disasters, especially the destruction of both Temples, for which Jews mourn on *Tishah B'Av*, the fast of the Ninth of *Av*. *Aba*, of course, means father. We may say, therefore, that loss of the father represents a personal "*Av*," that is, a time of mourning for the absent *Aba*. At the utterance of that word, the poem ends; the father has gone into the void, which is also the place (or non-place) where there is no language.

But the absolute silence of the void is a condition that no poet can tolerate (and here the poet is like God, who also, perhaps, found that emptiness and silence intolerable, and therefore spoke Creation into being). As I mentioned above, "Lamentation" *anticipates* the death of the father; it is "*for my father, on his dying*" – not, significantly, on the occasion of his death, though that too is formally memorialized later in the book. Back actually invokes the presence of her father, especially his commanding physical presence ("Six feet tall and bearded... He's a large man, he *fills* / the room") as much as his absence.[43] Watching him lay tefillin, she poignantly wonders "If you bind the straps / tight enough / might // they hold you / to this world / awhile longer?"[44] Even when she imagines her brothers already saying Kaddish for him, she makes a point of reminding us that the Kaddish prayer ("*raised / lauded extolled // adored and / blessed*") is not really a prayer of mourning, but

---

42. For a related view of this legend, see my discussion of Robert Duncan's references to it in Chapter 9.

43. *A Messenger Comes*, 43.

44. Ibid., 45.

a prayer in praise of "the Name," containing "not a word / on Death."[45] Here, it is not an accident that she calls God (who is Unnamable) by the English equivalent of the Hebrew reference to Him: *ha-Shem*. As a poet, a namer, she allies herself with the source of life, who is also the supreme user of language.

Be that as it may, Back still presents herself as a "Wayward daughter who imagines / the after before / even as you // wrestle disease / refuse surrender." Likewise, she thinks of the poem itself as "This wayward // writing." She is abashed at recording the vision of her father's death and of her family's mourning, despite the inevitability. Wayward means difficult to control, unpredictable, obstinate, contrary, disobedient; it implies a certain capriciousness and defiance of social convention. It comes from the earlier Middle English "awayward," ultimately meaning a turning from what is assumed, established, ordered. A wayward writing will never settle into a single meaning, just as a wayward individual never settles into conventional behavior. The wayward daughter, the wayward poet, asks "what crimes / to the spirit / do I commit – // then I return / unrepentant / to the unrepenting // page."[46] If writing of this sort – if writing poetry – requires a wayward, unrepenting attitude, then Back is ready to accept the consequences. For the page, the demand of the poem, is also unrepenting, always calling the poet to return to the task.

A Messenger Comes ends with the sequence *Elegy Fragments*, dedicated to Back's older sister Adina (1958–2008) who in died in Brooklyn of ovarian cancer. "As a public historian who specialized in the field of oral histories," Back writes of Adina, "she insisted on the multiplicity of voices as intrinsic to and essential for any historical retelling. This seems no less true for literary retellings. In this poem in particular, I adopt her inclusive approach, as strategy and faith, and in heartbroken memory."[47] To a greater extent than the poems to her father, this fragmentary sequence pushes Back to the border of silence.[48] She conceives of the work as

45. Ibid., 46.
46. Ibid., 48.
47. Ibid., 106. More on Adina Back can be found in her brother's moving obituary and tribute to her. See Aaron Back, "Adina Back," *Jewish Women's Archive*, https://jwa .org/weremember/back-adina.
48. In conversation with Back, she told me that she has never read this sequence at a public reading.

Love's ragged relics on the page:
what remains in the world wrestling

word and image to the ground
even as the definitive shape of your

light-boned embrace
disappears   Steadfast

sister, there is steady
unravelment

in the vastness of your
absence

We are solitary threads now
and know:

Silence tells it better.[49]

As in the poem about *aleph* and *bet,* Back again uses an image of unrav-
eling: the fabric of being comes apart as personal loss is experienced as
cosmic loss "in the vastness of your / absence." However much the poet
may wrestle with word and image, she is compelled to admit that in some
instances, "Silence tells it better." We are exiled in the silent void before
Creation. Yet somehow, out of that void comes a name:

Sometimes in the birds' flash
of white-winged flight

I think I see you
delicate delicate

your lovely name
in the winged instant written

across all the skies[50]

49. *A Messenger Comes,* 89.
50. Ibid., 100–101.

Adina in Hebrew means "delicate," "graceful," or "refined." The name of the lost sister is thus inscribed in the Book of Nature. Nature as the source of being, and as the source of the poem, is confirmed. The last words of the book echo, however faintly, the original divine creative act: "As though I am not / in Secret and / with every breath // Waiting for your return."[51]

Back's poetry of the last few years has been gathered in a volume called *What Use Is Poetry, the Poet Is Asking.* As the title indicates, the book is partly a return to the politically engaged work of *Azimuth* and *The Buffalo Poems,* as Back continues to speak as a poetic witness to the ongoing violence in Israel and Palestine. Even as the poet interrogates her own work, insistently questioning the value of her testimony in the face of almost ceaseless aggression and the loss of innocent civilians (she again focuses on the deaths of children, though she also depicts Israeli soldiers as children too), nevertheless she insists that the poem must continue to be written. The stakes are very high: Back's oldest son participated in the Gaza War of 2014 as a paramedic, and emerged deeply traumatized. In one remarkable poem, she appropriates the myth of Icarus and Dedalus to describe his situation. She gives us Icarus admiring his father's handiwork, "not realising that he was handling what would be his peril."[52] The scene shifts abruptly from the boy being instructed by his father on how to fly, to the Israeli paramedic *"carried aloft in the metal belly of / the roaring beast, unleashed into the sky."* The poem ends with shocking power, as the reality of Back's son is woven into the mythic son's fate:

> *His chest was weighted with vest and pack and gun. He rode the air*
>
> *until they landed in storming dust, into the bellowing battle.* Even as his mouth cried his father's name, *he wrapped bandages around the wounded,*

---

51. Ibid., 101.
52. Rachel Tzvia Back, *What Use Is Poetry, the Poet Is Asking* (Bristol, UK: Shearsman Books, 2019), 14.

staunched bleeding, placed morphine in ravaged mouths of pain.
the sky *was orphaned of birds;* there were *no feathers, not on land
   or waves. Imagined*

wing-span of the fallen.[53]

Mythic vision in a Hebraic rather than a Greek mode informs another poem in the sequence, this one focused on the mother rather than the son:

> The mother
> Who didn't stop her son
> From going
> To war –
>
> Was called before the High Court
> Of mothers held on full moon nights
> At undisclosed Celestial sites, Stars of the Light
> Not yet evident on earth the only ones
> In attendance.
>
> There they argued her case in silver-tinged
> Syntax, crystalline intonations, verbed
> Asterisms composed wholly from the black holes
> Of her heart[54]

At the end of the poem, the mother "Was found to be / Guilty. // She, and the High Court, found her / There where lost, and forever / Guilty."[55]

In Back's fantasy, the High Court of mothers are stars who judge the earthly mother's failure to act and prevent her son from going to war. An "asterism" is a group of stars smaller than a constellation, but these are "verbed," given words; thus the mothers argue the case in a sort of star-speech "composed wholly from the black holes / of her heart." The heavenly court is not really above her: it is within her; it

---

53. Ibid.
54. Ibid., 12.
55. Ibid., 13.

is she herself who judges herself lost and guilty. But Back has always been lost, never found, never grounded or rooted despite her and her family's generations-long connection to the land for which her son has risked his life. This remains the paradox that we have seen her identify as fundamental to her poetic being.

Another poem, however, directly confronts her lost or in-between state, but resolves itself differently:

> There were the tales being woven
> of others' lives, long narratives
> unfolding, crafted with devotion.
>
> She had been told, "This is the contract
> you make: you agree to believe,
> you agree to care." But she
>
> was already otherwhere: what pretend
> could hold through despair. Old
> vows were now disavowed.
>
> Shelves weighted with books, second-hand
> stores sought in strange cities, her
> ceaseless travelling
>
> through storied worlds created
> as though just for her, for she had agreed
> to believe –
>
> That was over now.
> Henceforth the heart would disallow all tales
> that weren't true.[56]

This poem crystallizes another significant moment of self-realization in Back's struggle to understand the paradox of her diasporic poetic. "Otherwhere" is the perfect coinage for Back's condition: at this moment she articulates her awareness of a situation that has always obtained, indeed, has always defined her work. But let us unpack this poem with

---

56. Ibid., 15.

care. What are "the tales being woven," the "long / narratives unfolding"? Just as importantly, what is the "contract" the poet has made, the "Old / vows…now disavowed"? One answer, I believe, has to do with her Israeli identity, and the kind of poet she has always chosen *not* to be. Again, from her crucial essay "A Species of Magic":

> Indeed, the Hebrew poets, through the better part of the twentieth century, were *expected* to speak the single narrative of the day, a narrative implicitly reflective and supportive of official government policies, which were – and too often still are – seen as synonymous with the desires of the people. Hebrew even has a term for this literary phenomenon: *shirah meguyeset* (mobilized poetry), poetry that speaks in the name of the nation, carrying the patriotic flag into battle. (The military terminology is hardly surprising; military language and military concepts have infiltrated and affected every aspect of Israeli life.) As a direct and predictable outcome of this phenomenon of mobilized poetry, the early modern Hebrew poets taught in schools, published in newspapers, anthologized and canonized – poets who were identified as "national poets" – were those who spoke the Zionist narrative most passionately and categorically: the absolute narrative of Return to the Homeland, of being a Chosen People, of the singular and always-righteous struggle of early Statehood, and so on.[57]

What Back identifies here is obviously not the sort of poetry she writes, and not only because she does not write in Hebrew (though this statement provides another important clue to her choice of English for her poetry): opposed to *shirah meguyeset*, she has never signed any "contract" that could lead to the "mobilization" of her poetry, or align the deep, conflicted desires we read in her work to any government policies whatsoever. The narratives of the State are explicitly disavowed in this work, and whatever vows she may have made when she chose Israel as her home have far more to do with her personal roots in the land than with any ideological narrative of Zionism.

Yet this poem complicates the matter to an even greater extent, and in

---

57. "A Species of Magic."

doing so, we may see Back becoming an even more important figure for modern Jewish poetry. The image of the poet wandering through second-hand bookstores in "strange cities" (and as I noted above, Back does not write her poetry in Israel, so a phrase such as this carries great weight) is one that would naturally be associated with a diasporic sensibility such as hers. But "her / ceaseless travelling // through storied worlds created / as though just for her" – which is to say, the paradoxical story she has told herself up until now, which has served as the engine for her poetry – "That was over now" as well. What then is left for her? "Henceforth the heart would disallow all tales / that weren't true." One may say that this has always been the case for Back, for given the complexities of the issues which she addresses, the truth of her testimony has been, and remains, her greatest priority. Perhaps we may venture to say that after repeated acts of witness, after giving testimony to such losses, even the myth, the story she tells herself of the "ceaselessly travelling" poet, must be put aside. In writing the poem, only the heart serves as judge.

At a number of points in Back's books, she turns to the *Modeh ani*, the prayer of thanks that observant Jews recite upon waking in the morning: "I give thanks before you, living and eternal King, for compassionately restoring my spirit to me, your faithfulness is great." It is a touchstone, providing reassurance despite her expressions of disbelief. In the *Envoi* of Back's latest book, a poem called "Like the Believer," the prayer is invoked yet again:

> And she –
> disbelieving
>
> poet of fallen faith –
> suspecting the word is
>
> barely if ever heard
> in the clamorous, the
>
> screaming world, wakes
> to another day of
>
> brokenness and praise –
> *modah ani breath to my body restored*

so compassionately –
and there as another

unbelieving believer
at prayer, she

puts one more poem
on the page.[58]

In the end, the poet's faith must reside in the poem's power to restore her, and in her power to restore the poem.

---

58. *What Is the Use of Poetry*, 93–94.

―――――

NINE

Dark Rabbis and Secret Jews

AS I MENTION IN MY INTRODUCTION, ONE OF THE QUESTIONS POSED
by Daniel Morris and Stephen Paul Miller to potential contributors
to *Radical Poetics and Secular Jewish Culture* was "how Jewish poetry
can be written by non-Jews." And as Jerome Rothenberg puts it in his
poem "The Connoisseur of Jews," writing out of what we might term
the present absence (or absent presence) of both pre- and post-war
Polish Jewry, if there were "no jews / there would still be jews ... / there
would still be someone to write the jewish poem."[1] These lines have
always served as a talisman for me, and I think about them whenever I
consider the vicissitudes of modern Jewish poetry.[2] It is especially that
phrase – "there would still be someone to write the jewish poem" – that
continually haunts me. More specifically, I am haunted by the question
(it echoes throughout this book, and much of my other work on Jewish
poetry) of what makes a Jewish poem, and who is the poet writing it.
Allen Grossman begins his crucial essay "Jewish Poetry Considered as a
Theophoric Project" by refusing to answer that very question, declaring
instead that "The poetry of a nation or a world is whatever comes to
pass in its domain in the name of poetry, and can neither succeed nor
fail."[3] This is a clever feint, since Grossman then proceeds to present his

1. *Triptych*, 12.
2. I discuss the poem at some length in *Not One of Them in Place*, 93–95.
3. *The Long Schoolroom*, 159.

conception of Jewish "theophoric" poetry in great detail. Yet however persuasive – indeed, I would venture to say, definitive – his working through may be, I am still led to wonder about the identity of that "someone" who is there to write the Jewish poem.

In "Shekhinah in America," a foundational essay in the field of Jewish American poetry, Eric Murphy Selinger discusses Grossman's call for Jewish American poets to engage in a deeper study of traditional texts, including Kabbalah, in order to escape the parochialism of ethnicity. Grossman's critique of Jewish parochialism is found in "The Jew as an American Poet: The Instance of Ginsberg," his elaborately argued review of Allen Ginsberg's "Kaddish," a poem which, for Grossman, acknowledges but also transcends the limits of Jewish ethnic writing.[4] For Grossman, "Judaism is an ahistorical religion" (a truly contrarian notion), and the return to traditional texts that he calls for will, as Selinger puts it, "make every Jewish age simultaneous."[5] What would this reconfigured Jewish American poem that transcends mere ethnicity sound like? "Might such a poem sound something like this?" Selinger asks – and then, in a brilliant move, quotes "What Do I Know of the Old Lore?," the opening poem in Robert Duncan's collection *Roots and Branches!*[6]

We will look at Duncan's poem later in this chapter, but for now, I simply want to note that when I reflect upon what makes a poem "Jewish," this moment in Selinger's essay comes to mind. His point is well taken: the "Jewish" wisdom of Robert Duncan – gentile, theosophist, syncretist, gnostic – makes "What Do I Know of the Old Lore," among a number of Duncan's works, into an uncannily "Jewish" poem. So if you don't have to be Jewish to love Levy's rye (as old New York City subway ads declared), maybe it's true that you don't have to be Jewish to write a Jewish poem.

Joking aside, what happens when American poets who are not Jewish choose to engage with identifiably Jewish concepts and beliefs? What motivates them to do so? What sort of (Jewish?) poems result?

4. In *The Long Schoolroom*, 150–58.
5. Selinger, 255.
6. Ibid.

As I have indicated, these are questions that have intrigued me for many years. My first exploration of these matters was "The Case of Michael Palmer" (1988), which I wrote about the great avant-garde poet Michael Palmer (b. 1943). In that essay, I examine the kabbalistic qualities of Palmer's poetry in two of his early books, *Notes for Echo Lake* (1981) and *First Figure* (1984), contrasting these qualities with the post-structuralist linguistic play which also features significantly in his poetry of that period.[7] I return to his later work and discuss it in more broadly religious terms, focusing on the notion of heresy, in my book *On Mount Vision*.[8] More recently, in a magisterial essay called "How to Write Poetry after Auschwitz: The Burnt Book of Michael Palmer," the poet and critic Patrick Pritchett expands on the Jewish dimension of Palmer's work, providing what I take to be a paradigm for the study of the "Jewish imaginary" in the work of a non-Jewish poet. Pritchett quotes Susannah Heschel from her article "Imagining Judaism in America": "the cultural boundaries in America are so porous that Jewishness has become a free-floating signifier open to appropriation by non-Jews as well."[9] Focusing on Palmer's response to Adorno's famous concern for the fate of poetry after Auschwitz, Pritchett argues that "The Jewish imaginary is so pronounced in Palmer's work because it is the discourse with the greatest resources for engaging in the subject's plight in history."[10] As Pritchett demonstrates, in order for Palmer to respond in the most meaningful way to these urgent historical concerns, he follows a number of important Jewish poets (George Oppen, Paul Celan, and most importantly, Edmond Jabès), and "purposefully adopted Judaic textual models," including talmudic and kabbalistic writing practices under the specific rubric of the "Burnt Book."[11] The style which Palmer

---

7. "The Case of Michael Palmer," *Contemporary Literature* 29, no. 4 (Winter 1988), 518–37.

8. *On Mount Vision*, 138–82.

9. Quoted in Patrick Pritchett, "How to Write Poetry after Auschwitz: The Burnt Book of Michael Palmer," *Journal of Modern Literature* 37, vol. 3 (Spring 2014), 137.

10. Ibid.

11. Here, Pritchett draws on Marc-Alain Ouaknin's *The Burnt Book: Reading the Talmud*, which has become an important influence on poets and theorists concerned with questions of Jewish representation and textuality, especially after the Shoah (Stephen Fredman draws extensively on it in his book on Reznikoff, *A Menorah for Athena*.) See

develops as he adopts these models not only transforms him into one of the most important "Jewish" poets writing today, but also confirms the overall value of thinking "Jewishly" about poetry which we would not necessarily read in this context.

In this final chapter, therefore, I will consider the role of the "Jewish imaginary" in a number of other non-Jewish poets, extending my study of modern Jewish poetry to the furthest and most porous border of what Grossman calls the "domain" of that "nation's" ("people's"? "culture's"?) poetry. I will look closely at three poets, Wallace Stevens (1879–1955), Robert Duncan (1919–1988), and Joseph Donahue (b. 1954) as important instances of this phenomenon. In Stevens' case, we shall see how a single Jewish notion threads its way through one of the most complex and elaborate poetic oeuvres in all of high modernism. In regard to both Duncan and Donahue (as is true of Palmer), we will examine works which consistently demonstrate a pervasive fascination and strong affinity with Jewish spirituality and Jewish texts. When we look at these poets, we must ask, as might Rothenberg: who, exactly, is writing the Jewish poem? As we shall see, dark rabbis and secret Jews gather about these poets as they write, and their presence – their absent presence – produces uncanny results.

Wallace Stevens' Rabbinic Romance

One of the most provocative and enigmatic words in the famously flamboyant lexicon of Wallace Stevens is "rabbi." According to *The Online Concordance to Wallace Stevens' Poetry*, the word appears seven times in Stevens' poetic oeuvre.[12] Its first appearance is in "Le Monocle de Mon Oncle" (1918, republished in Stevens' first volume, *Harmonium* [1923]); its last is in "Things of August" (1950), in the volume *The Auroras of Autumn*. Stevens has recourse to the word in such crucial poems as "The Sun This March" (the poem he writes in March, 1930, following six years of poetic silence), *Notes Toward a Supreme Fiction* (often regarded as

---

Marc-Alain Ouaknin, *The Burnt Book: Reading the Talmud*, trans. Llewellyn Brown (Princeton, NJ: Princeton University Press, 1995). For my thoughts on *The Burnt Book*, see "Secular Jewish Culture and Its Radical Poetic Discontents."

12. http://www.wallacestevens.com/concordance/WSdb.cgi.

his greatest poetic sequence), and the poem "The Auroras of Autumn" itself (one of Stevens' most sublimely esoteric works, in which the word appears after an earlier invocation of "that crown and mystical cabala").[13] In 1953, Stevens writes to the distinguished Italian critic Renato Poggioli, who was in the midst of translating a selection of Stevens' poems into Italian. Stevens, answering Poggioli's inquiry concerning the rabbi in "The Sun This March," informs him that "The rabbi is a rhetorical rabbi. Frankly, the figure of the rabbi has always been an exceedingly attractive one to me because it is the figure of a man devoted in the extreme to scholarship and at the same time to making some use of it for human purposes."[14] Even more revealing is this passage from a letter the previous year to Bernard Herringman, a graduate student writing a dissertation on Stevens at Columbia: "I have never referred to rabbis as religious figures but always as scholars. When I was a boy I was brought up to think that rabbis were men who spent their time getting wisdom. And I rather think that that is true. One doesn't feel the same way, for instance, about priests or about a Protestant pastor, who are almost exclusively religious figures."[15]

The rabbi in Stevens, distinguished from priests and pastors, is engaged in a scholarly search for wisdom, which in turn is useful "for human purposes." He is, then, a more secular figure, not "religious," and his scholarship has an engaged and active mission centered in what Stevens, throughout his work, tends to call "reality." "Reality is the spirit's true centre," he announces in his *Adagia*; likewise, he counsels that "In poetry at least the imagination must not detach itself from reality."[16] Furthermore, he insists that "After one has abandoned a belief in god, poetry is that essence which takes its place as life's redemption."[17] Putting these and many similar observations together, we can deduce

13. Wallace Stevens, *Collected Poetry and Prose* (New York: Library of America, 1997), 360.
14. Wallace Stevens, *Letters of Wallace Stevens*, ed. Holly Stevens (New York: Alfred A. Knopf, 1966), 786.
15. Ibid., 751.
16. Wallace Stevens, *Opus Posthumous*, ed. Milton J. Bates (New York: Vintage, 1990), 201, 187.
17. Ibid., 185.

that Stevens' attraction to the figure of the rabbi has a sort of double charge: as an engaged, worldly, imaginative scholar, the rabbi is of use in a secular world – but that use hearkens back to an older religious order, when the spirit was not centered in, but transcended "reality," and when "redemption" was a matter of divinity, not poetry. Whether this is in any way a *Jewish* understanding of a rabbi is an open question.

Given the poet's idiosyncratic understanding of the term as he explains it to others late in his life, and what may be regarded as its pivotal role in a number of his major poems over nearly the entire length of his career, it is curious that few critics have commented on Stevens' rabbi. Harold Bloom, with his pervasive interest in Jewish literature and culture, quotes from the letter to Poggioli, and equates "rabbi" specifically with the figure of the "scholar" in Emerson: "Stevens uses the two words interchangeably, and like Emerson he uses 'scholar' to mean 'poet.'"[18] In short, Bloom takes Stevens at his word, and oddly does not question whether Stevens is actually thinking of a specifically Jewish figure when a rabbi is invoked.

A more nuanced consideration of the question is offered by Joseph G. Kronick, who confirms that in Stevens, "Unlike the priest, or the priestly scholar, the rabbi is the secular reader of man and his text."[19] Kronick argues that "The scholar's search for the total book is a substitute for faith in God," and by "turning the poem into scripture, the scholar is tempted to substitute the illusion of God for the abyss opening up between the poet and his subject.... The scholar would be content with a poetry that affirms the One in face of the chaos of experience. This is what Stevens cannot accept."[20] For Kronick, it is this rejection on Stevens' part that leads him to privilege the figure of the rabbi as a secular – not a religious – scholar. Indeed, in a typically deconstructive turn (Kronick draws extensively on Derrida's essay on Edmond Jabès, and sees an affinity between Stevens' rabbis and those of Jabès in this

18. Harold Bloom, *Wallace Stevens: The Poems of Our Climate* (Ithaca, NY: Cornell University Press, 1977), 89.
19. Joseph G. Kronick, "Of Parents, Children, and Rabbis: Wallace Stevens and the Question of the Book," *boundary 2* 10, no. 3 (Spring 1982): 149.
20. Ibid., 146, 147.

respect), the rabbi in Stevens seeks "a book that can never be possessed but only traced in the path of writing."[21] "Poetry is the scholar's art," writes Stevens in the *Adagia*, which we may now translate so as to read "Poetry is the rabbi's art" too.[22]

Thus Stevens' rabbi may be "secular," given that the poet understands "religious" to define institutionalized negotiations between the human and the divine as they are ordinarily conceived; indeed, it is looking more and more that Stevens' rabbi is an idealized version of the poet himself. But *pace* Kronick, I still see Stevens as one of a number of modern poets who do indeed turn at least some of their poems into "scripture," a scripture intended to serve modern readers partly in the way that older religious texts served believers. How might this be the case? Traditional religious scripture provided believers with moral guidance; it structured their daily lives; and perhaps most importantly, it served as a binding power within communities where religious institutions played a fundamental social role. Modern poetry, especially difficult modern poetry like that of Wallace Stevens, certainly does not function in anywhere near the same respects.[23] Nevertheless, for Stevens' deepest readers, those relatively few individuals who seek a renewed sense of inwardness that is congruent with an intense awareness of what we have seen him call "reality," Stevens' "rabbinic" poems are the proof they need that "Poetry is a means of redemption."[24]

In his memorial essay on Stevens in *Poetry*, William Carlos Williams,

---

21. Ibid., 151.

22. *Opus Posthumous*, 193. This "translation" was originally proposed to me by Alan Golding.

23. Cf. T.S. Eliot's famous remark in "The Metaphysical Poets": We can only say that it appears likely that poets in our civilization, as it exists at present, must be *difficult*. Our civilization comprehends great variety and complexity, and this variety and complexity, playing upon a refined sensibility, must produce various and complex results. The poet must become more and more comprehensive, more allusive, more indirect, in order to force, to dislocate if necessary, language into his meaning." *Selected Prose*, 65. Among the modernists, Stevens and Eliot are frequently seen at odds, but in this matter I suspect they would agree.

24. *Opus Posthumous*, 189. I further address the idea of modern poetry as "scripture" in *On Mount Vision*, particularly in the introduction, 24–26, and in the first chapter, "Robert Duncan: From Poetry to Scripture."

his friend and sometime rival, notes "a cryptic quality to his verses that was never resolved, a ritualistic quality as though he were following a secret litany that he revealed to no man. Over and over again, as he reached his later years and suddenly began to be recognized for what he was, a thoroughly equipped poet, even in such a late book as *The Auroras of Autumn*, he could be detected to the surprise of the world, in this secret devotion."[25] Apropos of this "ritualistic quality," this "secret devotion," one could also make the case (as I do below, in my discussion of *The Auroras of Autumn*) that Stevens' rabbi is also a seeker of hermetic or even occult wisdom, beyond the bounds of normative religion. In any case, it is clear that Stevens uses the term "rabbi" for his own idiosyncratic poetic purposes, purposes which involve the creation of a highly imaginative liminal space located somewhere *between*, if not *beyond*, the religious and the secular. This use would be another instance of Steven M. Wasserstrom's "Religion After Religion," which, as we saw in regard to Michael Heller, is "is equivocal, dialectical, inside and outside history, and thus thickly ambivalent."[26] For Stevens, the rabbi's scholarly pursuits are a means of dialectally negotiating this liminality. As we shall see shortly, Stevens calls upon him in moments of crisis, when the burden of reality in one respect or another is about to prove too much for the poet's imaginative capacity. Stevens' rabbis, psychologically speaking, are figures in a *fantasy*, a defensive fantasy of imaginative empowerment, "Like an hallucination come to daze / The corner of the eye."[27]

These lines come from "The Sun This March," which, as I mentioned previously, is the poem Stevens writes to break six years of poetic silence following the publication (and to Stevens, the unsatisfactory reviews) of his first book, *Harmonium*. The lines refer to "a turning spirit of an earlier self," the self that wrote such grand early poems as "Sunday Morning," in which Stevens boldly declares himself free of the Christian mythos and embraces a passionate secular humanism. This is the spirit "that used to turn / To gold in broadest blue" in those verbally luxurious earlier poems, and now "returns from out the winter's air." Associated with the

---

25. William Carlos Williams, "Wallace Stevens," *Poetry* 87, no. 4 (Jan. 1956): 235.
26. Wasserstrom, 110.
27. *Collected Poetry*, 109.

imaginative power of the sun in March, this bright spirit of the former self appears to "Make me conceive how dark I have become." Can the poet bear to assume his imaginative identity and visionary powers of illumination once again? Seemingly out of nowhere, Stevens cries out in the last couplet of the poem, and this is his cry: "Oh! Rabbi, rabbi, fend my soul for me / And true savant of this dark nature be."[28]

Here, Stevens reaches toward the rabbi, the idealized scholar/poet and a projection of the self he wishes to become once again. Harold Bloom usefully comments on the word "fend," meaning "both to ward off and to shift or venture, and both meanings work here."[29] The rabbi as Stevens' ego ideal inspires the poet to venture forth into the realm of the imagination again, while at the same time defending him from the dark, the mundane reality which has kept the poet blocked within himself, a self which has gone dark too. Poetry, for Stevens, is *illumination* ("A poem is a meteor," he tells us) and as a savant of the poet's dark nature, the rabbi will bring his scholarship to bear and, in effect, teach Stevens what he needs in order to write poetry once more.[30]

It was not always thus. If we look back to the first appearance of the rabbi in Stevens' work, in "Le Monocle de Mon Oncle," we see how much bravura goes into this figure. This substantial poem – one hundred thirty-two lines, divided into twelve eleven-line stanzas – is generally understood to be a poem of mid-life crisis. Stevens is close to forty when he writes it, and it is a poem that deals at length with love, sex, and poetic inspiration. Its extravagant language and lofty rhetoric often dazzle, and it is replete with images of erotic intensity drawn from both nature and art. Addressed, with little kindness, to a muse or lover ("And so I mocked her in magnificent measure"), the poem is also severely if humorously self-critical ("Or was it that I mocked myself alone?"), noting that "When amorists grow bald, then amours shrink / Into the compass and curriculum / Of introspective exiles, lecturing."[31] Vacillating between tropes of self-denigration and self-excitement, Stevens tells us that "Like

28. Ibid., 108–9.
29. *Wallace Stevens*, 89.
30. *Opus Posthumous*, 185.
31. *Collected Poetry*, 10, 12.

a dull scholar, I behold, in love, / An ancient aspect touching a new mind": erotic desire continually renews itself, but where does that leave the middle-aged poet?

> In verses wild with motion, full of din,
> Loudened by cries, by clashes, quick and sure
> As the deadly thought of men accomplishing
> Their curious fates in war, come, celebrate
> The faith of forty, ward of Cupido.
> Most venerable heart, the lustiest conceit
> Is not too lusty for your broadening.
> I quiz all sounds, all thoughts, all everything
> For the music and manner of the paladins
> To make oblation fit. Where shall I find
> Bravura adequate to this great hymn?[32]

With "verses wild," the poet at forty tries to celebrate himself as a "ward of Cupido," and find "Bravura adequate to this great hymn" – perhaps the poem itself, but just as likely, the poems he hopes are still to come. Sex, however, is insufficient for inspiration: "If sex were all, then every trembling hand / Could make us squeak, like dolls, the wished for words."[33] The poet resolves his dilemma as best he can, asserting at last that he is no "dull scholar" but rather a rabbi capable of negotiating the binarisms of creativity and exhaustion that he has posed for himself throughout the poem:

> A blue pigeon it is, that circles the blue sky,
> On side-long wing, around and round and round.
> A white pigeon it is, that flutters to the ground,
> Grown tired of flight. Like a dark rabbi, I
> Observed, when young, the nature of mankind,
> In lordly study. Every day, I found
> Man proved a gobbet in my mincing world.
> Like a rose rabbi, later, I pursued,

32. Ibid., 13.
33. Ibid., 14.

And still pursue, the origin and course
Of love, but until now I never knew
That fluttering things have so distinct a shade.[34]

I find it curious that Stevens tells us that he *was* "like a dark rabbi" who "Observed, when young, the nature of mankind / In lordly study," when it seems that this would be the stance of an older poet. I would assume that the younger poet would be like the "rose rabbi" who pursues "the origin and course / Of love." Stevens, however, claims still to be like the rose rabbi, still pursuing knowledge of love, but his similarity to the dark rabbi has dropped away. "Man proved a gobbet in my mincing world": a gobbet is a piece of meat (which may get caught in one's throat), and to mince, in this instance, is to cut up finely. So in Stevens' world, the scholarly analysis, the necessary study or "mincing" of humanity, is superseded by the study of love, which may indeed be the origin and course of life. The blue pigeon remains in the blue sky, the white pigeon flutters to the ground: life and love are a great circle encompassing both imaginative flight and exhausting ground. This is what the rabbi always recalls.

It is because of this knowledge, dialectical and boldly investigatory, that the rabbi appears in Stevens' late masterpiece, *The Auroras of Autumn*. This sublime meditation on fate, death, and the origins of human life and human creativity, has as its great symbol a vision of the aurora borealis, what Stevens names "the serpent," "the bodiless," "form gulping after formlessness." The serpent is a transcendental entity almost beyond human imagining, "the master of the maze / Of body and air and forms and images, / Relentlessly in possession of happiness" – happiness that humanity can rarely experience, and only in moments of metaphysical insight, when such happiness is closely akin to the terror of the sublime.[35] As Stevens works his way through the ten sections of the poem, each consisting of eight tightly composed tercets, he reviews the origins of human life, meditating on the security of home, the mother as muse ("She makes that gentler that can gentle be"), and the father as stern

34. Ibid.
35. Ibid., 355.

but imaginative mage, a kind of Prospero who "fetches pageants out of air."[36] Yet these parental tropes unmake themselves, leaving the poet to face a more awe-inspiring and daemonic power:

> Is there an imagination that sits enthroned
> As grim as it is benevolent, the just
> And the unjust, which in the midst of summer stops
>
> To imagine winter? When the leaves are dead,
> Does it take its place in the north and enfold itself,
> Goat-leaper, crystalled and luminous, sitting
>
> In highest night? And do these heavens adorn
> And proclaim it, the white creator of black, jetted
> By extinguishings, even of planets as may be,
>
> Even of earth, even of sight, in snow,
> Except as needed by way of majesty,
> In the sky, as crown and diamond cabala.
>
> It leaps through us, through all our heavens leaps,
> Extinguishing our planets, one by one,
> Leaving, of where we were and looked, of where
>
> We knew each other and of each other thought,
> A shivering residue, chilled and foregone,
> Except for that crown and mystical cabala.
>
> But it dare not leap by chance in its own dark.
> It must change from destiny to slight caprice.
> And thus its jetted tragedy, its stele
>
> And shape and mournful making move to find
> What must unmake it and, at last, what can,
> Say, a flippant communication under the moon.[37]

36. Ibid., 356, 358.
37. Ibid., 360.

To be sure, the divine imagination, or imagination as divinity, has a distinctly kabbalistic quality in these lines.[38] More specifically, it is a vision of the imagination as emanation. The serpentine northern lights are an inhuman force of fate or destiny, just and unjust, projecting or jetting itself outward in acts of uncanny creativity. Like God writing the Torah in letters of black fire upon white fire, this force creates through cosmic "extinguishings"; being and nothingness are the materials of its scripture; hence its "majesty / In the sky, as crown and diamond cabala."[39] At the highest point in the kabbalistic tree of the sefirot, just below the utterly inscrutable Ain Sof (Without End), is the first emanation, Keter (Crown), associated with the force of Divine Will. In Stevens' poem, "It leaps through us," and in doing so, empties us, "Extinguishing our planets," leaving us as "shivering residue," empty shells (what the Kabbalists call the kelipot), "Except for that crown and mystical cabala." We are, in other words, the ruined remains of a failed, lifeless creation, unless we are animated by the imagination. Yet this breaking of the vessels, as the Kabbalists would put it, can itself be unmade by "a flippant communication under the moon": in the face of cosmic catastrophe, we answer the divine imagination with a poem of our own, and that may suffice.

This is why the poem, as it moves toward its conclusion, inclines toward "a time of innocence" that is "Like a book at evening beautiful but untrue, / Like a book on rising beautiful and true." After witnessing the auroras, the power of our own imagination is renewed in our innocence, which means both free of guile and without knowledge, so that what we write is both true and untrue, "in the idiom of an innocent earth."[40] When the rabbi appears in the last section of the poem, he is

38. Cf. Stevens' even later poem, "Final Soliloquy of the Interior Paramour," in which he simply states, "We say God and the imagination are one..." Ibid., 444.
39. The image of the Torah written in letters of black fire upon white fire appears in various traditional Jewish texts, including Midrash and the Zohar. Gershom Scholem notes that in its esoteric interpretation, "the white fire is the Written Torah in which the letters are not yet formed; only by means of the black fire, which is the Oral Torah, do the letters acquire form." *Messianic Idea*, 295. Stevens also echoes Psalm 19:1, "The heavens proclaim the glory of God," in his lines "And do these heavens adorn / and proclaim it..."
40. *Collected Poetry*, 361.

called upon to explain our imaginative condition, which, as the poet has it, is that of "An unhappy people in a happy world – / Read, rabbi, the phases of this difference." "Now, solemnize the secretive syllables," asks the poet of the rabbi; "Read to the congregation, for today / And for tomorrow, this extremity, / This contrivance of the spectre of the spheres…"[41] I take this "contrivance" to be the auroras, the vision of the sefirot to which he has previously referred, but most of all to the poem itself, ruled by the ego ideal, a figure of imaginative power, "The vital, never-failing genius, / Fulfilling his meditations, great and small."[42] Poet, rabbi, and poetic genius have merged here; this figure both writes and reads the meditation that is *The Auroras of Autumn*, a vision of the sublime that both terrifies and empowers, providing the "congregation" of readers what it always needs and always desires.

The last appearance of the rabbi in Stevens' work is section v of "Things of August," another sequence of lyrics from *The Auroras of Autumn*:

> We'll give the week-end to wisdom, to Weisheit, the rabbi,
> Lucidity of his city, joy of his nation,
> The state of circumstance.
>
> The thinker as reader reads what has been written
> He wears the words he reads to look upon
> Within his being,
>
> A crown within him of crispest diamonds
> A reddened garment falling to his feet,
> A hand of light to turn the page,
>
> A finger with a ring to guide his eye
> From line to line, as we lie on the grass and listen
> To that which has no speech,
>
> The voluble intentions of the symbols,
> The ghostly celebrations of the picnic,
> The secretions of insight.[43]

41. Ibid., 362–63.
42. Ibid., 363.
43. Ibid., 419–20.

It is difficult to read this as anything other than the summation of what we may call Stevens' rabbinic romance. Here, the rabbi is equated to wisdom, to *Weisheit*, "Lucidity of his city, joy of his nation." He is the embodiment of reading as writing, writing as reading, a noble thinker who now internalizes the crown "of crispest diamonds" which in *The Auroras of Autumn* was seen, at least until the end of the poem, as an externalized force of creative will.[44] Once again we see, in the "hand of light to turn the page," that poetry is illumination; once again we enter the presence of an ideal poem, "that which has no speech," but is rather "The voluble intentions of the symbols."[45] The reading to the congregation becomes a picnic (whenever we find ourselves on the grass, Stevens is communing with Whitman, his great precursor), and what we hear are "secretions of insight" – not only in the sense of releasing a substance, but of separating, keeping something apart, hiding it away except to those who are initiated or privy to the truth. Poetry is a life-long initiation into the secret wisdom of things, of reality, of the "state of circumstance." Whatever that circumstance may be, we may turn to the rabbi for his insight.[46]

44. Charles Berger offers a more specifically historical and sociological reading of Weisheit, post-Holocaust, that complements my own. Berger observes that "to use the German name for wisdom and then to mark that German as Jewish is to construct a profound equation between wisdom, exile, and survival in 1949 and, perhaps, perpetually. ... His German name signals the possibility that he is a refugee; since he is first identified as 'wisdom', we can accept as well the hint that, beyond the political sphere, this figure bodies forth the palpable image of wisdom-in-exile. ... Weisheit is in possession of his place wherever he is placed, partly because wisdom is at home everywhere and nowhere, partly because his ethno-religiosity has trained him to survive the cataclysm of exile, and partly because there is room for him in the American city of Hartford, room to picnic in peace among others for whom his marked alterity, at their best moments, raises no fears, but encourages thought to move in the direction of lucidity and joy, for at least as long as the still season of August lasts." Charles Berger, "Reading the Alien in American Scenes: Henry James and Wallace Stevens," *The Wallace Stevens Journal* 34, no. 1 (Spring 2010): 34–35.

45. Cf. another of Stevens' *Adagia*: "Every poem is a poem within a poem: the poem of the idea within the poem of the words." *Opus Posthumous*, 199.

46. A comparable poem of even greater power, centered on the figure of the poet as reader, is "Large Red Man Reading," ibid., 365. For my kabbalistic (or "Scholemesque")

Robert Duncan's Universal Kabbalah

Like Wallace Stevens, Robert Duncan associates "rabbis" with the search for wisdom. Stevens' rabbis are figures, tropes, part of a great set of symbols deployed in his career-long working through of the relationship of belief and imagination. Duncan, on the other hand, is a poet for whom Judaism, especially Jewish mysticism, is fundamental to his conception of the poetic vocation and to the act of writing poetry: "It seemed to me that in mystical traditions of Judaism, religion was passing into imagination."[47] For Stevens, rabbis symbolize those who seek wisdom, whereas for Duncan, rabbis are actual teachers whom one may read and study in order to gain the wisdom one seeks.

Adopted as an infant into a family of Theosophists, Duncan spent his childhood listening to his elders conducting séances after he had been put to bed. Upon hearing Eugene Field's children's poem "Wynken, Blynken, and Nod," he associated its imagery with the belief he was taught that his "soul . . . went out to the stars or to other worlds."[48] Deeply immersed in the work of Madame Blavatsky and other Theosophical writers, Duncan's grandmother "was an elder in a provincial expression of this Hermetic movement, far from its center in London."[49] Her goal, like that of other initiates in this order, was occult wisdom; they claimed Hermes as their teacher, which "meant the same as a god." As Duncan tells us, "the real image of the god was the picture Grandmother showed me in *The Book of the Dead*. In Egypt was the hidden meaning of things, not only of Greek things but of Hebrew things. The wand of Hermes was the rod of Moses, and my grandmother studied hieroglyphics as she studied Hebrew letters and searched in dictionaries for the meaning of Greek roots, to come into the primal knowledge of the universe that had

consideration of the poem, see *The Ritual of New Creation*, 58–61. This passage also includes my preliminary thoughts on rabbis in Stevens, which I have elaborated here.

47. Robert Duncan, "Realms of Being," interview with Rodger Kamenetz, in *A Poet's Mind: Collected Interviews with Robert Duncan, 1969–1985*, ed. Christopher Wagstaff (Berkeley, CA: North Atlantic Books, 2012), 394.

48. Robert Duncan, *The H.D. Book*, ed. Michael Boughn and Victor Coleman (Berkeley: University of California Press, 2011), 124.

49. Ibid., 145.

been lost in the diversity of mankind."[50] When his family moved from the Bay Area to Bakersfield in 1928, Duncan recounts that "My parents, living far from the center of things, were concerned now with security and status, the politics and business opportunities of Bakersfield. Our religion became something we did not talk about to everybody. I talked to myself about it."[51]

Although Duncan goes beyond the Theosophical beliefs of his family, incorporating not only hermetic and occult thought, but Freudian psychoanalysis (which he sees as the continuation of kabbalistic hermeneutics), anthropology, linguistics, and even genetics into his poetic theorizing, he holds to that one goal of his grandmother – "to come into the primal knowledge of the universe that had been lost in the diversity of mankind." That diversity is cultural and linguistic: all peoples, all languages, share in this knowledge, which, according to gnostic and kabbalistic myth, is now fallen and scattered, like the body of the primal Adam itself. Poetry, understood in very broad terms, becomes the means to achieve that primal knowledge, as well as its enactment. The study of Kabbalah, as one part of that body of primal knowledge, proves essential to Duncan's quest. Throughout his extensive critical prose, Duncan makes frequent reference to kabbalistic texts, especially the *Zohar*, but also to *The Tree of Life* of Hayyim Vital and *Sefer Yetzirah*. Additionally, he studies modern scholars of Jewish mysticism, such as Gershom Scholem and R.J. Zvi Werblowsky. But Duncan does not study Jewish mysticism for its own sake. Not only is Kabbalah a part of this universal body of ancient wisdom – which, given its hermetic nature, can be regarded as *gnosis* – but it is an active mode of poetry, engaged in a process of *poesis*, or creative making.[52] In this respect, for Duncan,

---

50. Ibid., 126. "Occult Matters," Chapter 5 of *The H.D. Book*, from which this and the two previous quotations are drawn, is Duncan's most complete discussion of his Theosophical upbringing.

51. Ibid, 148. Duncan also describes his family's beliefs in "The Truth and Life of Myth," in his *Collected Essays*, 142–43. For a biographical account of Duncan's early years, including his family's Theosophical beliefs and practices, see Lisa Jarnot, *Robert Duncan: The Ambassador from Venus* (Berkeley: University of California Press, 2012), 3–39.

52. The influence of Gnosticism on Duncan's poetics (apart from the influence that

Kabbalah, especially the language magic of "practical Kabbalah," is an important model of poetic language – which is in itself magical. As Burton Hatlen explains, "Versed in the lore of Judaism and Christianity and Buddhism and Theosophy, Duncan never became a believer in any of these religions. Rather he cultivated *writing itself* as a magical act... a systematic procedure for drawing together opposing forces, with the goal of healing and renewing both the self and the world."[53]

Duncan's Kabbalah, therefore, is to be understood as part of a universal, cross-cultural set of beliefs and practices which together constitute, as he puts it in "Rites of Participation" (one of the most influential chapters of *The H.D. Book*), "the coming of all men into one fate." Thinking of the kabbalistic trope of Adam Kadmon, Duncan declares that "Our secret Adam is written in the script of the primal cell."[54] To gather together "a symposium of the whole, such a totality, all the old excluded orders must be included." These excluded orders, such as the "female, the lumpen-proletariat, the foreign" also include the Jew, not only given the importance Duncan places on esoteric Jewish wisdom, but also his consideration of the long history of Western antisemitism, culminating in the Holocaust.[55] Jewish culture and learning as an excluded order

Gnosticism has on Kabbalah) is fully documented and examined in Peter O'Leary, *Gnostic Contagion: Robert Duncan and the Poetry of Illness* (Middletown, CT: Wesleyan University Press, 2002). See also my chapter on Duncan in *On Mount Vision*.

53. Burton Hatlen, "Duncan's Marriage of Heaven and Hell: Kabbalah and Rime in *Roots and Branches*," in *World, Self, Poem: Essays on Contemporary Poetry from the "Jubilation of Poets,"* ed. Leonard M. Trawick (Kent, OH: Kent State University Press, 1990), 208–9.

54. *The H.D. Book*, 153. The mystical concept of the cosmic Adam permeates Duncan's poetry. As he notes in the interview with Rodger Kamenetz, "Through the mysticism in Scholem, I was also very fascinated, right away, with the giant figure of Adam... There was an Adam before there was an Adam, and so forth..." "Realms of Being," 394.

55. Ibid., 154. It is worth noting that Duncan's interest in Jewish mysticism and his sympathy with Jewish culture as one of the "excluded orders" leads to his encouraging Jerome Rothenberg to explore his Jewish roots as part of his comprehensive development of ethnopoetics. This results in Rothenberg's crucial anthology, *A Big Jewish Book* (*Exiled in the Word*). As Rothenberg notes in the Pre-Face, "And the Jew too [is] among the 'old excluded orders'... a primal people, then, as an instance of those cultures of the old worlds..." *Exiled in the Word: Poems & Other Visions of the*

requires inclusion and intense study. Kabbalistic lore and ritual serve as an important instance of Duncan's "Rites of Participation": one of the first extended examples he gives in that chapter is taken from the *Zohar*, specifically the myth of the Hebrew letters, which appear before God prior to Creation and, in effect, compete for the honor of being the first in the alphabet, since, in kabbalistic tradition, God speaks (or writes) the world into being. The modesty of the *Aleph* (which cannot be sounded orally) leads to God rewarding it, as He proclaims "My unity shall not be expressed except through thee, on thee shall be based all calculations and operations of the world, and unity shall not be expressed save by the letter *Aleph*."[56] Duncan then comments that "In this primal scene, before the beginning of the world that is also here before the beginning of a writing, the Self contemplates and toys in a rite of play until the letters present themselves and speak."[57] Some pages later, Duncan quotes Scholem from *Major Trends In Jewish Mysticism*: "The world of the Sefiroth is the hidden world of language … the world of divine names."[58] The initiate, mystic, or poet, seeks this hidden world, and in gaining knowledge of the divine names, writes the esoteric text or hermetic poem.

Jews from Tribal Times to Present, ed. Jerome Rothenberg and Harris Lenowitz (Port Townsend, WA: Copper Canyon Press, 1989), 4. Another of Rothenberg's anthologies, *The Symposium of the Whole* (1983), takes its title from Duncan's phrase in *The H.D. Book*. For more on Duncan and Rothenberg, see Stephen Fredman, "Symposium of the Whole: Jerome Rothenberg and the Dream of 'A Poetry of All Poetries,'" in *Reading Duncan Reading: Robert Duncan and the Poetics of Derivation*, ed. Stephen Collis and Graham Lyons (Iowa City: University of Iowa Press, 2012), 151–71.

56. *The H.D. Book*, 158–59. Duncan owned a copy of the five-volume first edition of the Soncino Press *Zohar* (1931–1934), translated by Harry Sperling and Maurice Simon; in this instance, the passages he quotes come from the Prologue, Volume 1 (Bereshith), 2b–3a. The importance of this edition to Duncan's identity can be judged from Jess's portrait of Duncan, *The Enamord Mage: Translation #6*. In this heavily impastoed oil painting, the five books of the Soncino *Zohar* are positioned prominently in the right foreground, along with G.R.S. Mead's *Thrice Greatest Hermes* (1906) and Mead's edition of the Gnostic *Pistis Sophia*. Very thick daubs of paint are applied to four of the five volumes, as if to indicate the spiritual weight or perhaps the archaic, magical power of the text.

57. Ibid., 159.

58. Ibid., 164.

Duncan's study of kabbalistic language mysticism is complemented by his attempts to understand Jewish culture as a product of diaspora. Here, the mediating figure is that of the Shekhinah. Again, from the "Rites of Participation" chapter: "The esoteric tradition of Jewish mysticism again had its intensity in the loss of the home-land and in the long wandering in exile as children of a spirit-Mother, the Shekinah. She was the Glory, but She was also the Queen or Mother or Lady, and She might appear, as She does in *The Zohar*, as a great bird under whose celestial wings the immortal spirit-children of Israel nestled."[59] Duncan may sound unusually syncretic here, drawing on both pagan and Christian spirituality, but in fact, his emphasis on the Shekhinah as a separate divine entity as much as an emanation of the Godhead is entirely valid. As Scholem notes in *Major Trends*, in the *Zohar*, the Shekhinah is "identified with the 'Community of Israel', a sort of Invisible Church, representing the mystical idea of Israel in its bond with God and in its bliss, but also in its suffering and its exile. She is not only Queen, daughter and bride of God, but also the mother of every individual in Israel... In the symbolic world of the Zohar, this new conception of the Shekhinah as the symbol of 'eternal womanhood' occupies a place of immense importance and appears under an endless variety of names and images."[60] As a number of commentators on Jewish American poetry argue, the Shekhinah functions as a crucial muse figure, and as we observed with Eric Murphy Selinger at the beginning of this chapter, one of the most revealing and ironic folds in the history of that poetry is the role Duncan plays in leading his Jewish colleagues to come to terms with their Jewish roots, including a recognition of the Shekhinah's imaginative potential, especially in portraying a diasporic condition.[61]

59. Ibid., 174.

60. Gershom G. Scholem, *Major Trends in Jewish Mysticism* (New York: Schocken Books, 1961), 230.

61. For Allen Grossman in "Jewish Poetry Considered as a Theophoric Project," "The Jewish poet who invokes the Shechinah has an obligation to construct the place where 'Light and Law are manifest', to which the nations may come because it is where they are." *Long School Room*, 166. For Maeera Y. Shreiber, who, like Selinger, surveys a range of poets who invoke the Shekhinah, she "signifies a poetics that is about a culture in flux, under negotiation." *Singing in a Strange Land*, 28.

But Duncan considers the Jewish diaspora historically and mystically in contexts apart from the Shekhinah as well, and it is here that his vision of what I am calling a universal Kabbalah becomes somewhat problematic. Duncan is very much the philosemite, with all the ambivalence that this term implies. As recent scholarship indicates, the phenomenon of philosemitism is extremely complicated, with a history that extends back to antiquity. Jonathan Karp and Adam Sutcliffe point out that philosemitism has frequently been seen as "sharing with antisemitism a trafficking in distorted, exaggerated, and exceptionalist views of Jews and Judaism."[62] Be that as it may, Jews have also been genuinely idealized "for such imputed virtues as their superior intelligence, economic acumen, ethnic loyalty, cultural cohesion, or familial commitment."[63] Given Duncan's Theosophical upbringing, we should note that one strand of philosemitism is that of the "mystically inclined ecumenicists" of the sixteenth and seventeenth centuries, who considered "the Jewish mystical tradition as the key to uncontaminated and universal philosophical truth."[64]

Although the origin of Duncan's fascination with Jews and Judaism lies in the Theosophy of his family, it was compounded by his college friendship with a young Jewish woman, Cecily Kramer, and by his sensitivity to antisemitism as a gay man – a member of another persecuted minority. Duncan self-consciously describes Cecily Kramer, called "Athalie" in *The H.D. Book*, as a "Jewess," "for she impersonated a racial elegance, knowingly referring to old ideas of beauty from the Middle East, Levantine or Persian hints that had a mock seductiveness, exciting

62. Jonathan Karp and Adam Sutcliffe, "Introduction: A Brief History of Philosemitism," in *Philosemitism in History*, ed. Jonathan Karp and Adam Sutcliffe (Cambridge, UK: Cambridge University Press, 2011), 1.

63. Ibid., 2.

64. Ibid., 11. See also Julian Levinson, "Connoisseurs of Angst: The Jewish Mystique and Postwar American Literary Culture," in Karp and Sutcliffe, 235–256. This essay focuses on references to Jews and Judaism in the work of three "Confessional" poets contemporary with Duncan: Robert Lowell, Sylvia Plath, and John Berryman. While none of these poets had any particular awareness of Jewish mysticism, their interest in and specific appropriations of Jewish culture and history reveal a good deal about the receptivity of non-Jewish American poets to Jewish influences in the late fifties and early sixties, which is when Duncan's engagement with Kabbalah was at its height.

our sense of the exotic and taunting us in that sense. At the same time she had a bitter knowledge of what to be Jewish meant – it gave reality to her despair."[65] Kramer, along with the Italian-American Lillian Fabilli ("Lili" in *The H.D. Book*), was part of a group of young women who supported and mentored Duncan during his early days at Berkeley, despite some tension around Duncan's homosexuality.[66]

As his poetic vision of a "symposium of the whole" gradually comes into focus, Duncan, despite his genuine admiration for Jewish culture and belief, grows increasingly troubled by what he perceives to be Jewish exclusivism or tribalism, and he returns to the issue frequently in his prose and interviews. What Duncan calls "The Truth and Life of Myth" is to be found in religion, but this poetic or imaginative essence in effect must be refined and separated from normative religion, especially restrictive religious law. What Duncan "believes in," therefore, is poetry: as I write in *On Mount Vision*, "He is a *religious* poet: for him, poetry is a religion and the prophetic poet inherits from the religious and philosophical traditions of the past all that is necessary to bring spiritual insight or *gnosis* (which includes a renewed understanding of the social and political conditions of history and of one's own time) to his readers."[67] It is from this position that Duncan criticizes Judaism: "And all mankind share the oldest gods as they share the oldest identities of the germinal cell. This share is so real that even the most racial tribalism – the ethnocentric laws of Ezra – cannot render the Jews other than or more than men … The Gods men know are realizations of God.

65. *The H.D. Book*, 59–60. Presumably this "bitter knowledge" refers to Kramer's own experience of antisemitism.

66. See Jarnot, 47–54. As for Duncan's awareness of antisemitism, in his groundbreaking early essay "The Homosexual in Society," the figures of the Jew as victim of antisemitism and of the African-American as a victim of racism, both struggling for human rights, are explicitly compared to the situation of the homosexual and the need for gay liberation. See "The Homosexual in Society" in *Collected Essays and Other Prose*, 5–18. Additionally, the antisemitism of Ezra Pound, whom Duncan regarded as a crucial poetic influence, appalled him, and like other poets of his generation, Duncan wrestled frequently with the contradictions of this great poet succumbing to such a vicious ideology.

67. *On Mount Vision*, 28.

But what I speak of here in the terms of a theology is a poetics."[68] This attitude does not only apply to Judaism; in the Notes toward Book 3 of *The H.D. Book*, Duncan asserts that "It is part of the sad story of monotheism that where it first forbade worship of other gods it divorced its people from the communion of the human spirit... For the Jews, and after them, for the Christians and the Moslems, all that was not lawful and in the book was error and falsehood."[69]

As Duncan admits to Rodger Kamenetz, "it's no wonder that the Jew fascinates me." In order to "drive deep... in an art, you do a series of things that are the same [*as the Jews*]. You divide yourself off from others because you cease to read in a tolerant way. My readings in poetry are exceedingly fanatical. If I put on a tolerant mood, that's because I cease to wrestle with what I'm reading..."[70] Duncan makes this statement in a discussion of his poems "The Law I Love Is Major Mover" and "The Structure of Rime I." In both these poems, Duncan invokes the story of Jacob wrestling with the Angel, "*like a man reading a strong sentence.*"[71] For Duncan, the biblical Scene of Naming is also, metaphorically, a Scene of Reading: "Look! the Angel that made a man of Jacob / made Israël in His embrace / was the Law, was Syntax."[72] It would seem that the passionate, even "fanatical" nature of Jewish reading inspires Duncan, though it may also provoke a certain anxiety. Can he devote himself to the text – reading and writing – with the same religious intensity?

Duncan broods upon these matters throughout his entire career; indeed, the very last essay he writes, "The Delirium of Meaning," on the Egyptian-French-Jewish poet Edmond Jabès, is a full-blown consideration of Jewish identity, poetry, exile, and hermeneutical practices both mystical and otherwise. Forced to leave Egypt along with the rest of the Jewish community in 1956, Jabès moved to Paris and published the first volume of his groundbreaking work *The Book of Questions* in

---

68. *Collected Essays*, 154.
69. *The H.D. Book*, 641–42.
70. "Realms of Being," 405. Brackets in the original.
71. Robert Duncan, *The Collected Later Poems and Plays*, ed. Peter Quartermain (Berkeley: University of California Press, 2014), 8.
72. Ibid., 7. For more on Duncan's vision of Jacob and the Angel, see my essay "Robert Duncan, Poet of the Law," *Sagetrieb* 2, no. 1 (Spring 1983), 82.

French in 1963 (his work began to appear in English in 1976, translated by Rosemarie Waldrop). Duncan first met Jabès in 1979. His piece appeared in a collection of essays on Jabès, as the afterword to a selection of Jabès' poetry in English, and as the last piece in the *Selected Prose*, and I think this publication history indicates the degree of importance Duncan placed on it. For Duncan, the poetry of Jabès represents "an ancient allegiance of Poetry, even as it is an ancient devotional hermeneutics. Each world in Creation seeks to tell us of other worlds or is itself a sign of other worlds; and only as we read do we live." Yet even in his opening paragraph, while using this kabbalistic mode of discourse, Duncan still expresses self-doubt: *The Book of Questions* "reaches still to resonances both of French language and of Jewish soul in my own imagination of my deep self – who am neither French nor Jewish."[73] Nevertheless, in his encounter with Jabès, "I take this French to be my 'Hebrew', as my temenos and dwelling in language."[74] In other words, Duncan regards his encounter with this writing as a sacred act and a mystical communion.

Duncan's tendency, in reading Jabès, is again, insistently, a universalizing one, and he poses the question of Jewish exclusivity directly. Meditating on the tragedy of Yukel and Sarah (the Jewish couple separated in the concentration camps) in *The Book of Questions*, Duncan states that the poem becomes their "Song of Songs... of the utter humanity of being Jewish for us who are not Jewish." He then asks "Why is this Jewishness – that for many Jews is a racism – somehow in its covenant, in its dwelling apart, so the ground essential to the discovery of our own selves in our apartness? Is it that the Jews have taken the full burden, the extremity, of an apartness at the root of Life itself?"[75] Why indeed? Duncan answers his own question: in recognizing Jewish "apartness," we recognize human apartness; in recognizing Jewish reading and writing, the mystery of what Jabès repeatedly calls "the Book," we recognize a poetics and a hermeneutics that are part of the heritage of the entire human collective; and in recognizing Jabès' personal loss of Jewish Cairo and his embrace of "his Jewish universe in the universe of the French

73. *Collected Essays*, 416.
74. Ibid., 425.
75. Ibid., 430.

language," we discover that "This 'Jewishness' is the need for a new universal consciousness/conscience."[76] This is why, in the course of the essay, Duncan invokes Moses de Leon (purported author of the *Zohar*), Ferdinand de Saussure (founder of structural linguistics) and Freud. Each of these figures, like Jabès himself, is an exponent of unbounded signifying practices – the mystical language of the Godhead, the arbitrary relation of signifier to signified, the rebus of the dream's manifest content – all waiting to be deciphered. Like the many imaginary rabbis in *The Book of Questions* who offer an endless sequence of enigmatic statements about Jews, exile, writing and the Book, de Leon, Saussure, Freud, and Jabès are all engaged in parallel processes of interpretation, resulting, to use Duncan's title, in a "delirium of meaning."

Duncan, drawing on Scholem's *Major Trends*, notes that for the Kabbalist Abraham Abulafia, "every language, not only Hebrew, is transformed into a transcendental medium of the one and only language of God." Naturally, this concept would appeal strongly to Duncan; as he reads it, "what we know as Hebrew belongs also, one among all the languages of Man, to the Diaspora of Tongues."[77] Thus, "all languages belong to the nature of *the* language of the Book of Creation, all correspond. The drama of the Jews then is 'ours', as the undergoing of all peoples is 'ours.'"[78] Duncan's fascination with the way in which Jabès Hebraizes the French language, finding "his Jewish universe in the universe of the French language," is thus related to this kabbalistic idea of a "Diaspora of Tongues," and in turn to the Jewish diaspora as representative of a diaspora of the human collective in its totality.[79] We are all in exile, and we all speak fallen versions of an ur-Hebrew, which "the Book," in whatever language it may be written, both memorializes and impossibly seeks to restore. For Duncan, a poetry which mourns that loss and seeks that impossible restoration will be infinitely enriched by entering into "the currents of a Jewish mysticism, in which the spiritual alchemies of absence and exile, the Book and the Shekinah, the hidden

76. Ibid., 427.
77. Ibid., 424.
78. Ibid., 430.
79. Ibid., 427.

Tzaddik and the mute letter" may effect "a great change," even as the *Zohar* did when it made its way not only in the Jewish world, but the Christian and Islamic worlds as well.[80] Such is the message Duncan takes from the Kabbalah.

In turning to the "spiritual alchemies" of a few of Duncan's poems, it worth noting how Jewish tropes appear and disappear, but always palpably influence the weaving of the text. In his essay on Duncan's *Roots and Branches*, Burton Hatlen observes that "only occasionally is Duncan's poetry about Kabbalistic doctrines. Rather than presenting 'ideas', these poems are themselves magical acts that seek to unite opposites and thereby redeem the world. Duncan's poetry seeks to achieve the goals sought by all Kabbalistic ritual."[81] Such being the case (as Hatlen's article demonstrates), then much of Duncan's poetry up through *Roots and Branches* may be understood as kabbalistically influenced, whether references to Jewish mysticism appear in the poetry or not.[82] Still, it makes sense to first consider "What Do I Know of the Old Lore," the second poem in *Roots and Branches*, and Duncan's most direct poetic engagement with Kabbalah. Here are its opening lines:

> A young editor wants me to write on Kabbalah for his
> magazine.
> What do I know of the left and the right, of the Shekinah, of
> the Metatron?

---

80. Ibid., 426.

81. Hatlen, 211. Hatlen then quotes Gershom Scholem's list of these goals from his essay "Tradition and New Creation in the Ritual of the Kabbalists." See *On the Kabbalah and Its Symbolism*, 130.

82. Hatlen's essay may be the single best piece on Duncan's Kabbalism, though given my own reading of Duncan's career, I would argue that Duncan's desire to write a magical, redemptive poetry of this sort comes to a head with *Roots and Branches* (1964). In his last three books (*Bending the Bow* [1968] and the two volumes of *Ground Work* [1984, 1987]), especially in the serial poem *Passages*, Duncan's poetry changes into what I describe as a gnostic "scripture" that departs radically from his earlier poetry of "cosmos" by ritualistically unmaking itself. See *On Mount Vision*, 27–31. The poems I will consider here are from *The Opening of the Field* (1960) and *Roots and Branches*, written when Duncan's redemptive understanding of Kabbalah is shaping his poetry to the greatest extent.

It is an old book lying on the velvet cloth, the color of olive
    under-leaf and plumstain in the velvet;
it is a romance of pain and relief from pain, tale told of the Lord
    of the Hour of Midnight,
the changing over that is a going down into Day from the
    Mountain.

Ah! the seed that lies in the sweetness of the Kabbalah
is the thought of those rabbis rejoicing in their common
    devotions,
of the thousand threads of their threnodies, praises, wisdoms,
    shared loves and curses interwoven.[83]

As critics have pointed out, Duncan contradictorily indicates that
he has little knowledge of the Kabbalah, yet presents himself as quite
conversant with some of its most important figures and concepts. This
is to say that he feels both *inside* and *outside* the Jewish world of "those
rabbis rejoicing in their common devotions." To study the Kabbalah
is to study esoteric wisdom, but Duncan is uncertain whether he can
present himself as an initiate, and given the "pain and relief from pain,"
is not even sure whether he desires this status. As for the rabbis them-
selves, "There are terrible things in the design they weave, fair and unfair
establisht in one. / How all righteousness is founded upon Jacob's cheat
upon cheat..." Here is that same ambivalence we have already observed
regarding Jewish exclusivity and secretiveness; and when Duncan con-
siders the special access that the rabbis have to mystical truth, he declares
"O, I know nothing of the left and right," of the good and evil that are in
constant tension in the kabbalistic worldview.[84]

    Duncan's ambivalence and vacillation when asked to write about
the Kabbalah (and, since it is a young editor who makes the request, to
consider that he may be regarded as an older authority on the subject)
results in a move that he makes in a number of his kabbalistic poems,
especially regarding the figure of the Shekhinah – he brings in a legend
from another culture, in order to create a sort of magical comparative

83. *Collected Later Poems*, 101.
84. Ibid., 102.

ethnography. Presumably thinking of the *Zohar* or another kabbalistic text, he writes, "It is an old book of stories, the Bible is an old book of stories / – a mirror made by goblins for that Ice Queen, the Shekinah – / a likelihood of our hearts withheld from healing."[85] Eric Murphy Selinger remarks that "Duncan's ease with the Shekhinah leads him to treat her as a half-forgotten, richly syncretic, quite ambivalent figure...a figure for the links between Jewish and non-Jewish spark and divinity...On the other hand, however, she remains in part a frigid 'Ice Queen', trapped in the Jewish failure to escape belief in itself as (in Duncan's words) 'the incomparable nation or race' and thus envision a true 'symposium of the whole.'"[86] The poem ends, however, with the poet more at peace with his kabbalistic vision: he imagines "El Eljon walking in the cool of His garden," and then situates the rabbis similarly:

> The Rabbis stop under the lemon tree
> rejoicing in the cool of its leaves
> which they say is the cool of the leaves of that Tree of Trees.
>
> Look, Rabbi Eleazer says,
> the Glory of the Shekinah shines from lettuces
> in the Name of that Garden![87]

Like the rabbis beneath the "Tree of Trees" (the Tree of Life, which is also the Tree of Emanations), Duncan partakes of "the Glory of the Shekinah," if not in the Garden itself, then in its Name, the word of his poem.

As readers of Duncan know, this is by no means the first time he invokes the Shekhinah. Her presence is felt strongly in *The Opening of the Field*, the volume before *Roots and Branches*, and the book which

85. Ibid.
86. Selinger, 256. The "Ice Queen" refers to Hans Christian Anderson's story by that name. As Selinger explains, "The Jewish sparks of holiness spilled at Creation's Breaking of the Vessels look just like the shards of the distorting mirror made (in Anderson) for the Ice Queen, which made everything look stunted and ugly and small – and it turns out that [in Duncan's poem] the uglifying goblin mirror is the normative Bible itself!" Ibid., 255.
87. *Collected Later Poems*, 102, 103.

may be said to inaugurate the major phase of Duncan's career. "Often I Am Permitted To Return To A Meadow," the first poem of *Opening*, is probably Duncan's most famous, a lyric that by now has a long history of commentary, centering on "the First Beloved," "the Lady," "She it is Queen Under the Hill."[88] This conflated figure of mother, muse, and regal Fairy Queen is only tangentially related to the Shekhinah, insofar as she is not really a trope representing exile and mourning, but rather an imperious authority who grants permission for the poet to enter the space of the poem, which is a place of great psychic risk.[89] Yet she is also a Queen "whose hosts are a disturbance of words within words / that is a field folded," and in this respect she may be related to the turbulence of kabbalistic language mysticism and to the magical process of writing intended to bring about cosmic restoration and an end to exile.[90] As Duncan writes in "The Maiden," she is "precedent to that Shekinah, She / in whom the Jew has his communion."[91] To an even greater extent than "What Do I Know of the Old Lore" or "Often I Am Permitted To Return To A Meadow," "The Maiden" also moves from a specifically kabbalistic reference to what amounts to a catalogue of allusions to female archetypes and images from Western culture, mythologies and works of art – from Dante, Shakespeare, and Wordsworth, to Edith Sitwell and Marianne Moore, to the painters Millais and Bonnard. Thus Duncan insistently folds his kabbalistic vision of the Jewish muse into a universal expression of "unquenchable longing."[92]

What happens when Duncan brings an actual Jew – a Jewish poet – into his kabbalistic romance? As in the case of Edmond Jabès, the result is both complicated and revealing. "After Reading *Barely and Widely*," the penultimate poem in *The Opening of the Field*, invokes the Jewish-American poet Louis Zukofsky, to whom Duncan was devoted for many years.[93] Duncan was reading Zukofsky as early as the thirties,

---

88. Ibid., 3.
89. The best reading of the poem, and of Duncan's "Atlantis Dream" which shaped so much of his poetry and sensibility, is O'Leary, 85–92.
90. *Collected Later Poems*, 3.
91. Ibid., 23.
92. Ibid.
93. My consideration of this poem owes a good deal to Zukofsky scholar Jeffrey

and worked hard to bring him to the attention of a wider audience. In 1958, he arranged for the older poet's six-week summer residency at San Francisco State College (Duncan was disappointed by Zukofsky's lack of enthusiasm for the work of the students and local poets). A limited edition of Zukofsky's collection *Barely and Widely* was produced by Zukofsky's wife Celia when the Zukofsky family returned home to New York City. As Jeffrey Twitchell-Waas observes, "at the time Duncan composed his poem, Zukofsky's revival in the larger public consciousness had barely begun...and few readers of *The Opening of the Field* would have had access to or even heard of *Barely and Widely*."[94]

"After Reading *Barely and Widely*" is a poem about "the double-play of the mind," about the duplicity of language, about the related psychoanalytic phenomenon of repression, and about the vagaries of cultural and racial identification – all having to do with "Good and bad jews [*sic*]," including Zukofsky.[95] Typical of Duncan's mature style, it has a collage-like structure and moves by way of association and repetition of ideas and sounds (what Duncan calls "rime"), including complicated patterns of allusions, puns, etymologies, and direct but not necessarily acknowledged quotation. It employs various registers of discourse, from rhapsodic lyricism to scholarly explication to ordinary conversation. Yet it rarely loses sight of its intentions, one of which is Duncan's exploration of certain aspects of Jewishness, as initially provoked by Zukofsky and his poetry.

The poem begins "will you give yourself airs / from that lute of Zukofsky?" and immediately answers itself: "Yes, for I would have my share / in the discretion I read from certain jews..."[96] Here, the image

---

Twitchell-Waas, "The Airs of Duncan and Zukofsky," in *Reading Duncan Reading*, 67–87. This essay presents a detailed history of the two poets' relationship, both in their literary responses to each other and in their personal encounters; it includes an expansive reading of Duncan's poem, whereas I will concentrate on its specifically Jewish dimension.

94. Twitchell-Waas, 69. For more on Zukofsky's residency and his impact on the Bay Area poetry community at that time, see Mark Scroggins, *The Poem of a Life: A Biography of Louis Zukofsky* (Berkeley, CA: Shoemaker & Hoard, 2007), 289–92.

95. *Collected Later Poems*, 80, 83.

96. Ibid., 80.

of the lute and the reference to "airs" presents the two poets as figures out of the Renaissance (one thinks of such poems as Wyatt's "My Lute, Awake!"), indicating a shared literary tradition. Twitchell-Waas notes "a range of other meanings for "airs": "atmosphere, aura, impression, personal manner, or even an affected pose that in some sense Duncan will activate."[97] The question that Duncan is posing, therefore, may have to do with the extent that he adopts elements of Zukofsky's style, which, though Duncan greatly admired it, was also in some important respects antithetical to Duncan's own.[98] As for "discretion," Twitchell-Waas sees it as a

> term chosen to characterize Zukofsky's work, suggesting discreet/ discrete, both careful distinctions and reserved manner, as well as fine judgment...It is Zukofsky's rigorous and nuanced formalism that Duncan admires, but there is also a sense of distance that Duncan will tend to read psychologically as implying a certain fear of intimacy. That Duncan associates this "discretion" with Zukofsky's Jewishness will manifest itself in the sense of the Jew as outsider, "standing apart"...Duncan here touches on a stereotype, particularly virulent in his youth, of the Jews as overintellectual, as infected and infecting a cerebralism that has fatally alienated Western culture from itself.[99]

How does this analysis relate to what we have established as Duncan's fascination with ancient, esoteric Jewish wisdom, as well as his tendency to fold Jewish mysticism into a multicultural hermetic tradition, in opposition to Jewish exclusivism? Obviously, Duncan is a serious reader of Zukofsky; he admires Zukofsky's skills, and despite some important differences, learns a good deal from Zukofsky and his Objectivist poetics (it bears mentioning that the styles of both poets share a common origin in the work of Ezra Pound). But Zukofsky also contributes to Duncan's

---

97. Twitchell-Waas, 70.
98. Twitchell-Waas provides a useful contrast: "Whereas Duncan advocates mythopoetics, esoteric knowledge, romanticism, extravagant poetic rhetoric, and an insistent dramatization of the poem within a cosmic framework, Zukofsky is this-worldly, rationalist, rigorous, and restrained and projects a deheroicized role of the poet." Ibid., 67.
99. Ibid., 71.

Jewish fantasy, which plays itself out not only in his extensive study of Kabbalah, but in a racialized construction of "the Jew," however philosemitic. Twitchell-Waas rightly argues that Duncan presents a stereotype of the overly intellectual Jew in "After Reading *Barely and Widely*," but I would argue that Duncan does more than touch on it. The "cerebralism" of the "discrete" Jew is a quality that Duncan both admires and suspects, as we see in the following lines:

> *Do not touch.*
> Forbear if you respect the man!
> He who writes a touching line dares over much.
>
> He does not observe
> the intimate boundaries of natural speech
> – then we in hearing must have reserve.[100]

Respecting and heeding this marginalized, daring but thoughtful figure (whom I take to be related to Zukofsky if not Zukofsky himself) requires forbearance: like Christ after the resurrection (*"Noli me tangere"*) he cannot be touched, which is to say he maintains his distance, both physically and psychically, even though he writes "touching" poetry. Duncan identifies with him, for each poet in his own way does not write in observance of "natural speech."[101] Prior to this passage, Duncan asso-

---

100. *Collected Later Poems*, 81.
101. Duncan may identify with him in terms of sexual orientation as well, since rumors have long circulated that Zukofsky was a closeted gay man, at least prior to his marriage to Celia Thaew in 1939. See Libbie Rifkin, *Career Moves: Olson, Creeley, Zukofsky, Berrigan, and the American Avant-Garde* (Madison: University of Wisconsin Press, 2000), 87–91; Nick Salvato, *Uncloseting Drama: American Modernism and Queer Performance* (New Haven, CT: Yale University Press, 2010), 60–98. Duncan's advocacy of Zukofsky (and the lingering question of Zukofsky's sexual orientation) culminated in the now famous episode at the memorial for Zukofsky at the San Francisco Art Institute on Dec. 8, 1978. Duncan and the language poet Barrett Watten were to comment on Zukofsky, but shortly after Watten began his remarks, Duncan interrupted him, protesting Watten's approach to Zukofsky and fiercely, even violently, defending his own perspective. This argument between older and younger avant-gardes over Zukofsky's legacy is seen as a defining moment in both the canonization of Zukofsky and in the history of Language poetry. See Scroggins, 462–65 and Salvato, 91–94. A recording of the event can be heard online at *Dispatches from the Poetry Wars*, https://www

ciates the "discrete" difference of Jewishness with the difference of (his own) "peculiar" homosexuality, "queer // crossd, athwart, fated, fey."[102] In doing so, he draws on the longstanding stereotype of the effeminate male Jew, which complements that of the overly intellectual Jew. All of these figures are Christ-like insofar as they may become sacrificial victims. To complicate matters further, Duncan also introduces another antisemitic stereotype, the sexually aggressive, threatening "Jewess": "There's that avid Jewess / combing in the familiar address "dearie" // a careless hostility and affection." This "old battleaxe" is a "hag grasping, without discretion" who wishes "in one gesture to destroy and to retain."[103] Doubleness multiplies: discretion and avidness; hostility and affection; effeminate and/or gay Jewish men and aggressively masculine but heterosexual Jewish women. Duncan obviously takes a good deal of risk here, and the reader is certainly entitled to ask whether he is manipulating these stereotypes or falling prey to them. But for Duncan, this "double-play of the mind" (and the body) is a necessary condition for writing poetry: "Poetry, that must *touch* the string / for music's service / is of violence and obedience a delicate balancing." Duncan would balance all these qualities, and this becomes quite explicit in the poem's final movement:

> Good and bad jews, gods
> and *bæddel* mixtures,
> dwarves then, twisty-sexd men, cobs
>
> that survive in spite of man's best nature…
> so Shylock pleads
> eyes, hands, organs, pain and hunger

.dispatchespoetrywars.com/videos/special-dispatch-recovering-a-suppressed-and -vital-document-of-post-war-american-poetry/.

102. Ibid., 80. Duncan's use of the term "fey," as in feminized but also as in the supernatural "fairy" and/or one who is magically "fated" to behave in certain ways or possess certain knowledge, is elaborated in *The H.D. Book*, 125–28. Duncan's Aunt Fay, his mother's sister, was one of his early instructors in the family's Theosophical religion.

103. Ibid., 81.

– common life. He laughs, he bleeds,
he turns both ways, he is a man.
He's a troll and shares only the human need!

Shrunken Jehovah, cunning Pan!
("Good People we calld them – another folk
that work underground)

Of such double-dealings I would talk.
Of these are turnd from hostile threads
the round around of a single rope.[104]

In this section of the poem (which continues for another twelve stanzas), Duncan both acknowledges "racial," sexual, and cultural difference, while simultaneously showing how these variously stereotypical, mythological "threads" are all part of "a single rope." As Twitchell-Waas explains, "Duncan quickly accumulates a series of manifestations of this repressed other: dwarves, trolls, Pan, fairies, occult and alchemical traditions, and Shylock as the outsider who pleads his commonness with his accusers. Again Duncan sets in motion etymological connections, since the Old English *bæddel*, meaning hermaphrodite (Hermes + Aphrodite) or 'effeminate', with implications of homosexuality, is the root of the modern 'bad.'"[105] For Duncan, the poet is "Thomas the Rimer, Solomon the Wise," bringing pagan and Jewish figures together; "day's // child and night's too; may be jew and gentile ... / The words of the song are *mercurial*." Mercury or Hermes, standing for alchemical transformation, ancient wisdom, and verbal trickery, brings together and manipulates opposites; he, more than any other archetype, serves as the poet's model. The poem ends with another powerful set of contrasts:

Hate and love may in a song be held
as if they were a scale ... How well the fairy

minstrel sings of life eternal within his hill,
or, in exile, the Rabbi seeking the word
recalls David singing unto Saul

104. Ibid., 83.
105. Twitchell-Waas, 74.

sang in full faith, and sends into the air we share
a tradition, a caution, a string of the lute
from division and union whereon

    this air.[106]

The fairy minstrel and the Rabbi recalling "David singing unto Saul" come from different traditions (do they also represent Duncan and Zukofsky?) but are held in a single musical scale, like hate and love and the other opposites Duncan has named throughout his poem. Duncan identifies with them both, for they are both crucial participants in his symposium of the whole. Here, division and union do indeed produce a moving air.

Joseph Donahue's Secret Jews

Joseph Donahue writes in a number of idioms. Certain of his books, such as *Incidental Eclipse* (2003) and *Red Flash in a Black Field* (2014) feature what could be described as an aggressively fractured, post-New York School heteroglossia that, at its most intense, drops us in an unlikely space between the mundane and the apocalyptic. Here is a passage from the uncanny sequence "A Servant of God Without a Head":

> Children in a dream
> collect fingernails in a sachet
> and tie them to the cathedral door.
> However, the book of Numbers tells us
> holy toys are carried across Sinai
> wrapped in dolphin skin. Only
> one caste can pack them.
> For the rest, to look is to die.
> Words are flies, they live a day.
> In the morning, under the streetlights
> along the block, their bodies
> will be a fine black dust.
> Here at the hospital,

106. Ibid., 84.

Manhattan Gnostic, we call
the nativity ward the doom room.
But death can be misleading.[107]

A good deal could be said about these outrageous lines, with their weird
mixture of transgressive humor and (Manhattan) Gnostic wisdom –
as if a volume of John Ashbery's poetry had been found among the
manuscripts of Nag Hammadi. For our purposes, it is sufficient to note
Donahue's Jewish references: the scandalous image of the Tabernacle
in Numbers as "holy toys...carried across Sinai / wrapped in dolphin
skin," and perhaps even more scandalous, the ephemerality of words
as flies, since it is in language, passed from one generation to the next,
that Jewish tradition endures. To say the least, Donahue's Hebraism in
a poem like this is deeply disquieting.

But Donahue's major opus, the serial poem *Terra Lucida*, works
somewhat differently. Taking its title from the "Earth of Light," the
spiritual paradise that appears in various iterations of Iranian mysti-
cism, the poem encompasses a range of discourses, including personal
memories, historical and current events, reworkings of myth and par-
able, midrashic commentary, ecstatic prophecy, exhortation, hymn,
psalm, and prayer.[108] Written exclusively in terse but flexible couplets,
it looks back both formally and thematically to H.D.'s *Trilogy*, which is
arguably the first long American serial poem to present itself as much as
scripture as epic. *Terra Lucida*'s engagement with the sacred – and with
sacred texts – is often quite direct. Again like *Trilogy*, along with other
works in that tradition, such as Robert Duncan's *Passages* and Nathaniel
Mackey's *Song of the Andoumboulou*, its particular relation to the sacred
is through quest and recovery. Peter O'Leary describes *Terra Lucida*

---

107. Joseph Donahue, *Red Flash on a Black Field* (New York: Black Square Editions,
2014), 56.
108. See Henry Corbin, *The Man of Light in Iranian Sufism*, trans. Nancy Pearson (New
Lebanon, NY: Omega Publications, 1994), 5, 11. Particularly relevant to poetic inspi-
ration, the *terra lucida*, according to Corbin, "is the very place where the meeting
occurs between the pilgrim and the one who gave birth to him...his Perfect Nature,
the personal Angel, who reveals to him the mystical hierarch of all those who go
before him in the supersenory heights." (23–24).

as "as an epic trance of hypnopompic mythos," that is, an elaborately arranged mythos, or plot, leading up out of dream into an awakened state of visionary rapture.[109] Donahue's deep and abiding interest in the mystical traditions of Judaism, Christianity, and Islam leads frequently to passages of rhapsodic lyricism, and part of the work's great strength lies in its intertwined, sometimes conflicted patterns of allusion – an overdetermined revelation or hierophany that is paradoxically hidden by an overabundance of truths.

In the first volume of *Terra Lucida*, this sense of revelation, this trembling of the veil, often arrives with a particularly Jewish inflection. Consider this passage from Section 11, *in this paradise*:

> The souls left in the Garden
> roam at every full moon.
>
> They bow before the towers of
> Jerusalem, bathe in that radiance.
>
> They return to the Garden, and go out.
> They fly at night and wail before
>
> the gates of the fallen cities.
> They see the bodies of those
>
> suffering in punishment.
> They push on, remembering
>
> The agony of all they see.
> They fly back to Eden.
>
> They tell the Holy One, who
> grieves, there, in the Hall of Illness:
>
> *The world is a hollow,*
> *a ghost of water in a ditch...*[110]

109. Peter O'Leary, "An Imaginal Homage to Joseph Donahue," *Jacket 2*, Dec. 17, 2014, https://jacket2.org/article/imaginal-homage-joseph-donahue. Drawing on the work of Henry Corbin, O'Leary focuses on Donahue's connections to mystical Islam.

110. Joseph Donahue, *Terra Lucida* (Jersey City, NJ: Talisman House, 2009), 39. So far,

The source of these lines is the *Zohar* (2:212a), which, we should recall, presents itself as an extended commentary on the Torah, but actually constitutes an immense body of Jewish theosophical thought. Gershom Scholem's definition of theosophy (to distinguish it from the more modern, formal "religion" in which Robert Duncan was raised) is relevant to what Donahue seeks to achieve in *Terra Lucida*. As Scholem puts it, "*theosophy* signifies a mystical doctrine, or school of thought, which purports to perceive and to describe the mysterious workings of the Divinity, perhaps also believing it possible to become absorbed in its contemplation. Theosophy postulates a kind of divine emanation whereby God, abandoning his self-contained repose, awakens to mysterious life; further, it maintains that the mysteries of creation reflect the pulsations of this divine life."[111] I would argue that *Terra Lucida* as a whole is suffused with the idea that divine life mysteriously pulses through creation; it is a notion that informs the poem whether it addresses the mundane or the supernal.

The passage from the *Zohar* that Donahue reworks in the lines quoted above refers to the suffering of the Messiah, the "Holy One" who longs to redeem Israel, but is indefinitely held back by the world's wickedness. Like Duncan before him, Donahue assimilates and transforms kabbalistic discourse, creating a vision of loss, exile, and redemption in deferment that accords with Jewish mysticism's – and Donahue's own – gnostic impulses. The pathos of the Holy One grieving in the "Hall of Illness" is deeply moving; the idea of the Messiah's helplessness in the face of human wretchedness and cosmic disaster is expressed with wonderful tact and restraint.[112] In another passage that follows shortly thereafter, Donahue tells us that

three volumes of *Terra Lucida* have been published. The second and third are *Dissolves: Terra Lucida IV–VIII* (Greenfield, MA: Talisman House, 2012) and *Dark Church: Terra Lucida IX–XII* (Chicago, IL: Verge Books, 2015). I will limit my comments mainly to volume one.

111. *Major Trends in Jewish Mysticism*, 206.
112. In an email (December 29, 2016), Donahue informed me that he found the passage from the *Zohar* in Raphael Patai, *The Messiah Texts: Jewish Legends of Three Thousand Years* (Detroit, MI: Wayne State University Press, 1988), 115–16.

Orders, Songs, Laws,
have been hidden away.

We must try to find them.
We must, we say, go find them.

But we hide, ever more deeply,
clinging to an unreal glitter,

as these perfections
struggle to reach us.[113]

This vision of ambivalent students of the Law reminds me of the great debate between Walter Benjamin and Gershom Scholem over the status of tradition and transmissibility in Kafka. Benjamin asserts that Kafka's "students are pupils who have lost the Holy Writ," while Scholem counters that these students "are not so much those who have lost the Scripture . . . but rather those students who cannot decipher it."[114] And then there is Kafka himself, who, in "An Imperial Message," imagines the dying Emperor sending a message to "his pathetic subject" through the incalculable distances of the Imperial Court. "But you sit at your window when evening falls," the parable ends, "and dream it to yourself."[115] The predicament that Kafka, Benjamin, and Scholem describe is analogous to how, in Donahue's lyric, "we hide, ever more deeply," as "these per-fections / struggle to reach us." Thus Donahue includes himself in a tradition of esoteric textual interpretation made all the more troubling by the "unreal glitter" of modernity, and the nagging doubt that we are no longer inspired to persist with the hermeneutic quest.

Nevertheless, Donahue perseveres. Despite the popularization of Kabbalah among the Hasidim starting in the eighteenth century (to say nothing of its popularized New Age status today), the gnostic qualities of Jewish mysticism make it, in some respects, an initiatory belief system.

---

113. *Terra Lucida*, 40.
114. *Illuminations*, 126; *The Correspondence of Walter Benjamin and Gershom Scholem 1932–1940*, trans. Gary Smith and Andre Lefevere (New York: Schocken Books, 1989), 127.
115. Franz Kafka, "An Imperial Message," trans. Willa and Edwin Muir, in *The Complete Stories*, ed. Nahum N. Glatzer (New York: Schocken Books, 1983), 5.

Unlike normative Judaism, Kabbalah, either as a meditative practice or as text-based theosophy, calls for gradual progression into its mysteries: as Scholem puts it, Jewish mysticism strives "to detect successively new layers in the mystery of the Godhead," and it is that movement inward and upward that the student must follow.[116] The *Zohar* (3:152a) famously observes of its hermeneutic that "Just as wine must be in a jar to keep, so the Torah must be contained in an outer garment. The garment is made up of the tales and stories, but we, we are bound to penetrate beyond."[117] Donahue, as should be clear by now, is enamored (I'm tempted to say intoxicated) by the enduring possibility not only of a religious poetry in a secular age, but of a successively layered esoteric poetry in endless pursuit of mystical truth, a hermeneutic poetry dependent upon self-commentary to keep itself in motion. In this respect, *Terra Lucida* constitutes an ongoing process of unveiling, a continual departure and arrival, an endless sequence of revelatory moments: "*I can see, and can see myself here // where I'm transcribing the images… /* admits a scribe about to go blind. *// My life is a letter in a word rising / on the unrolling white of the sky.*"[118] The scribe sees himself self-reflexively in the act of writing, a metaphor for the composition of the poem and for the poet himself. Steeped in Kabbalah, he knows that all of creation is an endless Torah scroll, and that he himself is a single letter in one mere word.

But Donahue is also aware of the specific historical and material conditions which produce the religious texts and rituals which so fascinate him, and which in turn lead him to the gnostic insights for which he hungers. Thus Donahue's use of Kabbalah correlates to his understanding of the ambiguities of Jewish history itself. One concrete instance of this ambiguous, even hidden dimension of Jewish history is the "secret" Jews of the American southwest. These *conversos*, crypto-Jews of Sephardic descent, outwardly practiced Catholicism but would reveal, sometimes ritualistically, their hidden Jewish identity and beliefs to the next generation. Donahue's section about these Jews in *Terra Lucida* is

116. *Major Trends in Jewish Mysticism*, 207.
117. *Zohar: The Book of Splendor*, ed. Gershom Scholem (New York: Schocken Books, 1949), 122.
118. *Terra Lucida*, 45.

a crucial counterpoint to the kabbalistic passages of the poem, and is made all the more ironic because the poem presents the secret social, existential, and spiritual condition of this group as a subject of almost talmudic debate. After a vignette of a father telling his twelve-year-old child that the family is not Catholic, "that Christ / has never been their god," Donahue gives us three voices variously interpreting this discovery. The first observes the condition of the crypto-Jews as an "Exile within an exile"; the second speculates on the terror of the child as *"that new truth / becomes the task"*; but the third, as the poem ends, says *"No"*: *"What / an ecstasy. To be free, // in an instant, of / all you were…"*[119]

These lines can be read in terms of Donahue's relationship to the mystical traditions which he studies so intently and which provide so much important material for his poetry. What fascinates Donahue about Kabbalah, along with these other traditions, is its esotericism. As I see it, the very condition of some secret or hidden truth, is, for the poet, the *essence* of Judaism. The moment of revelation is, in effect, the most *poetic* moment, which is also an ecstatic moment of freedom, when all you were, all you previously believed, is shown to be an illusion, a disguise. This is what the poem may give us. The child is told that he or she is not a Catholic but a Jew, just as the religious scripture is shown to mean something other than what readers have assumed it to mean, what they have previously been taught or have believed. Is this not so with Donahue's poetry as well? We are, in effect, initiates in this poetry, as is the case when we read other poets in this tradition, such as H.D., Duncan, or Nathaniel Mackey.[120] The poem reveals a truth, and is in itself that revelation.

There is a wonderful section in *Terra Lucida* about the building of a new synagogue, presumably in Durham, where Donahue lives (he teaches at Duke):

> …the new temple takes
> a shape oddly reminiscent

119. Ibid., 86–87.
120. By way of comparison, especially in regard to mystical initiation, see my chapter on Mackey in *On Mount Vision*, 183–207.

of a barn built by slaves
on a local plantation,

ancient axe-blows plainly
visible in the vaulting beams

that rise to a cupola
– a visitor said it was like

the quaternity of prophets,
the holy Moslem box, the Ka'Ba.

Already, these girders
make this Carolina tract

a place not the place it was,
or no longer a place at all,

as Sinai is not, meant
never to be revisited...[121]

The religious identity of this structure is strangely unfixed. As the temple rises, it appears to resemble an antebellum barn built by slaves, whose faith would no doubt blend African and Christian belief. But it also reminds Donahue of the Ka'Ba, the holiest site of Islam. Its Jewish spirit is even more mysterious: its physical being unmakes the "Carolina tract" where it is being built, "as Sinai is not, meant / never to be revisited..." Both the Talmud and Midrash claim that all Jews who ever were or will be were gathered at Sinai when Moses received the Law. After that, the Law went forth in the Ark, and in the rest of the poem, Donahue envisions the ark of the new synagogue "like a floating altar // of silver, copper, crimson, / carried across a desert."[122] Like the Ark of the Covenant, the poem wanders ceaselessly through space and time, moving from one moment of revelation to another.

"Who can say for sure what / it is God gives to exiles?": again and again in his poem, Donahue returns to the uncertainty of faith and the

121. *Terra Lucida*, 106–7.
122. Ibid., 107.

instability of religious traditions, even as those moments of revelation continue to recur.[123] In *Dissolves*, the second volume of *Terra Lucida*,

> We sleep
>
> as Hindus,
> wake up Jews,
>
> drift off
> Christian
>
> rouse as Muslim.
> Sleep, wake, sleep,
>
> persecuted,
> now protected.
>
> Centuries are passing.
> Religions flare and fade.[124]

For Donahue, we fall asleep secure in one faith, but wake believing another. In the light of history, we are alternately persecuted and protected: that is the secret which in turn calls forth the necessity of a secret doctrine. "Religions flare and fade": I am reminded of stars, for Donahue's expansive vision is that of a mystical cosmos, a great constellation of religious systems, none of them complete, all of them somehow necessary. The Jewish contribution to this vision remains crucial to *Terra Lucida*, and to Donahue, still in the midst of one of the boldest and most compelling of contemporary poetic sequences.

123. Ibid., 114.
124. *Dissolves*, 41–42.

TEN

Afterword: "Diasporas of Imperfection"

A RECENT POEM BY PETER COLE CALLED "FOR A THEOPHORIC Figure," in memory of Allen Grossman, reminds us once again of the continuities and losses, the visions and revisions, that constitute the Jewish literary imagination. Cole is one of our most important contemporaries: not only is he a prolific and innovative translator of Jewish poetry from antiquity to the twenty-first century, his own verse demonstrates a mastery of an extraordinary range of English poetic forms. Like Grossman before him, Cole is equally at home with traditional rhyme and meter as well as a variety of open forms. Over the course of his career, he has addressed some of the most complex Jewish cultural, religious, and historical concerns, from esoteric kabbalistic conundrums to the current political struggles in Israel and Palestine. It makes a great deal of sense, then, that he should wish to pay homage to Grossman, specifically addressing him using the term "theophoric" (God-bearing, or bearing the name of a god), which, as we have seen, Grossman appropriates to describe the unique qualities of Jewish poetry in his essay "Jewish Poetry Considered as a Theophoric Project." In the title of Cole's poem, Grossman the poet becomes, in effect, congruent with Jewish poetry itself; Grossman is a "figure," that is, an individual person of stature, but he is also a trope, a synecdochic figure of speech standing for what he does and what he makes, which, given Grossman's poetics, is far greater than the person.[1] Here is the poem:

> Strange how first things dawn on us
>   late in the game,
> again and again.
> Just last week, for instance,
>   I learned
> of a young man's lines that appeared on a page,
> black flames on a blaze of white –
>   early June,
> the year I was born:
> *The bell pursues me*, they said, *it is time…*
>   *to sigh in the ears of my children.*
>   They did,
> and do still, though their maker has died,
>   and I, a scribe to that living word
> he carried toward his distant God
>   across diasporas of imperfection,
> try now to lift it ever
>   so slightly higher, or longer on high,
> to honor,
>   as I'm able, that force
>   he rode for the span of more than his life
> out of the Eden of his mind like a river…[2]

Beginning on a seemingly casual, almost conversational note, yet promising something "strange," Cole's free verse uses the space of the page to indicate his hesitancies of thought and speech as the poet gradually shapes the poem which he hopes will honor this theophoric figure. Cole's kabbalistic imagery ("black flames on a blaze of white")

---

1. Recall how Grossman argues that "Poems create poets.... One of the *consequences* of the existence of poetry is the existence of 'the poet'.... The poem is a thing made which makes its maker." *The Sighted Singer,* 260.

2. Peter Cole, *Hymns and Qualms: New and Selected Poems and Translations* (New York: Farrar, Straus and Giroux, 2017), 28.

refers to *another* poem, an early poem by Grossman, as if it were divine, like the Torah written in black fire upon white fire from which God read to enact Creation. Grossman's poem, "I Am in Babylon Dying," is first published in the June 1957 issue of *Poetry*, and Cole himself, as he notes in his poem, is born on August 19th of that year. Grossman dies on June 27, 2014; shortly thereafter, Cole encounters the poem again (he first read it years before in Grossman's *A Harlot's Hire*), "late in the game." Now Cole recognizes Grossman's poem to be one of his "first things," a primal utterance written in the year he was born, and, in effect, destined to bring him to birth *as a poet* – a realization which comes to Cole when he learns of Grossman's death, which in turn inspires his own poem.

This circulation of birth and death, presence and absence, poets, poems, and poetic incarnation, becomes even more complicated when we look at Grossman's poem, and how Cole works with it. Here is the text of "I Am in Babylon Dying," as it appears in *Poetry*:

> The bell pursues me. It is time to die.
> It is the hour when no man works. I feel
> My time fill up with leaves like a dry well
> With many autumns over it, leaves that I
> Leave to sigh in the ears of my children. My enemy
> Asks for a song, but I sing not. Let the willow
> Tell how many sons of them my sons will kill
> Before they forget Jerusalem. I cry
> Not though the bell pursues and the willow hangs over.
> This is vile captive food these my tears.
> I am in Babylon dying. In the leaves that cover
> The silent women by the river my fear
> And hate hang like a harp which the wind will play.[3]

This is a truncated Petrarchan sonnet: it has a complete octave but rather than a sestet (six rhyming lines), the second part of the poem has five lines, and the powerful thirteenth line, the last, has no rhyme. One could say, therefore, that the form is incomplete, or to use Cole's term in "For a Theophoric Figure," it is in a condition of "imperfection," which, insofar

---

3. Allen Grossman, "I Am in Babylon Dying," *Poetry*, vol. 90, 3 (June 1957): 146.

as it addresses the fall of Jerusalem and the Babylonian exile, is also what "I Am in Babylon Dying" is about.

Just as Cole's poem refers to Grossman's, so Grossman's poem refers to Psalm 137, probably in the King James Version (no poet writing in English, even if he or she is fluent in Hebrew, can escape the language of the KJV). It is one of a number of his early poems spoken in a voice from Jewish myth or history, in this case one of the Jewish exiles in Babylon. The intertextuality here is quite complicated. Grossman draws extensively from the text of the Psalm, borrowing the images of the Babylonian enemy asking for a song, the exiles' refusal to sing, the insistence that Jerusalem shall not be forgotten, the destruction of the enemy's children, and the hanging of the harps upon the willow trees. The images of the leaves, the dry well, and the bell are original to Grossman's poem, as is its overall insistence on dying in exile, though there seems to be some hope for the exiled children. It is an ambitious, rather traditional poem, but not much like the audacious work of Grossman's maturity, except that here we can see him reaching toward the prophetic voice that he will eventually transform and uniquely modernize in his greatest poems.

Psalm 137 is traditionally associated with Jeremiah, given his prophecies of Jerusalem's destruction and his relationship to the Babylonian exile (hence, perhaps, Grossman's image of the dry well, since Jeremiah's enemies tried to kill him by putting him in a cistern). If psalm and prophecy are poetic modes to which the young Grossman aspires, what can we say about Cole's poem to Grossman in terms of these modes, and more generally, in regard to becoming a Jewish poet, since psalm and prophecy are fundamental to that calling? Although "For a Theophoric Figure" is a poem of Cole's maturity, we still see him seeking to align himself with the Jewish poetic tradition and with a specific precursor who represents that tradition. Cole is a poet who broods a great deal upon his vocation; he even has a witty but very serious poem, a sort of self-interrogation, called "Quatrains for a Calling."[4] As we have seen, he is deeply concerned with his poetic birth or incarnation. He also depicts himself merely as Grossman's scribe "to that living word / he carried toward his distant God / across diasporas of imperfection." A scribe,

4. *Hymns and Qualms*, 48–50.

especially a Jewish *sofer* who has learned the high art of writing Torah scrolls, must transcribe the text perfectly, especially because he and the Jewish people dwell in "diasporas of imperfection." But Cole's transcription of Grossman's poem is not exactly perfect. Cole quotes Grossman: "*The bell pursues me*, they said, *it is time . . . / to sigh in the ears of my children.*" The first line of Grossman's poem reads "The bell pursues me. It is time to die": Cole has elided the reference to death! Instead, he conjoins the phrase "It is time" with the phrase in line five, "to sigh in the ears of my children," creating a new sentence with a different meaning from that which appears in Grossman's text. The new sentence – "It is time to sigh in the ears of my children" – describes precisely what Grossman's poem is doing to Cole. It is sighing in the younger poet's ear, breathing into him, and however mournfully, *inspiring* him.

Grossman's "bell" is almost certainly a passing bell, and we may argue, therefore, that in his poem, exile is virtually tantamount to death. Cole's poem in memory of Grossman (is it an elegy? a Kaddish? perhaps not quite either) revises this formulation: in exile, in the "diasporas of imperfection," Jewish poets, heeding the "living word" of those who have come before them, "try now to lift it ever / so slightly higher, or longer on high." They compete with their precursors but they also "honor" them, and they do so by trying to lift the word ever so slightly higher. What Cole calls "that force / he rode for the span of more than his life / out of the Eden of his mind like a river . . ." is the force of poetic inspiration, the force that flows out of the perfect Eden of mind into language, which is always fallen (since we are no longer in Eden), always imperfect, and yet still able to lead us to poetic utterance.

In *The Summer Conversations*, Grossman speaks of poetic vocation as "a story about a social person whose mortal voice is replaced by a transhistorical and, in the language of the West, an 'immortal' voice." Furthermore, "the social expression of that immortality is the continuity of a tradition, always older and other than the history of any moment of poetic practice, that constitutes an alternative genealogy to the genealogy contributed by the mortal family."[5] This is why, as Cole realizes, poets long to understand that genealogy, the "first things [that] dawn on us /

---

5. *The Sighted Singer*, 148.

late in the game, / again and again," especially when a "theophoric figure" of the previous generation passes away. Freud tells us that as children, we wish to penetrate the mystery of our "mortal family," and Harold Bloom tells us that poets wish much the same in regard to their poetic family, a wish that provokes anxiety but also strengthens their rhetorical power. Peter Cole is one of Bloom's favorite contemporary poets, and among Jewish American poets, one of the very strongest; in reciprocal acts of homage, Bloom wrote the introduction to Cole's book of poems *The Invention of Influence*, which plays on Bloom's famous critical work, *The Anxiety of Influence*. According to Bloom, "Peter Cole has become a writer in the Jewish wisdom tradition, building an open enclosure around a secularized scripture, which for him comprehends all of the Post-Exilic Jewish imaginative literature of the highest aesthetic and cognitive merit."[6]

The terms which Bloom uses in his praise of Cole, which Cole fully deserves, are of particular interest to me. The reader who has come this far with me here, or who has looked into my earlier books on modern Jewish literature, knows that I take issue with Bloom, as I seek a broader and more inclusive set of criteria for understanding and valuing Jewish American poetry. For me, Grossman and Cole are in the "Jewish wisdom tradition," but so are poets such as Charles Reznikoff and Harvey Shapiro. Indeed, the various approaches which modern Jewish poets take in formulating their "secularized scripture," and the remarkable range of styles which result, prove how surprisingly, refreshingly, open the tradition has become, without losing any of its dark and dialectical rabbinic wisdom.

Hu hayah omer, lo aleicha hammelachah ligmor, velo attah ben chorin libbatel mimennah: this famous saying of Rabbi Tarfon is found in Mishnah Avot 2:16, though the first time I came upon it was in an English translation in Bloom's foundational essay, "The Sorrows of American-Jewish

6. Harold Bloom, introduction to *The Invention of Influence*, by Peter Cole (New York: New Directions, 2014), x. This lively, freewheeling piece, written by Bloom at age eighty-three, is one of the most revealing statements he has made about poetry and Jewishness in a long career of meditating upon this subject.

Poetry."[7] It is usually translated as "He used to say: You are not required to complete the work, but neither are you free to desist from it." But the phrase *"ben chorin"* indicates a member of a group or class: you are not a free or unbound individual who has no obligations, and therefore you are bound to continue working.[8] Such is the fate of Jewish poets. Diasporas of imperfection, diasporas of incompletion...this, in the end, is the condition of Jewish poetry.

7. Harold Bloom, "The Sorrows of American-Jewish Poetry," in *Figures of Capable Imagination* (New York: Seabury Press), 262. Bloom has referred to this saying in many of his subsequent works.
8. The meaning of the phrase *"ben chorin"* was pointed out to me by my friend David H. Aaron of Hebrew Union College.

Bibliography

Ahearne, Barry, editor. *Pound/Zukofsky: Selected Letters of Ezra Pound and Louis Zukofsky*. New York: New Directions, 1987.

Alter, Robert. "Epitaph for a Jewish Magazine." *Commentary* 39, no. 5 (1965): 51–55.

Althusser, Louis. *Lenin and Philosophy and Other Essays*. Translated by Ben Brewster. New York: Monthly Review Press, 1971.

Ashton, Jennifer. "Lyric, Gender, and Subjectivity in Modern and Contemporary Women's Poetry." In *The Cambridge History of American Women's Literature*, 515–38. Edited by Dale M. Bauer. Cambridge, UK: Cambridge University Press, 2012.

Bachman, Merle L. *Recovering "Yiddishland": Threshold Moments in American Literature*. Syracuse, NY: Syracuse University Press, 2008.

Back, Rachel Tzvia. *Azimuth*. Riverdale-On-Hudson, NY: Sheep Meadow Press, 2001.

———. *Led by Language: The Poetry and Poetics of Susan Howe*. Tuscaloosa: University of Alabama Press, 2002.

———. *A Messenger Comes*. San Diego, CA: Singing Horse Press, 2012.

———. *On Ruins & Return*. Exeter, UK: Shearsman Books, 2007.

———. "'A Species of Magic': The Role of Poetry in Protest and Truth-telling (An Israeli Poet's Perspective)." *World Literature Today* (May–August 2014), https://www.worldliteraturetoday.org/2014/may/species-magic-role-poetry-protest-and-truth-telling-israeli-poets-perspective.

————. *What Use Is Poetry, the Poet Is Asking*. Bristol, UK: Shearsman Books, 2019.

Barron, Jonathan N. and Eric Murphy Selinger, editors. *Jewish American Poetry: Poems, Commentary, and Reflections*. Hanover, NH: Brandeis University Press / University Press of New England, 2000.

Barthes, Roland. *Mythologies*. Translated by Annette Lavers. New York: Farrar, Straus and Giroux, 1972.

Baudrillard, Jean. *Simulations*. Translated by Phil Beitchman. New York: Semiotext(e), 1982.

Benite, Zvi Ben-Dor. *The Ten Lost Tribes: A World History*. Oxford: Oxford University Press, 2009.

Benjamin, Walter. *The Correspondence of Walter Benjamin 1910–1940*. Edited by Gershom Scholem and Theodor W. Adorno. Translated by Manfred R. Jacobson and Evelyn M. Jacobson. Chicago, IL: University of Chicago Press, 1994.

————. *Illuminations*. Translated by Harry Zohn. New York: Schocken Books, 1965.

————. *The Origin of German Tragic Drama*. Translated by John Osborne. London: Verso, 1998.

————. *Reflections*. Translated by Edmund Jephcott. New York: Schocken Books, 1986.

Berger, Charles. "reading the Alien in American Scenes: Henry James and Wallace Stevens." *The Wallace Stevens Journal* 34, no. 1., 2010. (Spring 2010): 15, 36.

Bernstein, Charles. "Radical Jewish Culture / Secular Jewish Practice." In *Radical Poetics and Secular Jewish Culture*, 12–17.

————. "Reznikoff's Nearness." In *The Objectivist Nexus*, 210–39.

Biale, David. *Not in the Heavens: The Tradition of Jewish Secular Thought*. Princeton, NJ: Princeton University Press, 2011.

Bialik, Haim Nachman. "Revealment and Concealment in Language." Translated by Jacob Sloan. In *Revealment and Concealment: Five Essays*, 11–26. Jerusalem: Ibis Editions, 2000.

Bloch, Chana. "Commentary." In *Jewish American Poetry: Poems, Commentary, and Reflections*, 37–47.

————. *The Moon Is Almost Full*. Pittsburgh, PA: Autumn House Press, 2017.

————. *Swimming in the Rain: New and Selected Poems 1980–2015*. Pittsburgh, PA: Autumn House Press, 2015.

Bloom, Harold. *Figures of Capable Imagination*. New York: Seabury Press, 1976.

————. Introduction to *Musical Variations on Jewish Thought*, by Olivier Revault D'Allonnes. New York: George Braziller, 1984.

————. *Ruin the Sacred Truths: Poetry and Belief from the Bible to the Present*. Cambridge, MA: Harvard University Press, 1987.

————. *Wallace Stevens: The Poems of Our Climate*. Ithaca, NY: Cornell University Press, 1977.

Castle, Terry. *The Female Thermometer: Eighteenth-Century Culture and the Invention of the Uncanny*. New York: Oxford University Press, 1995.

Celan, Paul. *Breathturn into Timestead: The Collected Later Poetry*. Translated by Pierre Joris. New York: Farrar, Straus, and Giroux, 2014.

————. *Poems of Paul Celan*. Translated by Michael Hamburger. New York: Persea Books, 1988.

————. *Selected Poems and Prose of Paul Celan*, Translated by John Felstiner. New York: Norton, 2001.

Cole, Peter. *Hymns and Qualms: New and Selected Poems and Translations*. New York: Farrar, Straus and Giroux, 2017.

Collis, Stephen, and Graham Lyons. *Reading Duncan Reading: Robert Duncan and the Poetics of Derivation*. Iowa City: University of Iowa Press, 2012.

Corbin, Henry. *The Man of Light in Iranian Sufism*. Translated by Nancy Pearson. New Lebanon, NY: Omega Publications, 1994.

Curley, Jon, and Burt Kimmelman, editors. *The Poetry and Poetics of Michael Heller: A Nomad Memory*. Madison, NJ: Fairleigh Dickinson University Press, 2016.

Dante Aligheri. *The Divine Comedy of Dante Aligheri: Inferno*. Translated by Allen Mandelbaum. New York: Bantam Books, 1982.

Dembo, L.S. *The Monological Jew*. Madison: University of Wisconsin Press, 1988.

————. "The 'Objectivist' Poet: Four Interviews." *Contemporary Literature* 10, no. 2 (Spring 1969): 155–311.

Derrida, Jacques. *Speech and Phenomena and Other Essays on Husserl's*

Theory of Signs. Translated by David B. Allison. Evanston, IL: North-western University Press, 1973.

Donahue, Joseph. *Dark Church: Terra Lucida IX–XII*. Chicago, IL: Verge Books, 2015.

———. *Dissolves: Terra Lucida IV–VIII*. Greenfield, MA: Talisman House, 2012.

———. *Red Flash on a Black Field*. New York: Black Square Editions, 2014.

———. *Terra Lucida*. Jersey City, NJ: Talisman House, 2009.

Donin, Hayim Halevy. *To Pray as A Jew*. New York: Basic Books, 1980.

Duncan, Robert. *Collected Essays and Other Prose*. Edited by James Maynard. Berkeley: University of California Press, 2014.

———. *The Collected Later Poems and Plays*. Edited by Peter Quartermain. Berkeley: University of California Press, 2014.

———. *The H.D. Book*. Edited by Michael Boughn and Victor Coleman. Berkeley: University of California Press, 2011.

———. *A Poet's Mind: Collected Interviews with Robert Duncan, 1969–1985*. Edited by Christopher Wagstaff. Berkeley, CA: North Atlantic Books, 2012.

DuPlessis, Rachel Blau and Peter Quartermain, editors. *The Objectivist Nexus: Essays in Cultural Poetics*. Tuscaloosa: University of Alabama Press, 1999.

Eliot, T.S. *Selected Prose of T.S. Eliot*. Edited by Frank Kermode. New York: Harcourt Brace Jovanovich / Farrar, Straus and Giroux, 1975.

Finkelstein, Norman. "The Case of Michael Palmer." *Contemporary Literature* 29, no. 4 (Winter 1988), 518–37.

———. *Not One of Them in Place: Modern Poetry and Jewish American Identity*. Albany: State University of New York Press, 2001.

———. *On Mount Vision: Forms of the Sacred in Contemporary American Poetry*. Iowa City: University of Iowa Press, 2010.

———. "Orphic Explanations." *Denver Quarterly* 35.2 (Summer 2000): 73–80.

———. *The Ritual of New Creation: Jewish Tradition and Contemporary Literature*. Albany: State University of New York Press, 1992.

———. "Robert Duncan, Poet of the Law." *Sagetrieb* 2, no. 1 (Spring 1983): 75–88.

———. "Secular Jewish Culture and Its Radical Poetic Discontents." In *Radical Poetics and Secular Jewish Culture*, 225–44.

———, and Michael Heller. "On the Poetics of the Jewish God." In *Imagining the Jewish God*, 3–18. Edited by Leonard Kaplan and Kenneth Koltun-Fromm. Lanham, MD: Lexington Books, 2016.

Fredman, Stephen. "Judaism as Loss in the Poetry of Michael Heller." In *The Poetry and Poetics of Michael Heller*, 121–30.

———. *A Menorah for Athena: Charles Reznikoff and the Jewish Dilemmas of Objectivist Poetry*. Chicago, IL: University of Chicago Press, 2001.

———. "Symposium of the Whole: Jerome Rothenberg and the Dream of 'A Poetry of All Poetries.'" In *Reading Duncan Reading*, 151–71.

Freud, Sigmund. "The 'Uncanny.'" Translated by James Strachey. *The Standard Edition of the Complete Psychological Works of Sigmund Freud*. Volume XVII. London: The Hogarth Press, 1955.

Gilman, Sander L. *Jewish Self-Hatred: Anti-Semitism and the Hidden Language of the Jews*. Baltimore, MD: Johns Hopkins University Press, 1986.

Ginsberg, Allen. "Reznikoff's Poetics." In *Charles Reznikoff: Man and Poet*, 139–50.

Girard, René. *Violence and the Sacred*. Translated by Patrick Gregory. Baltimore: Johns Hopkins University Press, 1972.

Golding, Alan. "Recent American Poetry Anthologies and the Idea of the 'Mainstream.'" In *Poetry and Contemporary Culture: The Question of Value*, 123–40. Edited by Andrew Michael Roberts and Jonathan Allison. Edinburgh: Edinburgh University Press, 2002.

Greene, Daniel. *The Jewish Origins of Cultural Pluralism: The Menorah Association and American Diversity*. Bloomington: Indiana University Press, 2011.

Grossman, Allen. *Descartes' Loneliness*. New York: New Directions, 2007.

———. *The Ether Dome and Other Poems: New and Selected 1979–1991*. New York: New Directions, 1991.

———. *How to Do Things with Tears*. New York: New Directions, 2001.

———. *The Long Schoolroom: Lessons in the Bitter Logic of the Poetic Principle.* Ann Arbor: University of Michigan Press, 1997.

———. *The Sighted Singer: Two Works on Poetry for Readers and Writers.* Baltimore, MD: Johns Hopkins University Press, 1992.

Hartman, Geoffrey. *Criticism in the Wilderness: The Study of Literature Today.* New Haven, NJ: Yale University Press, 1980.

Hass, Robert. *What Light Can Do: Essays on Art, Imagination, and the Natural World.* New York: HarperCollins Publishers, 2012.

Hatlen, Burton. "Duncan's Marriage of Heaven and Hell: Kabbalah and Rime in *Roots and Branches.*" In *World, Self, Poem: Essays on Contemporary Poetry from the "Jubilation of Poets,"* 207–26. Edited by Leonard M. Trawick. Kent, OH: Kent State University Press, 1990.

Heller, Michael. *Conviction's Net of Branches: Essays on the Objectivist Poets and Poetry.* Carbondale: Southern Illinois University Press, 1985.

———. *Dianoia.* New York: Nightboat Books, 2016.

———. *Living Root: A Memoir.* Albany: State University of New York Press, 2000.

———. "Remains of the Diaspora: A Personal Meditation." In *Radical Jewish Poetics and Secular Jewish Culture,* 170–83.

———. *This Constellation Is a Name: Collected Poems, 1965–2010.* Callicoon, NY: Nightboat Books, 2012.

———. *Uncertain Poetics: Selected Essays on Poets, Poetry and Poetics.* Cambridge, UK: Salt Publishing, 2005.

Highman, John. "Social Discrimination Against Jews, 1830–1930." In *Antisemitism in America.* American Jewish History 6. Edited by Jefrey S. Gurock. New York: Routledge, 1998.

Hindus, Milton. *Charles Reznikoff: A Critical Essay.* Santa Barbara, CA: Black Sparrow Press, 1977.

———, editor. *Charles Reznikoff: Man and Poet.* Orono, ME: National Poetry Foundation, 1984.

Howe, Susan. *Singularities.* Hanover, NH: Wesleyan University Press / University Press of New England, 1990.

Idel, Moshe. *Messianic Mystics.* New Haven, CT: Yale University Press, 1998.

Jameson, Fredric. "Postmodernism, or the Cultural Logic of Late Capitalism." *New Left Review* 146 (July/August 1984): 53–92.

Jarnot, Lisa. *Robert Duncan: The Ambassador from Venus.* Berkeley: University of California Press, 2012.

Karp, Jonathan, and Adam Sutcliffe, editors. *Philosemitism in History.* Cambridge, UK: Cambridge University Press, 2011.

Kenner, Hugh. *A Homemade World: The American Modernist Writers.* New York: Knopf, 1975.

Kronick, Joseph G. "Of Parents, Children, and Rabbis: Wallace Stevens and the Question of the Book." *boundary 2* 10, no. 3 (Spring 1982): 125–44.

Levinson, Julian. "Connoisseurs of Angst: The Jewish Mystique and Postwar American Literary Culture." In *Philosemitism in History,* 235–56.

Longfellow, Henry Wadsworth. *Evangeline.* New York: Avon Books, 1971.

Mallarmé, Stéphane. *Collected Poems.* Translated by Henry Weinfield. Berkeley: University of California Press, 1994.

Mandelbaum, Allen. *Chelmaxioms.* Boston, MA: David R. Godine, 1977.

Miller, Stephen Paul, and Daniel Morris, editors. *Radical Poetics and Secular Jewish Culture.* Tuscaloosa: University of Alabama Press, 2010.

Mossin, Andrew. "Against Witness as Such," *Jacket* 35 (early 2008), http://jacketmagazine.com/35/r-back-rb-mossin.shtml.

O'Leary, Peter. *Gnostic Contagion: Robert Duncan and the Poetry of Illness.* Middletown, CT: Wesleyan University Press, 2002.

———. "An Imaginal Homage to Joseph Donahue," *Jacket* 2, Dec. 17, 2014, https://jacket2.org/article/imaginal-homage-joseph-donahue.

Omer-Sherman, Ranen. *Diaspora and Zionism in Jewish-American Literature.* Hanover, NH: Brandeis University Press / University Press of New England, 2002.

Oppen, George. *New Collected Poems.* Edited by Michael Davidson. New York: New Directions, 2002.

Osherow, Jacqueline. *Dead Men's Praise.* New York: Grove Press, 1999.

Ouaknin, Marc-Alain. *The Burnt Book: Reading the Talmud.* Translated by Llewellyn Brown. Princeton, NJ: Princeton University Press, 1995.

Parfitt, Tudor. *The Lost Tribes of Israel: The History of a Myth*. London: Weidenfeld & Nicolson, 2002.

Patai, Raphael. *The Messiah Texts: Jewish Legends of Three Thousand Years*. Detroit, MI: Wayne State University Press, 1988.

Pound, Ezra. *Literary Essays of Ezra Pound*. New York: New Directions, 1935.

Pritchett, Patrick. "How to Write Poetry after Auschwitz: The Burnt Book of Michael Palmer." *Journal of Modern Literature* 37, vol. 3 (Spring 2014): 127–45.

Reznikoff, Charles. *The Poems of Charles Reznikoff 1918–1975*. Edited by Seamus Cooney. Boston, MA: Black Sparrow / David R. Godine, 2005.

Rifkin, Libbie. *Career Moves: Olson, Creeley, Zukofsky, Berrigan, and the American Avant-Garde*. Madison: University of Wisconsin Press, 2000.

Roth, Philip. *The Counterlife*. New York: Farrar, Straus & Giroux, 1986.

———. *Portnoy's Complaint*. New York: Modern Library, 1982.

Rothenberg, Jerome. *A Big Jewish Book: Poems and Other Visions of the Jews From Tribal Times to Present*. Harris Lenowitz and Charles Doria, editors. Garden City, NJ: Anchor Press / Doubleday, 1978.

———. *Poetics and Polemics 1980–2005*. Tuscaloosa: University of Alabama Press, 2008.

———. *Triptych*. New York: New Directions, 2007.

Royle, Nicholas. *The Uncanny*. Manchester, UK: Manchester University Press, 2003.

Salvato, Nick. *Uncloseting Drama: American Modernism and Queer Performance*. New Haven, NJ: Yale University Press, 2010.

Scholem, Gershom. *Major Trends in Jewish Mysticism*. New York: Schocken Books, 1961.

———. *The Messianic Idea in Judaism and Other Essays on Jewish Spirituality*. New York: Schocken Books, 1971.

———. *On the Kabbalah and Its Symbolism*. Translated by Ralph Manheim. New York: Schocken Books, 1965.

———, editor. *Zohar: The Book of Splendor*. New York: Schocken Books, 1949.

Scroggins, Mark. *Louis Zukofsky and the Poetry of Knowledge*. Tuscaloosa: University of Alabama Press, 1998.

————. "Objectivist Poets." In *A History of Modernist Poetry*. Edited by Alex Davis and Lee M. Jenkins, 381–97. New York: Cambridge University Press, 2015.

————. *The Poem of a Life: A Biography of Louis Zukofsky* (Berkeley, CA: Shoemaker & Hoard, 2007.

Selinger, Eric Murphy. "Shekhinah in America." In *Jewish American Poetry: Poems, Commentary, and Reflections*, 250–71.

Shandler, Jeffrey. *Adventures in Yiddishland: Postvernacular Language and Culture*. Berkeley: University of California Press, 2006.

Shapiro, Harvey. *A Momentary Glory: Last Poems*. Edited by Norman Finkelstein. Middletown, CT: Wesleyan University Press, 2014.

————. "I Write Out of an Uncreated Identity." In *The Writer in the Jewish Community: An Israeli-North American Dialogue*. Edited by Richard Siegal and Tamar Sofer, 21–23. Rutherford, NJ: Fairleigh Dickinson University Press, 1993.

————. *The Sights Along the Harbor: New and Collected Poems*. Middletown, CT: Wesleyan University Press, 2006.

Shapiro, Karl. *Poems of a Jew*. New York: Random House, 1958.

Shreiber, Maeera Y. "Embracing the Void: A Short Essay in Memory of Chana Bloch." *Shofar* 36, no. 2 (Summer 2018): 42–54.

————. "The End of Exile: Jewish Identity and Its Diasporic Poetics." *PMLA* 113, no. 2 (March 1998): 273–87.

————. "Secularity, Sacredness, and Jewish American Poets 1950–2000." In *The Cambridge History of Jewish American Literature*. Edited by Hana Wirth-Nesher, 182–201. New York: Cambridge University Press, 2016.

————. *Singing in a Strange Land: A Jewish American Poetics*. Stanford, CA: Stanford University Press, 2007.

Stevens, Wallace. *Collected Poetry and Prose*. New York: Library of America, 1997.

————. *Letters of Wallace Stevens*. Edited by Holly Stevens. New York: Alfred A. Knopf, 1966.

————. *Opus Posthumous*. Edited by Milton J. Bates. New York: Vintage, 1990.

Syrkin, Marie. "Charles: A Memoir." In *Charles Reznikoff: Man and Poet*, 37–67.

Terman, Philip. "The Poetry of a Jewish Humanist." *Tikkun* (Summer 2015): 56–58.

Twitchell-Waas, Jeffrey. "The Airs of Duncan and Zukofsky." In *Reading Duncan Reading*, 67–87.

Wasserstrom, Steven M. *Religion After Religion: Gershom Scholem, Mircea Eliade, and Henry Corbin at Eranos*. Princeton, NJ: Princeton University Press, 1999.

Weinfield, Henry. *The Music of Thought in the Poetry of George Oppen and William Bronk*. Iowa City: University of Iowa Press, 2009.

———. *The Poet Without a Name: Gray's Elegy and the Problem of History*. Carbondale: Southern Illinois University Press, 1991.

———. *A Wandering Aramaean: Passover Poems and Translations*. Loveland, OH: Dos Madres Press, 2012.

———. *Without Mythologies: New & Selected Poems & Translations*. Loveland, OH: Dos Madres Press, 2008.

———. "'Wringing, Wringing His Pierced Hands': Religion, Identity, and Genre in the Poetry of Charles Reznikoff." *Sagetrieb* 13, no. 1–2 (1994): 225–32.

Wieseltier, Leon. *Kaddish*. New York: Vintage, 1998.

Williams, William Carlos. "Wallace Stevens." *Poetry* 87, no. 4 (Jan. 1956): 234–39.

Wirth-Nesher, Hana. *Call It English: The Languages of Jewish American Literature*. Princeton, NJ: Princeton University Press, 2006.

Yeats, W.B. *The Poems: A New Edition*. Edited by Richard J. Finneran. New York: Macmillan, 1983.

Yerushalmi, Yosef Hayim. *Zakhor: Jewish History and Jewish Memory*. Seattle: University of Washington Press, 1982.

Zukofsky, Louis. *Prepositions+: The Collected Critical Essays*. Edited by Mark Scroggins. Hanover, NH: Wesleyan University Press / University Press of New England, 2000.

Index

Abulafia, Abraham, 243.

Adorno, Theodor, 192, 221.

Aggadah, 153–54.

Aldington, Richard, 43.

Althusser, Louis: "Ideology and Ideological State Apparatuses," 174.

American Jewish Historical Society, 1.

Amichai, Yehuda, 133.

Antisemitism, 51, 62–64, 239–40, 251; British, 5; Christian, 8; European, 116; Western, 236. *See also* Pound, Ezra.

Anzaldúa, Gloria, 141.

Arafat, Yasser, 175.

Ashbery, John, 254.

Ashton, Jennifer, 139n17; "Lyric, Gender, and Subjectivity in Modern and Contemporary Women's Poetry," 141.

Auster, Paul, 1, 49.

Bachman, Merle, 18, 35n35.

Back, Rachel Tzvia, 193–218. Works: "A Broken Beginning," 206–8; *A Messenger Comes*, 206, 208, 211; "A Species of Magic," 216; *Azimuth*, 196–98, 213; "Bringing the Buffalo Back Home (October 2005, Adirondacks NY)," 204–6; *Elegy Fragments*, 211; "Lamentation," 208, 210; *Led by Language*, 195n6,

197n10, 201nn22–23, "Like the Believer," 217; *On Ruins & Return*, 200–201, 204; *The Buffalo Poems*, 200–201, 213; "This Bequest of Wings*", 194n3; "What is Still Possible (6 Love Poems)," 204; *What Use Is Poetry, the Poet Is Asking*, 213; *With an Iron Pen*, 194.

Barthes, Roland, 173–74; *Mythologies*, 173.

Battle of Adobe Walls, 202.

Baudrillard, Jean, 107.

Beckmann, Max, 120–22.

Bellow, Saul, 29.

Benjamin, Walter, 41–42, 81, 92, 104, 112–13, 153n43, 257; Messianic Kingdom, 41–42.

Berger, Charles, 233n44.

Bernstein, Charles, 1–2, 5n11, 40, 138; "The Academy in Peril," 138.

Berryman, John, 239n64.

Biale, David, 3–4; *Not in the Heavens*, 3n5.

Bialik, Haim Nahman: "Revealment and Concealment in Language," 126.

Blake, William, 32, 94; influence on Reznikoff, 61; *The Marriage of Heaven and Hell*, 61.

Blavatsky, Madame Helena Petrovna, 234.

281

Bloch, Chana, 131–60; "Jewish humanist," 137, 156. Works: *Blood Honey*, 136, 155; "Covenant," 155–58; "Death March, 1945," 154; "Exile," 145–46, 153; "Furniture," 143; "Hester Street, 1898," 131–35, 152; "Instructions for the Bridegroom," 152n42; "Commentary," in *Jewish American Poetry*, 134; *Mrs. Dumpty*, 136, 151, 154; translation of *Song of Songs*, 133, 151, 152n42; "Spell," 154–58; *Spelling the Word*, 136; *Swimming in the Rain*, 136, 151; "The Converts," 147–49; "The Kiss," 151–53; *The Moon Is Almost Full*, 136, 159; *The Past Keeps Changing*, 136, 149, 151; "The Real Truth," 137n11; "The Revised Version," 142; *The Secrets of the Tribe*, 136, 145; "White Petticoats," 149–53.

Bloom, Harold, 38, 63, 72, 224, 227, 268; *The Anxiety of Influence*, 268; "The Sorrows of American-Jewish Poetry," 63, 268–69.

Bonnard, Pierre, 247.

Bronk, William, 170–71; "About Dynamism, Desire, and Various Fictions," 170.

Buddhism, 104, 122–23, 236. *See also* Heller, Michael. *See also* Segalen, Victor.

Byron, Lord George Gordon, 172.

Castle, Terry, 87: *The Female Thermometer*, 88n32.

Celan, Paul, 104, 116–17, 155–59, 221; hermeticism, 116; *Der Niemandrose*, 159; "Psalm," 158–59.

Christianity, 7, 13, 34, 63, 148, 165, 167–68, 170, 183, 189, 238, 255, 260; Catholicism, 258–59; Jesus, 34, 62, 165, 250–51, 259; Mary, 189.

Cohen, Elliot, 44.

Cole, Peter: "For a Theophoric Figure," 263–68; "Quatrains for a Calling," 266–67; *The Invention of Influence*, 268.

Coleridge, Samuel Taylor: "Kubla Kahn," 83.

Commentary, concept of, 119–20, 122.

Corbin, Henry, 124, 254n108; *The Man of Light in Iranian Sufism*, 254n108.

Cordovero, Moses, 208.

Covenant, 67–68, 79, 95; linguistic, 111, 113.

Crane, Hart, 61.

Creation, 70, 85, 94, 109, 169–70, 206–12, 237, 242, 265.

Creeley, Robert, 49.

Dante, 13, 165, 168–69, 183–84, 247; *Commedia*, 14; *Inferno*, 183–84.

De Chirico, Giorgio: "The Uncertainty of the Poet," 105.

De Leon, Moses, 243. *See also* Zohar.

De Lestrange, Gisèle, 116.

De Saussure, Ferdinand, 243.

Dembo, L.S., 41, 49; "The 'Objectivist' Poet: Four Interviews," 49–51.

Derrida, Jacques, 106–7, 224.

Descartes, René, 99 – 100.

Diaspora, 38, 40, 60, 66, 69, 109, 113–14, 117, 180–81, 193–95, 199, 238–39, 243, 264, 266–67, 269.

Diasporism, 8, 40, 66, 70, 73, 146, 166–67.

Dickinson, Emily, 195–97.

Donahue, Joseph, 222, 253–61. Works: "A Servant of God Without a Head," 253; *Dark Church*, 256; *Dissolves*, 256, 261; *Incidental Eclipse*, 253; *Red*

Flash in a Black Field, 253; *Terra Lucida*, 254–61.

Donin, Hayim Halevy: *To Pray as a Jew*, 86.

Donne, John: "Holy Sonnet 7," 144–45n32.

Doolittle, Hilda (H.D.), 42–43, 259; *Trilogy*, 254.

Dorf, Carol, 139.

Duncan, Robert, 210n42, 220, 222, 234–54, 256, 259; function of Judaism in poetry, 234; mythopoesis, 107; Theosophism, 234–35, 239. *See also* Judaism. *See also* Kabbalah. *See also* philosemitism. Works: "After Reading *Barely and Widely*," 247–53; *Bending the Bow*, 244n82; *Collected Essays and other Prose*, 235n51; *Ground Work*, volume 1, 244n82; *Ground Work*, volume 2, 244n82; "Often I am Permitted To Return To A Meadow," 247; *Passages*, 244n82; "Rites of Participation," 236, 238; *Roots and Branches*, 220, 244, 246; "The Delirium of Meaning," 241; *The H.D. Book*, xvii, 235–37, 240; "The Homosexual in Society," 240n66; "The Law I Love Is Major Mover," 241; "The Maiden," 247; *The Opening of the Field*, 244n82, 246–48; "The Structure of Rime I," 241; "What Do I Know of the Old Lore?" 220, 244, 247.

DuPlessis, Rachel Blau, 141.

Egyptian myth: Isis, 203; Osiris 203.

Eliade, Mircea, 124.

Eliot, T.S., 173; influence on Reznikoff and Objectivists, 40, 63; "The Metaphysical Poets," 225n23; "*Ulysses*, Order, and Myth," 173.f

Emerson, Ralph Waldo, 224.

Engels, Friedrich: *Anti-Dühring*, 164.

Fabilli, Lillian, 240.

Feminism, 141, 150, 197.

Field, Eugene: "Wynken, Blynken, and Nod," 234.

Finkelstein, Norman: "Disputation," 34–35; *Inside the Ghost Factory*, 34; Introduction to *A Momentary Glory: Last Poems*, 14; *Not One of Them in Place*, 31n28, 37n1, 44n13, 56n42, 63n55, 77n2, 95n65, 104n1, 132n2, 140, 173n18, 219n2; *On Mount Vision*, 61n52, 221, 225n24, 240, 244n82, 259n120; "On the Poetics of the Jewish God," 125; *Passing Over*, 72; "Prayer," 72; *Restless Messengers*, 72n65; Review of *The Sorrow of Eros*, 161–62; "The Case of Michael Palmer," 221; *The Ritual of New Creation*, 38n3, 184n35, 233n46; "Total Midrash," 59n48; "Tradition and Modernity, Judaism and Objectivism," 37n1.

Fredman, Stephen, 27–28n21, 44nn12–13, 45, 50–51, 54n38, 66, 70; *A Menorah for Athena*, 221n11; "Judaism as Loss in the Poetry of Michael Heller," 123n43.

Freud, Sigmund, 34, 179, 243, 268.

Gates of Repentance, 71.

Gaza War of 2014, 213.

Gilman, Sander, 29.

Ginsberg, Allen, 46n17, 49, 220; "Kaddish," 220.

Girard, René, 176–77n25.

Glatstein, Jacob (Glatshteyn, Yankev), 19, 135.

Gnosticism, 235–36n52, 254, 256–57.

Gold, Ben-Zion, 154.

Goldberg, Lea, 194. *See also* Back, Rachel Tzvia.

Golding, Alan, 139–40.

Greek Myth: Aphrodite, 252; Hermes, 234, 252; Icarus and Dedalus, 213; Mercury, 252; Philomela, 95, Orpheus, 95, 203.

Grossman, Allen, 77, 126–29, 154, 222, 263–68; as a theophoric figure, 263–65, 268; on Objectivists, 127–28; poetry as socially interactive, 79–83; poetry as manifestation and countenance, 79, 80, 100; poetry as the covenant of language, 77–84; theory of poetry, 78. *See also* Cole, Peter. Works: *A Harlot's Hire*, 265; "At Sunset," 102; *Descartes' Loneliness*, 98–102; "Holiness," 86–87, 90; *How to Do Things with Tears*, 97–98, 126, 128; "I Am in Babylon Dying," 265–67; "Jewish Poetry Considered as a Theophoric Project," 54n39, 219–20, 238n61, 263; "Poland of Death," 85–98; *Summa Lyrica*, 78, 80, 90–91; *Sweet Youth*, 98; *The Ether Dome and Other Poems*, 81–83, 98; "The Famished Dead," 100–101; "The Jew as an American Poet," 220; *The Philosopher's Window and Other Poems*, 98; "The Piano Player Explains Himself", 81, 98; *The Sighted Singer*, 92–93, 127; *The Summer Conversations*, 267; *White Sails*, 97.

Haggadah, 34, 72, 191.

Halliday, Mark, 78– 81, 102, 127.

Hamburger, Michael, 116n33, 159.

Hartman, Geoffrey, 71.

Hass, Robert, 47. *See also* Oppen, George.

Hatlen, Burton, 236, 244.

Hegel, G.W.F., 113, 162–65; *Phenomenology of Spirit*, 162; *Philosophy of Right*, 113.

Hellenism, 115.

Heller, Michael, 38, 40, 41, 49, 70–73, 103–29, 137, 195, 226; philosophical poet, 104–5, 107–8; secular Jewish poet, 109, 115; secular poetry, 106, 108. Works: "Abide with Me a Moment," 126; *Accidental Center*, 103; "Afikomens" (sequence), 118; "Armand Schwerner: The Semiotician of Self Work," 111n18; "Aspects of Poetics," 41n9, 107, 111; "Avant-Garde Propellants of the Machine Made of Words," 41n9, 110, 112; *Bandelette de Torah*, 113–17; "Beyond Zero," 118; "Commentary Is the Concept of Order for the Spiritual World," 119; *Constellations of Waking*, 104, 112; *Conviction's Net of Branches*, 37n1, 104; *Dianoia*, 104, 123, 126; "Diasporic Poetics" 41n9, 70, 138, 140; "Encountering Oppen," 105; "For Uncle Nat," 132n2; "In the Builded Place," 114; "In a Dark Time, On His Grandfather," 132n2; *Knowledge*, 105; *Living Root*, 106; "Mappah," 123, 125–26; "Notes on Stevens," 104; "Remains of the Diaspora," 38, 108–9, 114, 118, 195; *Speaking the Estranged*, 104; "The American Jewish Clock," 132n2; *The Poetry and Poetics of Michael*

Heller, 104; *This Constellation Is a Name*, 103, 112, 120, 122, 132n2; "To Postmodernity," 111; "Winter Notes, East End," 110.

Heller, Zalman: *The Just Man and the Righteous Way*, 106.

Hellerstein, Kathryn, 1.

Herbert, George, 136, 143n28. *See also* Bloch, Chana.

Herringman, Bernard, 223.

Heschel, Susannah: "Imagining Judaism in America," 221.

Hindus, Milton, 37n1, 53; *Charles Reznikoff: A Critical Essay*, 39n5; *Charles Reznikoff: Man and Poet*, 37n1, 39n5.

Hirschfield, Robert, 136.

Hirschhorn, Norbert, 137.

Holocaust, the, 6, 15, 18, 29, 31, 38, 93, 116, 154, 157, 236.

Homer: *Odyssey*, 100; *Nekuia*, 100.

Horkheimer, Max, 192.

Howe, Susan, 141, 193, 195, 197, 201, 203. *See also* Back, Rachel Tzvia.

Ignatow, David, 49.

Imagism, 39, 43, 47, 50; influence on Reznikoff, 43.

Intifada, Second, 174, 200.

Islam, 177, 244, 255, 260; Ka'Ba, 260; Koran, 176.

Israel, 3, 5, 55, 58, 61, 65–68, 90, 157, 175, 193–94, 205–6, 216–17, 238, 256; Palestinian conflict, 174–79, 196, 199–202, 205, 213, 263.

Jabès, Edmond, 221, 224, 241–43, 247; *The Book of Questions*, 241–43.

Jameson, Fredric, 106–7.

Jarnot, Lisa: *Robert Duncan: The Ambassador from Venus*, 235n51.

Jess: *The Enamord Mage: Translation #6*, 237n56.

Johnson, Ellen Fishman, 104.

Joris, Pierre, 157.

Joyce, James: *Ulysses*, 6, 173

Kabbalah, 3, 108–9, 118, 124, 148, 156, 206, 208–9, 220–21, 231, 233, 235–39, 242–47, 250, 257–59, 263–64; Lurianic Kabbalah, 82, 108, 206.

Kaddish, 86–90, 94–95, 102, 206, 210, 220, 267.

Kafka, Franz, 85, 97, 257; "An Imperial Message," 257.

Karp, Jonathan, 239.

Kenner, Hugh, 173.

King James Bible, 7, 43, 59, 60, 67, 266.

The Klezmatics, 34, 73n66; *Rhythm and Jews*, 34.

Koch, Kenneth, 103.

Kramer, Cecily, 239–40.

Kronick, Joseph G., 224–25.

Language poetry, 110, 138, 141.

Lazer, Hank, 1.

Levinas, Emmanual, 80, 104; *Totality and Infinity*, 80; "Exteriority and the Face," 80.

Longfellow, Henry Wadsworth: *Evangeline*, 91.

Lowell, Robert, 239n64.

Loy, Mina, 141.

Mackey, Nathaniel, 259; *Song of the Andoumboulou*, 254.

Maimonides, 197.

Malamud, Bernard, 29.

Mallarmé, Stéphane: "Sonnet" ("The virginal, vibrant, and beautiful dawn"), 185, 187–89.

Mandelbaum, Allen, 161, 184; *Chelmaxioms*, 184.

Mann, Thomas: characterization of Kafka, 85.

Martin, John, 49.

Marx, Karl, 113.

Marxism, 48, 164–65.

Mead, G.R.S.: *Pistia Sophia*, 237n56; *Thrice Greatest Hermes*, 237n56.

Meltzer, David, 31.

Midrash, 58–59, 66, 86, 162, 231n39, 260; on Rabbi Akiva, 86.

Millais, John Everett, 247.

Miller, Stephen Paul, 1–2, 219.

Milton, John, 61, 162, 170–71; *Paradise Lost*, 61, 162, 170.

Mishkan HaNefesh, 71–73.

Mishnah Avot, 268.

Modernism, 110, 164–65, 173, 222; female, 141; modernists, 39, 164, 173, 225; poetry, 43, 165, 171–73; poets, 2, 37; poetics, 40; Yiddish, 17.

Monroe, Harriet, 43–44.

Moore, Marianne, 247.

Morris, Daniel, 1–2, 219.

Mossin, Andrew, 200–201.

Nag Hammadi, 254.

Nazis, 89, 120, 154, 168.

Nietzsche, Friedrich, 34.

Objectivists, 17, 37, 39–41, 104, 109, 119–20, 122, 127–28, 136–38, 164–65, 198, 249; "diasporic poetics" of, 40, 58, 203, 213; history of, 40–49; influence on other poets, 49; Jewish, 106, 173; principles of, 57–60, 63–64, 73–74.

Objectivist Press, 47–48.

Old Testament, 51; influence on Western poetry, 61; Luther's German, 51.

Omer-Sherman, Ranen, 40, 53, 58, 66.

Oppen, George, 37, 47–49, 104–6, 125, 136–37, 164–65, 168, 173, 189–90, 221; Jewishness of, 70. *See also*

Objectivist Press. Works: *Discrete Series*, 47; *Of Being Numerous*, 189–90; "Psalm," 120, 168; "Route," 136–37; *The Materials*, 49, 105; "World, World," 125.

Osherow, Jacqueline, 21–22; "Ch'vil Schreibn a Poem auf Yiddish," 21, 132.

Ouaknin, Marc-Alain, 221–22n11; *The Burnt Book*, 221–22. *See also* Palmer, Michael; Pritchett, Patrick.

Oz, Amos: "Two Stubborn Men, and Many Dead," 174–75.

Ozick, Cynthia: "Envy; or Yiddish in America," 19.

O'Leary, Peter, 254; *Gnostic Contagion*, 235n52.

Palmer, Michael, 221–22.

Parfitt, Tudor, 146.

Perelman, Bob, 138n15, 139n17; *The Marginalization of Poetry*, 139n17.

Perloff, Marjorie, 1.

Phantasmagoria, 87–89.

Philosemitism, 148, 239, 250.

Plath, Sylvia, 239n64.

Poggioli, Renato, 223–24.

Poetry, midrashic, 66, 70, 72, 136, 206.

Poetry, prophetic, 41, 81–83, 85, 87, 94, 99, 127–28, 154–58, 166–67, 206, 240, 266. *See also* Grossman, Allen and Reznikoff, Charles.

Poetry, theophoric, 87, 95, 219–20.

Poetry, publication, 4, 43–44, 47, 49, 225, 265.

Postmodernism, 104–7, 110–11, 163; poetry, 77, 140, 171–72; skepticism, 138.

Pound, Ezra, 44, 173, 249; American poet-prophet, 61; antisemitism, 44,

240; influence on Reznikoff and
Objectivists, 40, 42, 63; "Imagist
Manifesto" 43.

Pritchett, Patrick: "How to Write
Poetry after Auschwitz: The Burnt
Book of Michael Palmer," 221–22.
See also Ouaknin, Marc-Alain.

Profane, category of, 123–25.

Rabbinic literature, 14.

*Radical Poetics and Secular Jewish
Culture,* 1–4, 219.

Rakosi, Carl, 49, 104.

Rang, Florens Christian, 113.

Ravikovitch, Dahlia, 133.

Reznikoff, Charles, 4, 10, 27–30, 37–75,
104, 147, 195, 198, 268; as a pro-
phetic or psalmist poet, 39, 41–42,
54, 60–66, 68–69, 72–73; influ-
ence of Romantic poets on, 61,
64; Jewish identity of, 62, 68, 70;
midrashic poetry, 58–59, 66, 70;
modern revisionist, 58, 66. *See also*
Objectivist Press; Syrkin, Marie;
Weinfield, Henry. Works: *A Fifth
Group of Verse,* 53–54; *By the
Waters of Manhattan,* 49; "Early
History of a Writer," 43n10, 55n40,
60; *Five Groups of Verse,* 64; "Heart
and Clock," 49; "Hellenist," 10n28;
"How difficult for me is Hebrew...,"
73; "I went to my grandfather's
to say good-bye...," 73, 132; *In
Memoriam: 1933,* 47; *Jerusalem the
Golden,* 41n8, 47, 55–57; "Joshua at
Shechem," 67–70; "Obiter Dicta,"
42, 50; *Rhythms,* 44, 61; "Samuel"
64–65; *Separate Way,* 47–48; *Testi-
mony,* 47–48; *Testimony: Recitative,*
49; "The Hebrew of your poets,
Zion...," 73; "Wringing, Wringing
His Pierced Hands," 61–64.

Rich, Adrienne, 141.

Rosenzweig, Franz, 118–20; Free
Jewish School, 120; *The Star of
Redemption,* 119.

Roth, Henry, 29.

Roth, Philip, 5; *The Counterlife,* 5;
Portnoy's Complaint, 24.

Rothenberg, Jerome, 1, 29–31, 154, 157,
219, 222, 236. Works: *A Big Jewish
Book,* 54n39, 236n55; "Cokboy"
31–32; "Das Oysleydikn (The
Emptying)," 32; "Die Toyte Kloles
(The Maledictions)," 32–33; "Dos
Geshray (The Scream)," 32; *Exiled
in the Word,* 236–37n55; "Harold
Bloom: The Critic as Extermi-
nating Angel," 63–64; *Khurbn,* 29,
32–33, 157; "Poets & Tricksters:
Innovation & Disruption in
Ritual & Myth," 31; *Poland/1931,*
29–33; "The Connoisseur of Jews,"
219; *The Symposium of the Whole,*
236n55; *Triptych,* 29, 31.

Ruebner, Tuvia, 194. *See also* Back,
Rachel Tzvia.

Russ & Daughters, 25–27; appetizing,
26–27.

Sacred, category of the, 4, 39–41, 52–53,
61, 71–72, 77–78, 117, 123–27, 129,
180, 205, 242, 254.

Schiffer, Reinhold, 27, 51, 59.

Scholem, Gershom, 3, 104, 108, 124,
127, 153, 206, 208, 231, 235, 237, 244,
256–57; definition of Theoso-
phy, 256; *Major Trends In Jewish
Mysticism,* 237–38, 243; *On Jews
and Judaism in Crisis,* 108; *The
Mystical Shape of the Godhead,*
127; "Tradition and New Creation
in the Ritual of the Kabbalists,"
244n81.

Schwerner, Armand, 110–11; *The Tablets*, 111.

Scroggins, Mark, 37, 44, 48; *Louis Zukofsky and the Poetry of Knowledge*, 44n13; *The Poem of a Life*, 248n94, 250n101.

Secular Jewish Culture, 1, 6, 9–14, 108–9, 114, 116–18, 124, 166, 222–25.

"Secular Jewish Culture / Radical Poetic Practice," 1, 30.

Sefer Yetzirah, 235.

Segalen, Victor, 122.

Seidman, Hugh, 103.

Selinger, Eric Murphy, 220, 238, 246; "Shekhinah in America," 54n39, 220.

Shakespeare, William, 247; *Hamlet*, 164.

Shandler, Jeffrey, 18–21, 35n35; *Adventures in Yiddishland*, 18.

Shapiro, Harvey, 11–15, 22–27, 30, 49, 118, 143, 268; Jewish masculinity in a secular world, 11–13; secular Jewish identity, 9, 14. Works: "According to the Rabbis," 13; "Book Group," 15; "For the Yiddish Singers in the Lakewood Hotels of My Childhood" 22–25; "Psalm," 73; "The Generations," 11–13, 132; *The Sights Along The Harbor*, 13; "Three Flights Down the Stairs," 25.

Shapiro, Karl, 4–11; *Poems of a Jew*, 4, 10; secularism, 9; "The 151st Psalm," 6; "The First Time," 9; "The Synagogue," 7.

Sharon, Ariel, 175.

Shekhinah, 54–56, 95–96, 101, 238, 243–47.

Shelley, P.B., 122, 165; influence on Grossman, 85; influence on Reznikoff, 61; "Ode to the West Wind,"84; "Ozymandias," 177.

Shoah, 5, 136, 157, 166.

Shreiber, Maeera Y., 4, 10–11, 27, 54–55, 95n65, 141–43, 149–51, 238n61.

Silliman, Ron, 138.

Singer, I.B., 19, 30.

Sitwell, Edith, 247.

Stein, Gertrude, 31.

Stevens, Wallace, 3, 42, 96, 104, 222–33; American poet-prophet, 61; influence on Grossman, 85; secular humanism, 226–27; use of "rabbi" in his poetry, 222–34. Works: *Adagia*, 223, 225, 233n45; "Final Soliloquy of the Interior Paramour," 96, 231n38; *Harmonium*, 222, 226; "Large Red Man Reading," 233n46; "Le Monocle de Mon Oncle," 222, 227–29; *Notes Toward a Supreme Fiction*, 222; *The Auroras of Autumn*, 222, 229–32; "The Auroras of Autumn," poem, 223, 226; "The Sun This March," 222–23, 226; "Things of August," 222, 232–33.

Straus, Nathan, 23.

Sutcliffe, Adam, 239.

Syrkin, Marie, 40, 51, 58.

Talmud, 14, 28, 221, 260.

Tarfon, Rabbi, 268.

Ten Commandments, 147–49.

Tikkun, 108.

Tisha B'Av, 210.

Torah, 3, 109, 115, 117, 125, 208–9, 231, 256, 258, 267.

To Press, 47; *An "Objectivist" Anthology*, 47.

Trungpa, Rinpoche Chögyam, 104.

Twitchell-Waas, Jeffrey, 248–50, 252.

Tzara, Tristan, 31.

Vital, Hayyim: *The Tree of Life*, 235.

Waldrop, Rosemarie, 242. *See also* Jabès, Edmond.

Wasserstrom, Steven, 124, 226; *Religion after Religion*, 226.

Weimar period, 120.

Weiner, Hannah, 103.

Weinfield, Henry, 62–63, 162–92, 195; humanism, 169; secularism, 169, 178, 181, 183, 192. Works: *A Wandering Aramaean*, 191–92; "Adam and Eve," 162, 165; "An Essay on Violence," 168–71, 176; "August: The Lake at Notre Dame," 182–85, 188–89; *Hebrew Melodies*, 172; *In the Sweetness of the New Time*, 162; "My Father Was a Wandering Aramaean," 190–91; "Praise and Lamentation," 177–82; *Sonnets Elegiac and Satirical*, 165; "The Crisis in the Middle East," 174–77; *The Poet Without a Name*, 184n34; *The Sorrows of Eros*, 161; "The Sorrows of Eros," poem, 185; "The Unicorn Tapestries," 163–65.

Werblowsky, R.J. Zvi, 235.

Whitman, Walt, 32, 43, 61, 233; mythopoesis, 107.

Wieseltier, Leon: *Kaddish*, 86, 89.

Williams, Galen; interview with Harvey Shapiro, 74.

Williams, William Carlos, 164, 225–26; *Collected Poems: 1921–1931*, 47; influence on Reznikoff; and

Objectivists 40, 42, 63. *See also* Objectivist Press.

Wirth-Nesher, Hana, 20–22, 50; *Call It English: The Languages of Jewish American Literature*, 20.

Wordsworth, William, 24, 55, 247; "Ode: Intimations of Immortality," 55n40.

Wyatt, Thomas, 249.

Yeats, W.B., 166, 173; influence on Grossman, 85. Works: "Adam's Curse," 166; "All Souls' Night," 100–101; *Per Amica Silentia Lunae*, 121; "Sailing to Byzantium," 186n39; "The Second Coming," 177; "The Wild Swans at Coole," 185–89.

Yerushalmi, Yosef Hayim, 38.

Yiddish, 17–19, 39, 46, 50, 116, 134–35; as vernacular, 19–22, 135; hidden language, 29; in Jewish-American literature, 34; in translation (Yiddishisms), 26, 30; literature, 19; modernists, 17; postvernacular, 19–20, 35–36; post-Yiddish worldview, 25; secular literature, 18, 30.

Yom Kippur, 147–48.

Zionism, 5, 40, 66, 72, 166–67, 216.

Zohar, 231, 235, 237, 243–44, 256, 258.

Zukofsky, Louis, 37, 44–50, 103–4, 128, 247–50, 252; "A", 48; "An Objective," 128; *Barely and Widely*, 248; "Sincerity and Objectification," 44.

About the Author

NORMAN FINKELSTEIN IS A POET AND LITERARY CRITIC. BORN IN New York City in 1954, he received his B.A. from Binghamton University, and his Ph.D. from Emory University. He is the author of eleven books of poetry, including *The Ratio of Reason to Magic: New & Selected Poems* (Dos Madres Press, 2016) and *From the Files of the Immanent Foundation* (Dos Madres Press, 2018). Widely published in the fields of modern American poetry and Jewish American literature, he is the author of five previous books of literary criticism. He is a Professor of English at Xavier University, where he has taught since 1980.